The
Negro American
Family

Report of a social study made principally by the college classes of 1909 and 1910 of Atlanta University, under the patronage of the trustees of the John F. Slater Fund; together with the Proceedings of the 13th Annual Conference for the Study of Negro Problems, held at Atlanta University on Tuesday, May the 26th, 1908.

The Atlanta University Publications Series

The
Negro American
Family

Edited by
W. E. Burghardt Du Bois

The M.I.T. Press
Cambridge, Massachusetts, and London, England

Foreword

History, it has been remarked, is an antidote to hysteria. This is more, perhaps, an observed than a derived truth. Why anyone looking back should wish to look forward is not especially self-evident, but the phenomenon is unmistakable. A sense of the past lends an air of reasonableness to the present that is at once reassuring *and energizing* A people, as J. H. Plumb has argued, without a past can have no future. Two points make a line — and a projection. Absent that, the future takes on a formless universality: everything is possible; nothing likely. Individuals and societies alike regress to an infantile dependence on whatever is Now.

It was thus to be expected, and altogether to be welcomed, that the civil rights movement of the 1950's and 1960's was followed not only by the rise of black militancy but equally by a growing demand from Negro youth for the establishment of black studies curricula in universities and colleges, for the development and enrichment of a specific black culture, and perhaps most especially for a rediscovery of the Negro past. A people intent on moving forward in directions *they* would choose had to establish whence they had come.

That this should be an urgent, pressing need for black Americans, especially young ones, at this time will seem hardly an occasion for comment. The destruction of the Negro past was surely the primal horror of slavery in America. Yet as a nation we are too eager by half at this moment to view American society as a Beckett play with two characters, Whitey and Blacky, trapped — nay sentenced — to an unending, unendable dialogue of abuse, repentance, misunderstanding, and abuse. Reality is more complex. African studies will surely, before long, begin to differentiate with some precision the many and varied *ethnic* streams that flowed into the vast transatlantic movement of African populations from the seventeenth to the nineteenth century (such that black Americans will begin, one would imagine, to acquire by various clues, real or imagined, some sense of a specific tribal or regional past that associates them with some "black" Americans, and distinguishes them from others). Similarly white America is now and has always been made up of wildly heterogeneous and disputatious tribal groupings. (And then there are indigenous American Indians.) Only about a third — 38.6 percent to the best knowledge of the Bureau of the Census — of the American population is descended from inhabitants of Great Britain and Northern Ireland, and of course of these probably not many more than half would qualify for the honorific middle term in the acronym WASP. For the remainder, with respect to one another, and to the presumed but illusory White Anglo-Saxon Protestant majority, there has been little but contention and strife. Again to cite Plumb, "Political stability is a comparatively rare phenomenon in the history of human society. When achieved, it has seldom lasted."[1]

---

[1] J. H. Plumb, *The Origins of Political Stability, England* 1675–1725 (Boston: Houghton Mifflin Co., 1967), p. xvi.

The pressures toward political instability in the United States today, and in nations the world over, are singularly associated with the reassertion of ethnic distinctiveness. A surprisingly similar pattern seems to recur. In the great centuries of nation forming and empire building, vast amalgams of ethnically distinct peoples were combined into political entities of one kind or another, whereupon for many generations a process took place in which ethnic distinctiveness was a concomitant to the subordination of one ethnic group by another. Taffy was a Welshman and therefore a thief. After a time the weakening of will, the onset of satiation, or whatever, leads the superordinate group to ease the barriers to assimilation, even to proclaim the abolition of all such distinctions as the only true and proper foundations of the social contract. This in turn produces a dual reaction: at first, and for some members of the oppressed group, a measure of gratified, even eager acquiescence. But then, usually somewhat later, a reaction of contemptuous rejection — aimed not least at the hapless early beneficiaries of the policy of nondiscrimination. (One recalls as a child being puzzled by the frozen resentment directed against seemingly unoffending — and assuredly equally unprosperous — neighbors whose unforgivable crime it was to have been descended from peasant ancestors who "took the soup," that is, converted to Protestantism, in some remote Irish village, trading any small immediate gain for a progeny doomed to ostracization amidst the railroad flats of Manhattan's West Side.) Students of American ethnic history for some time have been labeling this phenomenon, this process of rejection, as the "grandfather effect." Third-generation immigrants reject the conformity of their all-too-Americanized parents in favor of the now acceptable "strangeness" of the first-generation immigrants.

Something very like this appears to be taking place among Negro Americans at this time. Dissatisfaction with the liberal doctrine of equality of opportunity was easy enough to forecast. The permissiveness of dominant groups toward suppressed classes or castes is not always as permissive a gesture as it might appear. To offer equal competition to persons who are not equally competitive is no great risk. And it takes no great wit to see as much. Thus the Civil Rights Act of 1964 was in ways the high-water mark of Social Darwinism in America. Little wonder that within months, almost, of requiring the total exclusion of racial, religious, or ethnic identification from the official and semiofficial record keeping of the nation, the Federal government was specifically requiring census and quotas of black Americans and other such groups as a condition of Federal aid, even as a precondition of legitimacy in a wide range of activities. Less easily foreseen was the rise of a militant, assertive black identity among the young. These things continually surprise, for they require the assumption that the social stability that seemed to exist, based on subordination or assimilation, either would not last or, indeed, did not even in fact exist. But for certain it has come to pass, and just as certainly it can be explained, welcomed, facilitated.

It is in this context that the reappearance of W. E. B. Du Bois's *The Negro American Family* is an event of moment. Two considerations, at very least, are involved.

The first has to do with the plain, if painful, fact that the professional standards of ethnic history when it first begins to appear are rarely reassuring.[2] Typically, the purpose of such history is to create a past that did not quite exist. The resulting documents characteristically serve an uneasy role somewhere between myth and analysis: their purpose not so much to explain as to celebrate. Above all, the purpose is rarely, if ever, to lay to rest ancient quarrels. *Tout comprendre, c'est tout pardonner* is a maxim for victors rather than vanquished. There is no necessary harm in this, and indeed much good to the extent that establishing a place in the past enables any group to assume a more self-confident and purposeful role in the present: even a less self-preoccupied role. But where the social present requires the management of large and pressing problems which have special historical roots not likely to be generally understood, it is a matter of consequence that those who would explain this do so accurately. Hence it is all the more a matter of consequence that the beginnings of serious ethnic history of the Negro American should have been so largely presided over by someone like W. E. B. Du Bois. The *too* well known debate between Du Bois and Booker T. Washington in his early career and his later radical rejection of American institutions tend to obscure the pioneering social scientist who not only helped begin the systematic study of the Negro American, in the Atlanta University monograph series that extended from 1898 to 1914 (*The Negro American Family* appearing about midway, in 1908), but also brought to those beginnings the highest credentials of American scholarship. A New England Brahmin in every useful sense of the word, Du Bois was a product not only of Harvard but of European universities as well. So much indeed, that Frazier would later describe him as every bit "a finished product of the aristocratic intellectual culture of the last decade of the nineteenth century." (And ever so slightly suggest he might not have been in as close communion with "the souls of black folk" as he imagined!)[3] This is not to say Du Bois escaped altogether the plight of those of whom he wrote. He was, for example, himself the product of a broken home. His father wandered off a year after his birth, never again to be heard from. In his *Autobiography* Du Bois writes, "I never saw him, and know not where or when he died." It happens in the best of families.[4]

A second and as important a ground for the revival of Du Bois's early work is, if anything, a more sensitive one. For nearly a decade now the position of the Negro American has all but preoccupied American intellectual life. Nothing save the war in Vietnam itself has aroused anything like the passionate commitment evoked by this issue Inevitably this preoccupation has been accompanied by an outpouring of books and articles. Alas, the great majority of these have been written by white Americans. If anything, this proportion has increased in recent years, at the very time when its inappropriateness has been becoming ever more evident. Increas-

[2] See Nathan Glazer and Daniel Patrick Moynihan, *Beyond the Melting Pot* (Cambridge, Mass.: The M.I.T. Press, 1963), passim.

[3] E. Franklin Frazier, ''The Du Bois Program in the Present Crisis,'' *Race*, Vol. 1, No. 1 (1935), p. 11.

[4] W. E. B. Du Bois, *The Autobiography of W. E. B. Du Bois* (New York: International Publishers, 1968), p. 73.

ingly one detects among blacks a rejection of such scholarship, however pure its motives, on grounds of *race* (that is, ethnicity) alone. This may be puzzling, even troubling, to white observers (not to say to white authors!), but surely it is an elemental accompaniment of a burgeoning sense of ethnic identity. It is all the more necessary, then, that young black students should have it made clear to them that the beginnings of scholarship in this great area of American studies were in fact the work of Negro American scholars. Moreover, in the 1930's, by far the most productive period to date of scholarship in this field, Negro scholars were also preeminent. Not only might this knowledge serve to make the later work of whites somewhat more acceptable, but it might serve as well to evoke a level of black effort worthy of what has gone before.

That is not to say that there are no difficulties with Du Bois's work. To the contrary, it appears we are entering a period of a massive redefinition of the entire "slavery" thesis of Negro American social structure. Just when this thesis first appeared I do not know, but as with so many elements in the analysis of American society, it will be found fully developed in the works of Alexis de Tocqueville. Not, however, in *Democracy in America*. Rather, in an obscure, almost wholly forgotten report prepared for the French Chamber of Deputies in 1839 and published, in English, in Boston a year later.[5] The British had emancipated some 700,000 slaves in their West Indian colonies as of 1834, providing a term of "apprenticeship," meaning indentured labor, for up to six years thereafter. France had done nothing and faced the prospect that the quarter million or more slaves in her West Indian possessions would shortly be surrounded by free British subjects, in an area from which memory of the massacres on Santo Domingo had hardly disappeared, A government commission was appointed to inquire into the subject, with de Tocqueville as chairman. Its view was unanimous in favor of abolition, but what distinguishes its report is de Tocqueville's passionate attachment to freedom, combined with his no less obdurate commitment to the social modes that make freedom possible. In deploring the horror of slavery, he turned first of all to its destruction of the husband-wife and parent-child relationships.

There exists, indeed, a profound and natural antipathy between the institution of marriage and that of slavery. A man does not marry when he cannot exercise marital authority, when his children must be born his equals, irrevocably destined to the wretchedness of their father; when, having no power over their fate, he can neither know the duties, the privileges, the hopes, nor the cares which belong to the paternal relation. It is easy to perceive that every motive, which incites the freeman to a lawful union, is lost to the slave *by the simple fact of his slavery*. The several means which the legislature or the master may use to attract him to that condition, which they have rendered him incapable of desiring, will always be without effect.

Du Bois followed de Tocqueville in this theme, and Frazier, Du Bois. Those others of us who have followed Frazier have simply taken the matter

---

[5]Alexis de Tocqueville, *Report made to The Chamber of Deputies on The Abolition of Slavery in the French Colonies*, July 23, 1839 (Boston: James Munroe & Co., 1840).

as settled. Now, however, new scholarship begins to call it into question. Professor Herbert G. Gutman, with associates such as Laurence A. Glasco, following the pattern of intergenerational studies of working-class families in the work of Stephen Thernstrom, have begun to show that, contrary to all that has been supposed, the actual family structure of free Negroes in the North prior to 1863 and of Southern Negroes in the decades immediately thereafter was very much the familiar, simple husband-wife-children arrangement. The nuclear family was dominant: as much as with white workers generally and more than in the case of certain ethnic groups such as, for example, the Buffalo Irish. (In his *Autobiography* Du Bois notes that in his boyhood in Great Barrington, Massachusetts, "None of the colored folk I knew were so poor, drunken and sloven as some of the lower class Americans and Irish." The distinction is repeatedly made between Americans *and* Irish, much as today black is distinguished from white. Of his college days he notes, "I was struck . . . when I came back from the South to New England, to find that the 'nigger' jokes of Tennessee were replaced at Harvard by tales of the 'two Irishmen' and songs like 'mush-mush-mush turliady.'")[6] The lower-class matriarchal form came later.[7] Gutman hypothesizes that it came about because of the increasingly narrowed employment opportunities of the immigrant in the city. Thus in 1865, 80 percent of the skilled artisans in the South were black. But by 1933, at the outset of the New Deal, twenty-four international unions — craft unions — of the American Federation of Labor excluded Negroes by constitutional provision. In that year the "Report of the President's Research Committee on Social Trends" offered one of the first extensive comments on what have become characteristic problems of social disorganization in the black slums.[8] It was reported, for example, that of the Negro families still remaining in the South a third were "being supported by aged widows, the aunts or grandmothers of the children of the household."[9] Also, it would appear that Negroes in factory work had gained almost no foothold prior to World War II, held only a precarious position during the economic ups and downs of the 1920's, and then were decimated by the great depression. It may well be that future generations will see *this* historical experience rather than earlier ones as the genesis of certain of the issues of the 1960's and 1970's; time will tell.

For the moment it is clear that the problems which Du Bois raised, whatever their exact etiology, do remain with the nation . . . indeed they grow more pressing. In the period 1960–1968 the number of male-headed Negro families in central cities grew by 172,000; the number of female-headed

---

[6] Du Bois, *Autobiography*, pp. 75, 82.

[7] Herbert G. Gutman and Laurence A. Glasco, ''The Buffalo, New York, Negro, 1855–1875: A Study of the Family Structure of Free Negroes and Some of Its Implications.'' Prepared for delivery at the Wisconsin Conference on the History of American Political and Social Behavior, May 16–17, 1968.

[8] Report of the President's Research Committee on Social Trends, ''Recent Trends in the United States'' (McGraw-Hill Book Company, 1933), pp. 553–601.

[9] *Ibid.*, p. 583.

families by 294,000. This was an increase of 11 percent in the former, 60 percent in the latter. In central cities with populations over one million, female-headed black families increased 83 percent. By 1967 the nonwhite illegitimacy ratio reached 293.8 per 1000 live births, while, again in central cities, in 1968 only 24 percent of Negro children in families with incomes under $4000 were living with both parents. Before reaching the age of twenty-one, between 50 and 60 percent of all Negro children are supported by the Aid to Families of Dependent Children Program. Who are these children? Overwhelmingly they are poor. In central city Negro families with incomes over $15,000 a full 95 percent — very near the biological maximum, as it were — of children were living with both parents in 1968. Have been and will be. This is not to reassert Frazier's theme of the two streams of Negro social structure — a hypothesis adopted by Jessie Bernard most recently. Indeed, it may be more useful to turn to Du Bois's striking image, cited by Professor Conyers, in the Introduction, of the forward movement of a people, not as the compact march of an army, but as the straggling, stretched-out affair of a great folk migration, with some very much to the fore, others to the rear, and the task of the social commentator being to find something like a true middle. Whatever the case, would that he were with us today to lend style to the inquiry! Surely in the company of such a man, the hysterics of so much present debate would diminish. What is, has in some measure been and will in some measure be. The great issue is which way things are heading, and on this point we have much to learn from this distinguished mind.

Daniel P. Moynihan

Cambridge, Massachusetts
January 19, 1969

Introduction

In 1895, W. E. B. Du Bois received the Ph.D. in history from Harvard University. Shortly thereafter he embarked upon a most illustrious and productive career. From 1897 to 1910, Du Bois served as director of the now famous Atlanta University Conferences. It was largely through the efforts of Du Bois and the Atlanta University Conferences that several studies on varied aspects of Negro life, popularly known as *The Atlanta University Publications,* were conducted. Published primarily from 1897 to 1914, they number slightly over twenty and are still highly sought by scholars in the social and behavioral sciences in America and abroad. When Dr. Du Bois retired from his post at Atlanta University in 1910 to become editor of *Crisis*[1] and Director of Publicity of the National Association for the Advancement of Colored People, he had already made history in the social sciences. *The Atlanta University Publications* represented one of the first serious attempts to examine the social context of the black experience in America, and Du Bois's *The Philadelphia Negro,* published in 1899, was one of the first empirical works in American sociology.

In 1933, Dr. Du Bois was requested to return to Atlanta University to become the first chairman of the Graduate Department of Sociology and Anthropology. In addition to training black men and women, in 1939–1940, he founded *Phylon* and became its editor. This journal, devoted to the analysis of racial and cultural relations, was until a few years ago the only major scholarly periodical in its field in the world. *Race, Civilization,* and *Freedomways* have come into existence recently.

If we add to these accomplishments the social action concerns of Du Bois and the numerous other famous books he wrote, it becomes quite clear why Afro-Americans and other black people, in searching for their identity and direction, find themselves discovering and rediscovering Dr. William E. Burghardt Du Bois.

The principal concern of this introduction is *The Negro American Family,* edited by Dr. Du Bois and published in 1908 as *The Atlanta University Publications, No. 13.* The present interest in the Negro American family, and in the family-connected problems explicit in such a concern, makes the republication of this work most welcome. Yet, it is doubtful whether this work, in its specific aspects, will provide solutions for any of the difficulties. It is not a description of contemporary black families or of the consciences of blacks as they interpret and respond to present circumstances. A most salient point about this study is that it was written prior to 1910. Aside from the question of the quality of the data on Negroes in 1900 and before, it is obvious they do not reflect current situations. In 1900, for example, about 90 percent of all Negroes lived in the South; presently, only a little more than one half reside there. In 1900, over three fourths of Negroes in the South lived in rural areas; in 1960, almost 60

---

[1] *Crisis* magazine is the official periodical publication of The National Association for the Advancement of Colored People.

percent lived in urban places in the South, and for the nation as a whole nearly three fourths of all Negroes live in urban places.

Similar changes are found in other areas of investigation. Thus, whereas Du Bois reports that illiteracy among Negroes in 1900 was 44.5 percent, in 1959 it was 7.5 percent. Du Bois reports home ownership for Negroes as 20.3 percent in 1900; today home ownership is about 40 percent. Du Bois reports an uncertain illegitimacy rate for Negroes of 25 percent, which is about the same as that reported today. (Illegitimacy rates might be too unstable an index to use for social planning. One author reports an illegitimacy rate of 16.8 percent for Negroes in 1940.)

Another reservation to be kept in mind while reading this book, or any pioneering work of this nature, relates to the changes brought about by the civil rights movement in recent years. The movement has altered the emphasis on, if not the substance of, the problem. Many present political and economic reforms did not exist when Du Bois wrote this work in 1908. Further, Du Bois was talking about integration — about the desirability of black families conforming to white American middle-class norms or European family norms. Many liberals, reformists, and militants of today suggest an attack on society's view of normative family structure as an alternative and more meaningful approach to social integration, contending that families are not undifferentiated entities, independent of the milieu in which they are contained.

What then is the principal contribution that this book makes to the social sciences and to contemporary America? It lets us know that some of the problems confronting blacks a long time ago still confront blacks, that is, problems of power, family stability, economic support, alienation, etc.; however, I feel the major contribution is methodological and theoretical. The following quote, taken from Ernest W. Burgess and Harvey J. Locke, *The Family*, 1945, is made especially understandable by Du Bois's work written forty years earlier:

> The Negro family more than that of any other race or nationality has been subject to social change. Its modifications under the successive crises of transplantation from Africa, slavery, sudden emancipation, and migration to cities must be studied to get an understanding of its present day status and problems in the United States.[2]

To Du Bois the Negro family just did not happen; it had a history. For this reason Du Bois begins practically every section of the book by attempting to connect present conditions with an African past. He does not do this "because Negro-Americans are Africans, or can trace an unbroken social history from Africa, but because there is a distinct nexus between Africa and America which, though broken and perverted, is nevertheless not to be neglected by the careful student." Although we know that it would be faulty logic to assume that the Negro American can be explained by African origins, it is equally erroneous to assume that black history *started* during or after slavery; therefore, even though we cannot attribute causal factors

---

[2] Ernest W. Burgess and Harvey J. Locke, *The Family* (New York: American Book Co., 1945), p. 148.

to history per se, it is important to know what the family life of the Negro tribes that furnished material for the American slave trade was like. How much family instability did they show? It is clear that the answer to this question puts the blame for family disorganization among American Negroes where it belongs — on the system(s). Slavery destroyed family life among blacks, and cultural genocide destroyed a sense of identity and history. Emancipation, though destroying legal slavery, issued in other types of political, social, and economic disabilities and exploitation, whose effects are attested to this day. Urbanization and technology have shifted the emphases and physical context of the problem by attenuating the whole process, thus making it appear more impersonal. The sting and substance of the problem continue to have their effects on black adults and their youth.

The type of differentiation into which Du Bois casts the Negro family in America is instructive. Many scholars feel that the lack of this concept has been one of the weaknesses of other works on black families in America. Thus, Du Bois characterizes some of the relevant family conditions of Africans, "family life" under slavery, the country home, the village home, and the city home. Further differentiation of black families is revealed by Du Bois's discussion of city homes — of the slums, and middle-class black homes in cities. From this treatment it is clear that Du Bois does not view the Negro family as static and undifferentiated. Thus he states:

> Few modern groups show a greater internal differentiation of social conditions than the Negro American, and the failure to realize this is the cause of much confusion. In looking for differentiation from the past in Africa and slavery, few persons realize that this involves extreme differentiation in the present. The forward movement of a social group is not the compact march of an army, where the distance covered is practically the same for all, but is rather the straggling of a crowd, where some . . . hasten, some linger, some turn back; some reach far-off goals before others even start, and yet the crowd moves on. The measure of the advancement of such a throng is a question at once nice and indefinite. Measured by the rear guard there may be no perceptible advance. Measured by the advance guard the transformation may be miraculous. Yet neither of these are reasonable measurements, but rather the point which one might call the center of gravity of the mass is the true measuring point, and the determination of this point in the absence of exact measurements may be for a long time a matter of opinion rather than proof. So with the Negro American. . . . It is begging and obscuring this question to harp on ignorance and crime among Negroes as though these were unexpected; or to laud exceptional accomplishments as though it was typical. The real crucial question is: What point has the mass of the race reached which can be justly looked upon as the average accomplishment of the group? (pp. 127–128)

It is conceivable that many readers of this work will try to gauge what Du Bois had to say about sexual morality among Negroes, family stability, and related topics. In several places in the book the disorganizing effects of late marriages among Negroes, high sex ratios under slavery (a preference for male slaves), and the preponderance of females in cities are examined; however, it is on the question of sexual morality that Du Bois shows moral ambivalence. Thus, while Du Bois understands the social and economic forces behind the sexual expression of blacks, he states: "Without doubt the point where the Negro American is furthest behind modern civilization is in his sexual mores." This leads Du Bois to postulate a notion of "widespread sexual irregularity" among Negroes, which his data do not demonstrate. Perhaps Du Bois reflected to a higher degree the puritanical norms so often surrounding sex than the ideology in his other works might suggest It is clear that Du Bois equates a high civilized status with female chastity and male continence. Du Bois, however, does not heartily condone the sex mores of modern European nations, though he sees them as having some degree of superiority over those of other peoples. Their relation to prostitution, divorce, and childlessness were among Du Bois's reservations about European marriage mores. It is in this regard that Du Bois feels that the Negro woman and race may teach the world something. In moving terms he says:

Just as . . . what is termed Negro ''laziness'' may be a means of making modern workingmen demand more rational rest and enjoyment rather than permitting themselves to be made machines, so too the Negro woman, with her strong desire for motherhood, may teach modern civilization that virginity, save as a means of healthy motherhood, is an evil and not a divine attribute. That while the sexual appetite is the most easily abused of all human appetites and deadly when perverted, that nevertheless it is a legitimate, beneficent appetite when normal, and that no civilization can long survive which stigmatizes it as essentially nasty and only to be discussed in shamefaced whispers. The Negro attitude in these matters is in many respects healthier and more reasonable. Their sexual passions are strong and frank, but they are, despite example and temptation, only to a limited degree perverted or merely commercial. The Negro mother-love and family instinct is strong, and it regards the family as a means, not an end, and although the end in the present Negro mind is usually personal happiness rather than social order, yet even here radical reformers of divorce courts have something to learn. (p. 42)

There is nothing in this work edited by Du Bois which would be against the general idea that the advancement of Negroes in America is related to the strengthening and development of family life. However, it appears that Du Bois was against using family disorganization indices to prove the disintegration of Negro family life. Family disorganization is an effect, and according to Du Bois, "These things all go to prove not the disintegration of Negro family life, but the distance which integration has gone and has yet to go."

The fact that Du Bois does not offer "solutions" and family policy programs for blacks or whites in America is understandable. The pioneering character of the book and its intent, except in a most general sense, are not programmatically focused. Some of the works since Du Bois do not achieve this objective either. The statement of a research problem and its "solution" as a social problem are not the same thing. This is particularly germane in the area of sex, marriage, and family life. Sometimes we have difficulty in agreeing on a condition as problematic; sometimes we disagree about means and/or goals implicit in problem-solving activity; still at other times we lack *power* and/or *knowledge* to act collectively. One thing is certain, however, social policy and family policy will take on more importance in the future. Questions about black families, lower-class families, family

stability, etc., will occupy increasing attention. Should we have a family
policy in the United States? If so, what form should it assume? How
much emphasis should be placed on family stability? Just how stable can
families be in an urban achievement-oriented culture? What is wrong with
female-headed families? Can broken families have positive consequences
for individual personalities because the families are broken? Here attention is called to the possibility that an unbroken family need not be intrin-
sically better than a broken family simply because it is unbroken. For many
persons a miserable unbroken family is far less desirable than a broken
one with some degree of happiness for individual family members, despite
norms which categorically sanction an unbroken family. How can the black
male be more fully incorporated into family units without destroying the
creativity and contributions of the black woman? Do children in father-
absent homes have lower aspirational levels than children in biparental
families? These and many many other questions are still being debated and
researched. Power, knowledge, and a sense of humanity will undoubtedly
contribute to the "answers" these and other questions will receive.

A final point is in order: The writer of this introduction looked through
several other books on the Negro family in America to see if the work by
Du Bois, *The Negro Family in America,* is cited or recognized. The answer
is negative. The prototype of works on the Negro family in America, E.
Franklin Frazier's *The Negro Family in the United States,* indicates no
awareness of Du Bois's publication, though Frazier's classic book was written some thirty years later. Perhaps Frazier was not aware of Du Bois's
work, although the parallels between the two are interesting.

James E. Conyers

Indiana State University
January, 1969

"The system produces general licentiousness among the slaves. Marriage, as a civil ordinance, they cannot enjòy. Our laws do not recognize this relation as existing among them, and, of course, do not enforce, by any sanction, the observance of its duties. Indeed, until slavery waxeth old, and tendeth to decay, there *cannot be any* legal recognition of the marriage rite, or the enforcement of its consequent duties. For, all the regulations on this subject would limit the master's absolute *right of property* in the slaves. In his disposal of them he could no longer be at liberty to consult merely his own interest. He could no longer separate the wife and the husband to suit the convenience or interest of the purchaser, no matter how advantageous might be the terms offered. . . . Hence, all marriages that could ever be allowed them, would be a mere contract, violable at the master's pleasure. Their present quasi marriages are continually thus voided. They are, in this way, brought to consider their matrimonial alliances as a thing not binding, and they act accordingly. We are then assured by the most unquestionable testimony that licentiousness is the necessary result of our system."

Address of the Presbyterian Synod of Kentucky, 1834.

"Chastity is no virtue among them; its violation neither injures female character in their own estimation, nor in that of their master and mistress. No instruction is ever given, no censure pronounced. I speak not of the world. I speak of Christian families generally."

Lexington (Ky.) Luminary, circa 1834.

"DIE weiblicher Tugend steht bei manchen Stämmen in viel höherer Achtung als die typischen Sittengemälde vermuthen lassen."

Schneider, on Negroes.

"THE contempt we have been taught to entertain for the blacks makes us fancy many things that are founded neither in reason nor experience."

Alexander Hamilton.

"AS fathers, husbands and brothers, you are summoned to rally around the standard of the Eagle to defend all which is dear in existence."

Andrew Jackson to the Negroes of Louisiana in 1814.

Contents

The Thirteenth Annual Conference

PROGRAMME

Subject: The Negro American Family

First Session, 10:00 a. m.

President Ware, presiding.

Subject: "The Home."

Address: Dr. G. F. Dickerman, Field Agent of the Trustees of the Slater Fund.

Address: Mr. W. T. B. Williams, Field Agent of the Trustees of the Slater Fund.

Second Session, 11:30 a. m.

Subject: "Health and the Family."

Special Talk to Men: Dr. J. W. Madison, of Atlanta.

Special Talk to Women: Miss L. S. Cathcart, of Lincoln Academy, N. C.

Third Session, 3:00 p. m.

Eleventh Annual Mothers' Meeting. (In charge of the Gate City Free Kindergarten Association), Mrs. Hattie Landrum Green, presiding.

Subject: "The Children."

1. Kindergarten songs, games and exercises by 150 children of the four free kindergartens:

> East Cain Street—Miss Ola Perry.
> Bradley Street—Mrs. J. P. Williamson.
> White's Alley—Miss Ethel Evans.
> Summerhill—Miss Hattie Sims.

2. Remarks by visitors.

3. Reports of the year's work and contributions.

Fourth Session, 8:00 p. m.

President E. T. Ware, presiding.

Subject: "The Negro American Family."

Paper: Archdeacon E. L. Henderson, of the Diocese of Georgia.

Address: Miss Jane Addams, of Hull House, Chicago.

ERRATUM

Page 122. To the table on the proportion of students paying their way, add,

1878-1879............37.4%...........62.6%

Preface

In 1897 the Atlanta University Negro Conference made an investigation into the "Social and Physical Condition of Negroes in Cities," which involved a study of 4742 individuals gathered in 1137 families, living in 59 different groups, in 18 different cities. These data were compiled by the United States Department of Labor and published in Bulletin number ten; and, as the editor said, "Great credit is due the investigators for their work." The object of the investigation was to study the mortality of Negroes and the social and family conditions. The study of Mortality was continued in 1906 by Atlanta University publication number eleven. The present study continues the study of social conditions from the point of view of the family group.

This study is therefore a further carrying out of the Atlanta University plan of social study of the Negro American by means of an annual series of decennially recurring subjects covering, so far as is practicable, every phase of human life. The object of these studies is primarily scientific—a careful research for truth conducted as thoroughly, broadly and honestly as the material resources and mental equipment at command will allow; but this is not our sole object : we wish not only to make the Truth clear but to present it in such shape as will encourage and help social reform. Our financial resources are unfortunately meagre: Atlanta University is primarily a school and most of its funds and energy go to teaching. It is, however, also a seat of learning and as such it has endeavored to advance knowledge, particularly in matters of racial contact and development, which seems obviously its nearest field. In this work it has received unusual encouragement from the scientific world, and the published results of these studies are used in America, Europe, Asia and Africa. Very few books on the Negro problem or any phase of it have been published in the last decade which have not acknowledged their indebtedness to our work.

On the other hand, the financial support given this work has been very small. The total cost of the 13 publications has been about $14,000, or a little over $1,000 a year. The growing demands of the work, the vast field to be covered and the delicacy and equipment needed in such work call for far greater resources. We need, for workers, laboratory and publications, a fund of $6,000 a year, if this work is going adequately to fulfill its promise. Last year a small temporary grant from the Carnegie Institution of Washington, D. C., greatly helped us, and this year our work was saved from suspension by an appropriation from the John F. Slater Fund.

In past years we have been enabled to serve the United States Bureau of Labor, the United States Census, the Board of Education of the

English Government, many scientific associations, professors in nearly all the leading universities, and many periodicals and reviews. May we not hope in the future for such increased financial resources as will enable us to study adequately this the greatest group of social problems that ever faced America?

A Select Bibliography of the Negro American Family

Bibliography

Atlanta University Publication No. 10—Bibliography of the Negro American. 1905.
Edwards, R. H.—Studies in American Social Conditions, No. 2: The Negro Problem, 1908 (See Section 4).

Books and Pamphlets

Atlanta University Publications—Mortality among Negroes in Cities. Atlanta. 1896. 51 pp. 8vo.
Atlanta University Publications—Social and Physical Condition of Negroes in Cities. Atlanta, 1897. 72, 14 pp. 8vo.
Atwater, Wilbur Olin, and Charles Dayton Woods—Dietary studies with reference to the food of the Negroes in Alabama in 1895 and 1896. Washington, 1897. 69 pp. 8vo. (U. S. Dept. of Agri.)
Bacon, Benjamin C.—Statistics of the colored people of Philadelphia. Phila., 1856.
Bacon, Benjamin C.—Ibid. Second edition with statistics of crime. Phila., 1859. 3–24 pp. 8vo.
Baltimore Association for the moral and educational improvement of the colored people. Annual report. 2d, 3d, 1866–67. Balt., 1866. 68, v. 8vo.
Brackett, Jeffrey Richardson—Notes on the progress of the colored people of Maryland since the war. Balt., 1890. 96 pp. (Johns Hopkins University Studies. Series 8, No. 7–9.) 8vo. Supplement to the Negro in Maryland.
Buford, Mrs.—Domestic missions among the plantation Negroes. N. Y., 189—? 4 pp. 8vo.
Chestnutt, Charles W.—The house behind the cedars. Boston, 1900. 8vo.
The marrow of tradition. Boston, 1901.
The wife of his youth. Boston, 1899. 12mo.
Clowes, W. Laird—Black America. Reprint from the Times. London, 1891. xiii, 240 pp. sm. 8vo. Map.
Condition of the people of color in Ohio. With interesting anecdotes. Boston, 1839. 48 pp. 12mo
Crummell, Alexander—The black woman of the South: her neglects and her needs. Cincin., 14 pp. 8vo.
Delaware association for the moral improvement and education of the colored people. An. Reps. 1867, 1869, 1870. Wilmington, Del.
DuBois, W. E. B.—The Philadelphia Negro. Publications of the University of Pennsylvania, No. 14. Phila., 1899. 20, 520 pp. Diagrams, 3 maps.
DuBois, W. E. B.—The souls of black folk. Chicago, 1903. viii, (1), 264, (1) pp. 8vo.
Edwards, Bryan—History, civil and commercial, of the British Colonies in the West Indies. Phila., 1806. 4 vols. 8vo. Portrs. Atlas, 4to. Folded table.
Elwang, Wm. Wilson—The Negroes of Columbia, Mo. Columbia, 1904. vii, 69 pp. 8vo. Plates. Map.
Frissell, Hollis Burke, and Isabel Brevier—Dietary studies of Negroes in eastern Va. in 1897 and 1898. Wash., 1899. 45 pp. 8vo. (U. S. Dept. of Agric.)

Goodell, Will—The American slave code in theory and practice. Judicial decisions and illustrative facts. N. Y., 1853. 431 pp. 12mo.

Haygood, Atticus Green—Our brother in black, etc. N. Y., 1881. 252 pp. 12mo.

Hickok, C. T.—The Negro in Ohio. 1802–1870. Cleveland, 1896. 182 pp. 12mo.

Hrdlicke, Ales—Anthropological investigations on one thousand white and colored children of both sexes, the inmates of the New York juvenile asylum, etc. N, Y., 189—? 86 pp. 8vo.

Ingle, Edward—The Negro in the District of Columbia, Johns Hopkins University Studies. Vol. XI. Balt., 1893. 110 pp. 8vo,

Johnson, Mrs. E, A.—The Hazeley family. Philadelphia, 1894.

Jones, C. C.—The religious instruction of the Negroes in the United States. Savannah, 1842. 277 pp. 12mo.

Kemble, Fanny—A journal of a residence on a Georgian plantation. N. Y., 1863. 337 pp. 12mo

Kingsley, M. H.—Story of West Africa, 1899.

   West African Studies.

   Travels in West Africa.

Laidlaw, Walter, editor—The federation of Churches and Christian workers in New York City. N. Y., Sociological canvasses, 1896—. 8vo. First, 112 pp., 2d, 116 pp.

Livermore, Mrs. Elizabeth D.—Zoe; or the quadroon triumph. A tale for the times. 1st vol., 327 pp. 2d vol., 306 pp. 12mo.

Majors, M. A.—Noted Negro women. Chicago, 1893.

Miller, Kelly—Race Adjustment. 1908. 306 pp.

Minutes of the Biennial Meetings of the National Association of Colored Women. Nos. 1–6, 1897–1908.

McDonald, Arthur—Colored children. Chicago, 1899. 14 pp. 16mo.

Mossell, Mrs. N. F.—The work of Afro-American women. Phila., 1894. 178 pp. 12mo.

Needles, Edward—Ten years' progress, or a comparison of the state and condition of the colored people in the city and county of Philadelphia from 1837 to 1847. Phila., 1849.

Negro mother's appeal, The—A poem. London, 185—? 4 pp. 8vo.

Negro young people's Christian and educational congress, Atlanta, 1902. The United Negro. Atlanta, 1902. 600 pp. 8vo.

Olmstead, F. L.—A journey in the back country. N. Y., 1861. 492 pp. 12mo.

Olmstead, F. L.—A journey in the seaboard slave states. N. Y., 1856. 723 pp. 12mo.

Olmstead, F. L.—A journey through Texas. N. Y., 1857. 516 pp. 12mo.

Payne, Daniel A.—A treatise on domestic education. Cincin., 1885.

Pollard, Edward A.—Black diamonds gathered in the darkey homes of the South. N. Y., 1859. 12mo.

Richmond, Leigh—The Negro servant. Boston, 1814. 16 pp. 12mo.

Robertson, John—On the period of puberty in the Negro. Edinburgh, 1848. 8 pp. 8vo.

Schneider, W.—Die Kulturfaehigkeit des Negers. Frankfort, 1885.

Scruggs, L. A.—Women of distinction. Raleigh, 1893.

Shorter, Susan L.—Heroines of African Methodism. Xenia, O., 1891.

Smith, Mrs. Amanda—Autobiography of Amanda Smith. Chicago, 1893.

Stowe, Harriet Beecher—Uncle Tom's Cabin. 1852.

Stowe, Harriet Beecher—Dred. 577 pp.

Truth, Sojourner—Sojourner Truth's narrative. Boston, 1875.

United States Census—References to the Negro-American family:

   1890: Vol. on Population, Part 1: sex, conjugal condition.

   1890: Vol. on Farms and Homes: ownership.

   1900: Vol. II: Sex, conjugal condition, homes owned.

   Vol. V, VI: Farms and Crops: ownership.

   Special Reports: Statistical Atlas.

   Bulletins:

      No. 8: Negroes in the United States by W. F. Wilcox and W. E. B. DuBois. Wash. 1904. 333 pp.

      No. 22: Birth rate.

United States Department (Bureau) of Labor Bulletins:

   No. 10. Condition of the Negro in various cities.

No. 14. The Negroes of Farmville, Va.: A social study, by W. E. B. DuBois, Ph.D.
No. 22. The Negro in the black belt: Some social sketches, by W. E. B. DuBois, Ph.D.
No. 32. The Negroes of Sandy Spring, Md. A social study, by W. T. Thom, Ph.D.
No. 35. The Negro landholder of Georgia, by W. E. B. DuBois, Ph.D.
No. 37. The Negroes of Litwalton, Va.: A social study of the "Oyster Negro," by William Taylor Thom, Ph.D.
No. 38. The Negroes of Cinclaire Central Factory and Calumet Plantation, La., by J. Bradford Laws.
No. 48. The Negroes of Xenia, Ohio, by Richard R. Wright, Jr., B.D.
Webster, Noah, Jr.—Effects of slavery on morals and industry. Hartford, 1793.

Periodical Literature

American Economic Association Publications:
   Race traits and tendencies of the Negro. F. L. Hoffman. 11: 1.
American Journal of Sociology:
   Special assimilation. S. E. Simons. 7: 539-56.
Annals of the American Academy of Political Science:
   Settlement work among colored people. C. B. Chapin. 21: 336.
Arena:
   Impossibility of racial amalgamation. W. S. McCurley. 21: 446.
Atlantic:
   Negroes: What they are doing for themselves. S. J. Barrows. 67: 805.
   Mulatto factor in the race problem. A. H. Stone. 91: 658-62.
   Intensely human. T. W. Higginson. 93: 588.
Chambers Journal:
   Family life in Negro town. 17: 12.
Charities Review:
   Colored children in the District of Columbia. H. W. Lewis. 5: 94.
   The make-up of Negro city groups. (L. Brandt.) Charities 15: 7.
   The Negro home in New York. M. W. Ovington. 15: 25.
   Fresh-air work among colored children in New York. M. W. Ovington. 17: 115.
Chautauquan:
   Negroes in Washington, D. C. M. W. Noble. 14 : 183.
   Southern Negro women. O. R. Jefferson. 18 : 91.
   Social life of Southern Negroes. W. T. Hewetson. 26 : 295.
Educational Review:
   Social and industrial capacities of Negroes of the South. 45 : 383.
Lend a Hand:
   The new Negro woman. B. T. Washington. 15 : 254.
Nation:
   Social problem in Baltimore. 77 : 497-8.
National Monthly:
   Advance of Negro women in the South. L. S. Orrick. 21 : 172.
Outlook:
   Gain in the life of Negro women. Mrs. B. T. Washington. 76 : 271-4.
   The Negro woman and the South. E. H. Abbott. 77 : 165, 689.
   Social and moral decadence of Negro women. E. Tayleur. 76 : 266.
American Statistical Association:
   The Negroes of St. Louis. VIII. Lillian Brandt.
Hampton Negro Conference:
   Nine reports. 1897-1905.
Slater Fund, Proceedings and Occasional Papers of:
   No. 9. Hobson and Hopkins: Colored women of the South.

The Negro American Family

Part 1. Marriage

Section 1. The Scope of this Study. This essay is an attempt to study the family among Negro-Americans—its formation, its home, its economic organization and its daily life. Such a study is at once faced by a lamentable dearth of material. There is comparatively little exact information on many important points. Nevertheless there is perhaps enough to give a tentative outline which more exact research may later fill in. In each case an attempt has been made to connect present conditions with the African past. This is not because Negro-Americans are Africans, or can trace an unbroken social history from Africa, but because there is a distinct nexus between Africa and America which, though broken and perverted, is nevertheless not to be neglected by the careful student. It is, however, exceedingly difficult and puzzling to know just where to find the broken thread of African and American social history. Accurate scientific inquiry must trace the social history in the seventeenth and eighteenth centuries of such Negro tribes as furnished material for the American slave trade. This inquiry is unfortunately impossible. We do not know accurately which tribes are represented in America, and we have but chance pictures of Negro social conditions in those times. Assuming, however, that the condition of Negro tribes in the nineteenth century reflected much of their earlier conditions, and that central and west Africa furnished most of the slaves, some attempt has been made to picture in broad outline the social evolution of the Negro in his family relations. For past American conditions the chief printed sources of information must be sought for in the vast literature of slavery. It is difficult to get a clear picture of the family relations of slaves, between the Southern apologist and his picture of cabin life, with idyllic devotion and careless toil, and that of the abolitionist with his tale of family disruption and cruelty, adultery and illegitimate mulattoes. Between these pictures the student must steer carefully to find a reasonable statement of the average truth.

For present conditions there are, in printed sources, only the Census reports, the eight studies of the United States Bureau of Labor, the previous studies of this series, and a few other sources noted in the bibliography. To supplement this, sixteen students of the college department of Atlanta University have made a study of 32 families. These studies are based on first-hand knowledge, and are unusually accurate. They do not, however, represent properly the proportion of different types among the mass of Negroes. Most of the families studied belong to the upper half of the black population. Finally, to repeat, this study is but a sketch with no pretense toward attempting to exhaust a fruitful subject. The main cause of its limitation is lack of material.

Section 2.   Africa. The data relating to African family life is fragmentary, relating to different times and places, and has all degrees of authority, from that of hurried passing travellers to that of careful students of local conditions like Ellis. In generalizing, then, one can never be very certain of his ground. Ratzel gives this general summary:

Marriage is concluded by purchase. This feature appears, to the suppression of all others, among those tribes who accumulate capital by the ownership of herds. The practice of wife-purchase is found, however, also among agriculturists, and a man's wealth is measured by the number of his wives. Polygamy is usual wherever there are means to support it. We sometimes find the young bridegroom living in his father-in-law's establishment till the birth of his first child. Only the ruling chief of the district has the right to take any man's daughter without the usual payment, just as the chief's daughter may select any man, who thereby from a peasant becomes a chief. [1] Many pretty features are met with in connection with the courtship. Among the Madis the daughter first takes the mother into her confidence, and she informs the father. He fixes the price, and the couple obey absolutely, whether "yes" or "no" be the end of the negotiations. The marriage ceremonies are almost entirely secular. Oxen are slaughtered and there is singing and dancing. Among tribes where good manners prevail, during all this time the bride never leaves the hut which her father has built for her, but sits surrounded by her new brothers and sisters-in-law, who extol the charms of married life. At the same time she may partake of the marriage-feast, but without letting herself be seen. The following picture of a ceremony in greater style is given by Cameron. First the bridegroom performed a solo-dance for half an hour; and when this was over, the bride, a girl of nine of ten years old, was placed, with all the state that could be mustered up, on the shoulders of a woman, and borne to the dancing-place, while a second woman supported her from behind. The bridegroom gave her two or three tobacco-leaves and beads, which she threw among the dancers. Then the bridegroom and bride danced together for ten minutes with very unseemly gestures, after which he snatched her up, and disappeared with her into his own hut. The dancing, yelling, and drumming went on all night.

Three pictures of betrothal and marriage may be given; the first is among the Tshi-speaking people of the west coast, after Ellis:

When a girl arrives at the age of puberty, usually in the eleventh or twelfth year, she is taken to the water-side by others of her sex, and washed. At the same time an offering, consisting of boiled ham, mashed and mixed with palm-oil, is scattered upon the banks of the stream by the members of her family, who call upon the local gods, and inform them that the child has reached a marriageable age. In Cape Coast the girl is taken to the rock of the goddess Ichar-tsirew, and there washed. After the washing, a bracelet, consisting of one white bead, one black, and one gold, threaded on white cord, is put on the girl's wrist. These three beads in conjunction are termed

---

[1] Innumerable fairy tales point to the prevalence of this rule among primitive races.

abbum, and their being taken into use is a sign to the Sassur that its protecting care is no longer required. In the interior, on such occasions, girls are streaked with white.

The natives seem to judge of a girl's fitness for the married state rather by the development of the bosom, than by the fact of menstruation having commenced; for if it be not developed at the time of performing the ceremony, they wait until it becomes so before taking the next step, which is for the purpose for announcing her eligibility for marriage to the men of the community. The girl is carefully adorned with all the ornaments and finery in the possession of the family, and frequently with others borrowed for the occasion. A silk cloth, in place of the ordinary cotton one, extends from the waist to the ankle, and is carefully arranged over a neatly-made attohfo, a kind of bustle made of rolled cloth, on which infants are carried, and which is kept in position by being attached to the girdle of beads worn by all females. The silk cloth is kept in position by a silk handkerchief, which is tied over it, round the waist. The hair is covered with gold ornaments, necklets, armlets, and anklets of gold and aggry beads encircle her neck, arms, and ankles; and her bosom and the upper part of her body, which is left uncovered, is marked with white clay in very fine lines.

Of course a girl thus attired would be a daughter of a wealthy family, but even the poorest people contrive to make some show on these occasions. Thus decorated, the virgin is escorted through the streets by a number of young people of her own sex, one of whom usually carries an open umbrella over her; while the remainder sing a song in honor of her maidenhood, and inform the men that their friend is now of a marriageable age. As the natives of the Gold Coast are a far handsomer people than any other Negro race with which I am acquainted, and possess usually superb figures, and an erectness of carriage which is no doubt due to the habit of carrying articles on the head, there is frequently something very attractive about these young girls, who, in their constrained and graceful movements, seem overflowing with youth and health.

Shortly after a virgin has thus advertised herself, she is married. Perhaps she has previously been betrothed; but, if not, the public advertisement of her charms and marriageable condition seldom fails to produce suitors. If the girl's family agree to the match, the amount to be paid for her is handed over by the suitor, and he at once prepares a marriage festival. Rum, gin, and other intoxicants, together with tobacco and pipes, are sent by him to the family of the bride, for the distribution amongst their kinsmen and intimate friends, and in notification of the approaching happy event. Sometimes it is announced with greater pomp, by means of a long train of people, bearing provisions of all kinds upon their heads, who parade through the town, singing songs in honor of the occasion. These preliminaries having been completed, the bride is led to the house of the bridegroom, where a feast is prepared for the friends of both families, who keep up an orgie until long after the husband has retired to his wife. Next morning, if the husband be satisfied concerning his wife's purity, he sprinkles her over the head, shoulders, and breast with a thick powdering of dried clay; and sends her to parade the streets, accompanied by a number of young girls, who sing songs in her honor. The day following, her life as a married woman commences. Should the husband be in doubt as to the virtue of his bride, he may, under certain conditions, repudiate her. [1]

---

[1] Ellis: The Tshi-Speaking Peoples of the Gold Coast of West Africa, pp. 234-7.

The second extract is from Tylor and relates to the Zulus:

Many Zulu girls are mere flirts, but when a girl finds that her father and brothers are seeking some one to recommend to her as a husband, she suddenly disappears, having hied away to her lover's kraal. If the family approves, in a day or two a party of men appear at the home of the future bride, driving two or three cows. They all act in a friendly manner and the visitors go away leaving the cattle.

When the eventful day arrives the bride and a party of friends set out for the bridegroom's kraal, which, however, they will not enter until night, singing and dancing as they go. Early in the morning they go to the nearest stream, and about noon come up and begin a dance, the bridegroom's party looking on. When both sides have finished, a cow slaughtered by the bridegroom's party is given to the bride's party.

At night the girl wanders about the kraal, followed by the female relatives of the bridegroom. She is supposed to be trying to run away and the girls to be preventing her. The next day the bridegroom, his brothers, sisters and friends, take their seats in the cattlefold and the last part of the ceremony takes place.

The bride comes in with her party of girls, carrying in her hand a spear. One girl bears a dish of water and a calabash, and another some beads. Then, coming up singing and dancing, the bride throws the water over her husband. She also sprinkles her brothers- and sisters-in-law, striking the latter, as a symbol that from that time she assumes authority over the girls in her husband's household. After this she breaks the staff of the spear and makes a run for the gate of the kraal. If she is not stopped by a young man appointed for the purpose it is a great disgrace, and the husband has to pay a cow to get her back. The marriage rites are then finished.

The third picture is from among the Yoruba-speaking peoples of the west coast:

When a man desires to marry a girl his parents visit her parents and make proposals of marriage. If they are accepted the suiter sends a present of native cloths and kola-nuts, and after consulting a *babalawo*, a day is appointed for the wedding.

The marriage feast is held at the house of the parents of the bridegroom, and the bride is conducted there by a procession of women, who sing an epithalamium. The bride is put in bed by a female of the bridegroom's family, who remains concealed in the apartment till the bridegroom has joined the bride; after which she receives the "tokens of virginity," and coming out of the room displays them to the assembled company. She then carries them to the house of the parents of the bride, who never attend a daughter's wedding feast, and next morning they are hung on the fence for the edification of the public. In this abstention of the bride's parents from the feasting and merry-making, we perhaps find a lingering survival from marriage by capture. The producer of the "tokens" is selected from the family of the bridegroom to ensure that there is no deception, because the husband's family has no interest in falsifying the facts, while the wife's family has; but virginity in a bride is only of paramount importance when the girl has been betrothed in childhood. The marriage feast is continued on the next day.

It is not uncommon for newly wedded couples to visit some celebrated shrine and offer sacrifices together, a practice which, together with the fixing of the wedding day by a *babalawo*, shows an increasing disposition on the part of the priests to control or interfere with matters that are purely social and quite beyond the domain of religion.

Of betrothals among these people, Ellis says:

Girls of the better classes are almost always betrothed when mere children, frequently when infants, the husband *in futuro* being sometimes a grown man and sometimes a boy. Betrothal confers upon the male all the rights of marriage except consummation, which takes place shortly after the girl arrives at puberty. Since the early age of betrothal makes ante-betrothal unchastity a physical impossibility, the absence of the *primitiœ* when the marriage is consummated proves that the girl has been unchaste after betrothal, that is, after the husband *in futuro* had acquired an exclusive right to her person, and consequently he has a right to repudiate her. In such a case he may dismiss her, sending a few broken cowries to her mother, and the girl's family must return the amount paid for her, and the value of all presents made; but it is more usual to effect a compromise.

In this custom of infant child betrothal we probably find the key to that curious regard for ante-nuptial chastity found not only among the tribes of the Slave and Gold coasts, but also among many other civilized people in different parts of the world, and which certainly cannot be attributed to any feelings of delicacy, since husbands lend their wives without compunction, and often merely as a sign of friendliness. In West Africa virginity in a bride is not valued *per se*, but because it is a proof that the betrothal has not infringed the exclusive marital privileges of the husband *in futuro ;* and non-virginity in a bride is only a valid ground for repudiation when the girl has been betrothed at a tender age, for unbetrothed girls can bestow favors upon whom they please. Thus no man who marries a girl without early betrothal feels aggrieved if she should prove not to be a virgin, for until she is married or betrothed she is perfectly free, and mistress of her own actions.

A great deal of evidence might be adduced to show that the custom of child-betrothal leads to virginity being expected in a bride, and its absence being regarded as a just ground for repudiation.[1]

By such ceremony the African family is formed. Of the rights thus obtained Ellis says, referring to the Yorubas:

By marriage the man acquires the services of his wife in domestic affairs and an exclusive right to her embraces. That is, she may not have intercourse with other men without his knowledge and consent, but there is no objection to his waiving his right in favor of some other person, and men sometimes lend their wives to their guests or friends, though more frequently their concubines, for in a household there are both wives and concubines, the latter usually being slaves. Each wife has her own house, situated in the "compound" of the husband, and her own slaves and dependants. The wife first married is the head wife, and is charged with the preservation of order among the women. She is styled *Iyale* (Iya ile), "Mistress of the house." The junior wives are called *Iyawo* (Iya owo), "Trade-wives," or "Wives of commerce," probably because they sell in the markets.

Family relationships in Africa are usually traced through the female line, a survival of the older matriarchal family. From this there is gradual change toward the fuller patriarchal type. Ellis says of the Yorubas:

---

[1] Ellis: Yoruba-Speaking Peoples, &c., pp. 153-4, 174-188.

We find a great change from the customs of the other tribal groups of this family of nations, in the Yoruba manner of tracing descent and blood relationship; descent and consanguinity being no longer reckoned exclusively in the female line, with succession to chiefdom, office, and property from brother to brother, and then to sister's son; but in the male line as far as succession to dignities is concerned, and on both sides of the house for blood descent. The Yoruba family—using the word family as meaning a group of persons who are united by ties of blood—is thus quite a different organization to that which we found existing among the Tshi and Ewe tribes, where a family consists solely of persons who are connected by uterine ties, and in which, as two persons of the same blood may not marry, the father is never related by blood to his children, and is not considered as belonging to the family. In the Tshi and Ewe tribes the clan-name is the test of blood-relationship, and as property follows the laws of blood-descent, it ensues that property never goes out of the clan; for, with descent in the female line, a family is only a small circle of persons, all of whom bear the same clan-name, within the larger circle of the clan itself.

Among the Yoruba tribes the blood-tie between father and child has been recognized, and the result of this recognition has been the inevitable downfall of the clan-system, which is only possible so long as descent is traced solely on one side of the house, as may be readily shown. Since two persons of the same clan-name may, under the clan-system, never marry, it follows that husband and wife must be of different clans. Let us say that one is a Dog and the other a Leopard. The clan-name is extended to all who are of the same blood; therefore, directly the blood relationship between father and child comes to be acknowledged, the children of such a pair as we have supposed, instead of being, as heretofore, simply Leopards, would be Dog-Leopards, and would belong to two clans. They in turn might marry with persons similarly belonging to two clans, say Cat-Snakes, and the offsprings of these unions would belong to four clans. The clan-system thus becomes altogether unworkable, because, as the number of clans is limited and cannot be added to, if the clan name still remained the test of blood-relationship and a bar to marriage, the result in a few generations would be that no marriages would be possible. Consequently the clan-name ceases to be the test of consanguinity, kinship is traced in some other way, and the clan-system disappears; or, as appears to have been occasionally the case, descent is boldly transferred unto the male line, and marriage in the father's clan is prohibited, that of the mother being ignored. The Yorubas have adopted what appears to have been the usual course, and blood relationship is now traced both on the father's and on the mother's side, as far as it can be remembered, and marriage within the known circle of consanguinity is forbidden.

When we consider the extraordinary vitality the system of descent through mothers possesses, so long as it is undisturbed by foreign influence, it seems probable that the acknowledgment of a father's blood-relationship to his children was brought about by the intercourse of the northern Yorubas with the Mohammedan tribes of the interior. That the Yorubas formerly had the system of female descents is known by an ancient proverb, which says, "The esuo (gazelle), claiming relationship with the ekulu (a large antelope), says his mother was the daughter of an ekulu." If the male system of descents had been in vogue when this proverb was invented, the esuo would have been made to say that his father was the son of an ekulu. Moreover, in spite of legal succession from father to son, children by different mothers, but by the same father, are by many natives still scarcely considered true blood relations.

It is no doubt in consequence of the change from kinship in the female line to kinship on both sides of the house that the family has become, to a certain extent, disintegrated. On tho Gold Coast, where the uterine family is the only one known, the family is collectively responsible for the crimes or injuries to persons or property committed by any of its members, and each mcm ber is liable for a proportion of the compensation to be paid. Similarly, each member is entitled to share the compensation received for injury to the person or property of one of the members. The head of the family can, if the necessity should arise, pawn, and in some cases sell, a junior member; while, on the other hand, the junior membeos have a right to be fed and clothed by the head of the family. Among the Yoruba tribes there is no collective responsibility in a family, except that parents are responsible for crimes committed by their children; the head of the family cannot pawn the younger members, the latter cannot claim, as a matter of right, to be supported by him.

When a man dies his sons divide all his property between them. The daughters have no inheritance in their father's house, but they divide between them the property of their mother, for here, as with the Tshi, Ya and Ewe tribes, the property of a wife is always separate and distinct from that of her husband. If a man has no sons his property falls to his brothers, or, if he has no brothers, to his sisters From these laws of inheritance there is no departure, and a man cannot disinherit a legal heir. A man can, within certain limits, give away property during his lifetime, provided it is purely personal and not family property; but he cannot make a will, or any arrangemcnr for its disposal after death. Succession to property entails the obligation of defraying the debts of the deceased.[1]

Marriages may be dissolved by divorce. Ratzel says:

Dissolution of marriage is not only rendered difficult by the business thread which runs through the bànd of wedlock, but apart from this, it comes into relation with legal institutions. Divorce is rare among tribes who lead a simple life undisturbed; nor is adultery so frequent among them as among those who have accumulated capital, possess numerous slaves, and have come into closer contact with Arabs or Europeans. But even among these a marriage is not dissolved without formality, as might appear on superficial observation. Among the corrupt tribes of the Gold Coast, only princesses have the privilege of separating from their husbands without coming before a tribunal. Some white clay, handed over by the husband, serves as a sign of dismissal. Common people on the other hand have to appear before the chiefs, who decide the case. If they allow the wife her divorce, her family keep the purchase money, and the chiefs present the woman with a piece of white clay, with which she marks the trees of the principal street as a sign that she is no longer a wedded wife. If the divorce is granted to the man, the wife's family have to return the sum received. An interesting example of innovation in this domain is given by Broyon in his description of Unyamwesi, where he relates how the Arabs had formerly from selfish motives introduced a law that a woman who broke anything of theirs became their slave. The Negro women had turned this to their own advantage. In order to get free from an uncongenial husband, they would break something of the chief's, and become his slaves.

Among West Coast tribes, Ellis says of the Yorubas:

---

[1] Ellis, Yoruba speaking peoples, *loc. cit.*

Adultery can only be committed with a married woman. Adultery in a wife is punishable by death or divorce, but as a rule the injured husband beats his erring wife and recovers damages (*oje*) from the adulterer. In extreme cases, where the husband is a man of rank and discovers the couple in fact, they are sometimes both put to death.

If a husband should divorce his wife for adultery, he can claim the restitution of the money he paid for her, but not if he sends her away for any other cause. When a wife is divorced or put away, no matter for what cause, the husband retains any children she may have borne him; but if a child be too young to leave the mother, it does not come to the father till ten or twelve years of age. We see here a great change from the Tshi tribes, among whom under every circumstance of divorce or separation the mother retains her children, though she is liable to her husband for a certain sum to compensate him for what he has paid for their maintenance. There children belong exclusively to the mother, but here they belong to the father, and the innovation is undoubtedly due to the alteration in the system of descents.

When a husband systematically neglects his wife and refuses to perform his marital duties, she can call upon her family to assemble and hold a palaver; when, if the husband promises to amend his ways, he is given an opportunity of retrieving his character. If after all there is no improvement, or if he refuses to treat his wife properly, she is at liberty to leave him, and sometimes, if he is of inferior rank, the indignant family tie him up and flog him.[1]

Some idea of African family government may be had from a study of the Gold Coast by a native:

The Headman, as his name implies, is the Head of a village community, a ward in a township, or of a family. His position is important, inasmuch as he has directly to deal with the composite elements of the general bulk of the people.

It is the duty of the Head of a family to bring up the members thereof in the way they should go; and by "family" you must understand the entire lineal descendants of a head *materfamilias*, if I may coin a convenient phrase. It is expected of him by the State to bring up his charge in the knowledge of matters political and traditional. It is his work to train up his wards in the ways of loyalty and obedience to the powers that be. He is held responsible for the freaks of recalcitrant members of his family, and he is looked to to keep them within bounds, and to insist upon conformity on their part with the customs, laws, and traditional observances of the community. In early times he could send off to exile by sale a troublesome relative who would not observe the laws of the community.

It is a difficult task that he is set to, but in this matter he has all-powerful helpers in the female members of the family, who will be either the aunts, or the sisters, or the cousins, or the nieces of the Headman; and as their interests are identical with his in every particular, the good women spontaneously train up their children to implicit obedience to the Headman, whose rule in the family thus becomes a simple and an easy matter. "The hand that rocks the cradle rules the world." What a power for good in the Native State System would the mothers of the Gold Coast and Ashanti become by judicious training upon native lines!

The Headman is *par excellence* the judge of his family or ward. Not only is he called upon to settle domestic squabbles, but frequently he sits as judge

---

[1] Ellis, *loc. cit.*

over more serious matters arising between one member of the ward and another; and where he is a man of ability and influence, men from other wards bring him their disputes to settle. When he so settles disputes, he is entitled to a hearing fee, which, however, is not so much as would be payable in the regular Court of the King or Chief.

The Headman is naturally an important member of his "company," and often is a captain thereof. When he combines the two offices of Headman and Captain, he renders to the community a very important service. For, in times of war, where the members of the ward would not serve cordially under a stranger, they would in all cases face any danger with their own kinsman as their leader.

The Headman is always succeeded by his uterine brother, cousin, or nephew—the line of succession, that is to say, following the Customary Law.[1]

The reasons for polygamy in Africa are social and economic:

Lichtenstein remarks of the Kaffirs that "there are fewer men than women, on account of the numbers of the former that fall in their frequent wars. Thence comes polygamy, and the women being principally employed in all menial occupation." Now, without accepting the inference that polygamy is initiated by the loss of men in war, we may recognize the fact which Lichtenstein does not name, that where the death rate of males considerably exceeds that of females, plurality of wives becomes a means of maintaining population.

Since in every society the doings of the powerful and the wealthy furnish the standards of right and wrong, so that even the very words "noble" and "servile," originally expressive of social status, have come to be expressive of good and bad in conduct, it results that plurality of wives acquires, in places where it prevails, an ethical sanction. Associated with greatness, polygamy is thought praiseworthy; and, associated with poverty, monogamy is thought mean. Hence the reprobation with which, as we have seen, the one-wife system is regarded in polygamous communities.[2]

Their ideas of right and wrong differ in no respect from our own, except in their professed inability to see how it can be improper for a man to have more than one wife.[3]

Parental affection is strong in Africa. Sweinfurth says:

Parental affection is developed among the Dyoor much more decidedly than among the other tribes. A bond between mother and child which lasts for life is the measure of affection shown among the Dyoor.

Parents [among the Dinkas] do not desert their children, nor are brothers faithless to brothers, but are ever prompt to render whatever aid is possible. Family affection is at a high ebb among them.[4]

Ratzel says:

Agreeably to the natural relation the mother stands first among the chief influences affecting the children. From the Zulus to the Waganda, we find the mother the most influential counsellor at the court of ferocious sovereigns like Chaka or Mtesa; sometimes sisters take her place. Thus even with chiefs who possess wives by hundreds the bonds of blood are the strongest. The father is less closely bound up with the family. He is indeed

---

[1] C. Hayford: Gold Coast Native Institutions, pp. 76-78.
[2] Spencer: Sociology I, pp. 671, 669.   [3] Livingstone, Zambesi, p. 309.
[4] Sweinfurth: Heart of Africa.

the head, and is recognised as such; it is said too that the Negro is in general a lover of children and therefore a good father. But even here he often rules more by force than by love. Among the institutions recalling Roman law which Hubbe-Schleiden, an expert on that subject, found among the Mpongwes, he mentions their domestic or family life: "We find among them the *patria potestas* equally comprehensive and equally strict, if not carried into such abstraction. Wives, children, servants, are all in the power of the *pater-familias* or *oga*. He alone is quite free; a degree of independence to which a woman among the Mpongwes can never attain." Yet that woman, though often heavily burdened, is in herself in no small esteem among the Negroes is clear from the numerous Negro queens, from the medicine-women, from the participation in public meetings permitted to women by many Negro peoples.

Out of some such ideas of marriage and married life the Negro was brought to America as a slave. The ideas were not those of the more highly developed modern nations. But they were definite and practicable, and evolved through long social struggle; the Africans who had invented them lived up to them and were, as Sumner shows so well, as moral as modern men; i. e., as faithful to their *Mores*.

Section 3. Slavery. The first fact which students of slavery must remember is the great disproportion among the sexes in the imported slaves. The first demand of the plantations was able-bodied male field hands. Edwards speaks

. of the great disproportion of the sexes in the yearly importations from Africa. It has been shown from unquestionable authority, that one-third only were females. Thus, notwithstanding every allowance for the Creoles, or natives, who may reasonably be supposed to have increased according to the general laws of nature, there was in the year 1789, in Jamaica alone, an excess in its Negro population of 30,000 males.[1]

Traces of this can be found in the census reports of the United States, which unfortunately separate the sexes among Negroes only as far back as 1820. [See chart on opposite page.]

Such a social derangement through violence, war, and severe economic competition is an effective cause of wide sexual irregularity, even with a people living under their own carefully elaborated moral code; but with a transplanted and broken nation the effect was indeed disastrous. The first instinctive effort of the transplanted group was to restore the ancestral *Mores*. Edwards says:

It is a truth well known, that the practice of polygamy, which universally prevails in Africa, is also very generally adopted in the West Indies; and he who conceives that a remedy may be found for this by introducing among them the laws of marriage as established in Europe, is utterly ignorant of their manners, propensities, and superstitions. It is reckoned in Jamaica, on a moderate computation, that not less than ten thousand of such as as are called Head Negroes (artificers and others) possess from two to four wives. This partial appropriation of the women creates a still greater proportion of single men, and produces all the mischiefs which are necessarily attached to the system of polygamy.[2]

---

[1] Edwards: West Indies, II, pp. 175-176.   [2] Edwards, *loc. cit.*

Sex of Negro Population.

CENSUS OF	1820	1830	1840	1850	1860	1870	1880	1890	1900
MALES....	902,991	1,166,276	1,432,998	1,811,259	2,216,744	2,393,263	3,253,115	3,725,561	4,393,221
FEMALES .	873,820	1,132,366	1,440,760	1,827,549	2,225,086	2,486,746	3,327,678	3,744,479	4,447,568
FEMALES TO 1,000 MALES	967	969	1,005	1,008	1,003	1,039	1,020	1,005	1,012

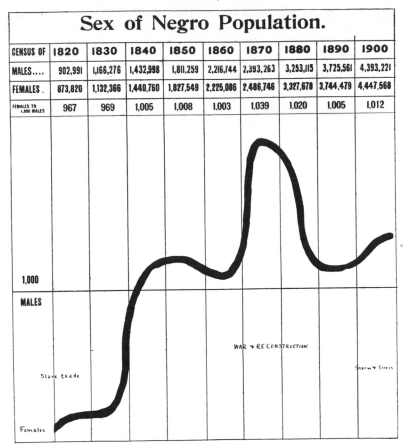

1,000

MALES

WAR + RE CONSTRUCTION

Storm + Stress

Slave trade

Females

Even under such conditions, however, traces of African family institutions persisted:

The men exacted a great show of respect from their families. I have often taken pleasure in watching a Negro carpenter at Guadaloupe when he ate his meals. His wife and children gathered around him, and served him with as much respect as the best drilled domestics served their masters; and if it was a fete day or Sunday, his sons-in-law and daughters did not fail to be present, and bring him some small gifts. They formed a circle about him, and conversed with him while he was eating. When he had finished, his pipe was brought to him, and then he bade them eat. They paid him their reverences and passed into another room, where they all ate together with their mother. I reproached him sometimes for his gravity, and cited him to the example of the governor, who ate every day with his wife; to which he replied that the governor was not the wiser for it; that he supposed the whites had their reasons, but they also had theirs; and if one would observe how proud and disobedient the white women were to their husbands, it would be admitted that the Negroes, who kept them always in respect and submission, are wiser and more experienced than the whites in this matter. The father says the Negroes were often very eloquent, and that they all spent much time in ridiculing the whites and their customs.[1]

When in any case these ancestral customs in family, clan, and tribal life could be preserved, revolt against slavery followed. This is the secret of the Haytian Revolution:

For many years there had been bands of runaway Negroes in the mountains under their chiefs. The earliest known of these chiefs was Polydorin, 1724; he was succeeded by Macandal, of whom the Negroes seemed to stand in superstitious dread. The great chief of these maroons at the time of the revolt was Jean Francais, and he was followed by another black called Biassou. One of their agents said to the French commissioner:

I am subject of three kings: of the King of Congo, master of all the blacks; of the King of France, who represents my father, and of the King of Spain, who represents my mother. If I passed into the service of the republic, I would perhaps be brought to make war against my brothers, the subjects of these three kings, to whom I have promised fidelity.[1]

When Christophe declared himself emperor,

Some writers have thought that this was purely an act of grandiloquence and mimicry on the part of Christophe, but it is truer to say that in it he was actuated by a clear insight into the needs and peculiarities of the people with whom he had to deal. There is nothing in the constitution which did not have its companion in Africa, where the organization of society was truly despotic, with elective-hereditary chiefs, royal families, polygamic marriages, councils, and regencies. But, undoubtedly, the form in which these things were put into writing was influenced very much by the language and systems which were known in Europe. Toussaint, Dessalines, and Christophe had ministers and others in their employ who were men educated in France.[2]

The government organized was founded on the ancient African clan:

But we have now to consider that which was the foundation of this system, which at once marks the insight of Toussaint and Christophe, and the African origin of their government. This is the system of agriculture. This system was adopted at the time of the reconciliation between the French and the blacks, under the advice of Toussaint. Some writers have called it an attempt to establish feudalism in the island, and the system does have a resemblance to it, but it also has many points of similarity with the organization of society in many African tribes. There was a division of the population into military and civil or laboring classes, the latter including both free and slave laborers. The territory was parcelled out to chiefs or lords, and the laborers were bound to the soil, which they were compelled to work under a rigorous system of inspection; for their support a part of the produce was set aside, the rest going to the chiefs, and for the support of the king or general government and the army. The army was kept under stern discipline, which made it possible to arm the free men and laborers; the women did a large part of the agricultural labor. Under Toussaint the administration of this labor system was committed to Dessalines, who carried it out with the

---

[1] Aimes; Journal of American Folk-Lore, p. 25.
[2] Aimes: Journal of American Folk-Lore, pp. 26-29.

utmost rigor, and it was afterward followed by Christophe in the same manner. The latter went so far as to import 4,000 Negroes from Africa, which he took means to bind to his person and form into a national guard, for patrolling the country. These regulations brought back for a time a large part of the prosperity which the island enjoyed.[1]

In Brazil "the Negroes brought their language and usages, which were found as original as on the coast of Africa." The patriarchal feeling remained very strong. The tribes seemed to be families, considering the prince as the father; the tie never died. "These princes are frequently seen sitting on a stone in the street, surrounded by a crowd who come to them for judgment. At the corner of the Travessa de S. Antonio, is a stone or post, for many years the throne of an African prince from Angola. . . . The natives of Congo elect a king among themselves, to whose decrees they submit in a similar manner."[2]

There is also a good account of an African funeral as practised in Jamaica. The person described above may be the Mumbo Jumbo of the Mandingoes, whose duty it was to execute public authority in the hall of the tribe upon the female offenders. The punishment was by whipping in public.[3]

In Lowndes county, Ala., in 1892, a description of a Negro country wedding tells of the chasing of the bride after the ceremony in a manner very similar to the Zulu ceremony described on a previous page. Careful research would doubtless reveal many other traces of the African family in America. They would, however, be traces only, for the effectiveness of the slave system meant the practically complete crushing out of the African clan and family life. No more complete method of reducing a barbarous people to subjection can be devised. The Indian could not be reduced to slavery because, being in his own home, he could not be permanently and effectively separated from his clan, and the clan fought for his freedom. Only in the isolated islands, then, was Indian slavery successful, and died out there for want of a slave trade. The essential features of Negro slavery in America was:

1. No legal marriage.
2. No legal family.
3. No legal control over children.

This is not inconsistent with much teaching of the morals of modern family life to slaves; the point is that the recognition of the black family from 1619 to 1863 was purely a matter of individual judgment or caprice on the part of the master. Public opinion and custom counted for much, and the law tended to recognize some *quasi* family rights— forbidding, for instance, in some cases the separation of mothers and very young infants—yet on the whole it is fair to say that while to some extent European family morals were taught the small select body of house servants and artisans, both by precept and example, the great body of field hands were raped of their own sex customs and provided with no binding new ones. Slavery gave the monogamic family ideal to slaves, but it compelled and desired only the most imperfect practice

---

[1] Aimes: Journal of American Folk-Lore, pp. 29-30.   [2] Ibid, p. 24.   [3] Ibid.

of its most ordinary morals. A few quotations will illustrate these conclusions:

A slave cannot even contract matrimony, the association which takes place among slaves and is called marriage being properly designated by the word contubernium, a relation which has no sanctity and to which no civil rights are attached.[1]

A slave has never maintained an action against the violator of his bed. A slave is not admonished for incontinence, or punished for fornication or adultery; never prosecuted for bigamy, or petty treason, for killing a husband being a slave, any more than admitted to an appeal for murder[2]

Slaves were not entitled to the conditions of matrimony, and therefore they had no relief in cases of adultery; nor were they the proper objects of cognation or affinity, but of quasi-cognation only.[3]

A necessary consequence of slavery is the absence of the marriage relation. No slave can commit bigamy, because the law knows no more of the marriage of slaves than of the marriage of brutes. A slave may, indeed, be formally married, but so far as legal rights and obligations are concerned it is an idle ceremony. . . . Of course these laws do not recognize the paternal relation as belonging to slaves. A slave has no more legal authority over his child than a cow has over her calf.[4]

In the slave-holding States, except in Louisiana, no law exists to prevent the violent separation of parents from their children, or even from each other.[5]

Slaves may be sold and transferred from one to another without any statutory restriction, as to the separation of parents and children, &c., except in the State of Louisiana.[6]

Slaves cannot marry without the consent of their masters, and then marriages do not produce any of the civil effects which result from such contract.[7]

A Brooklyn judge, in 1859, absolved a fugitive slave from bigamy,

Considering that marriage is a civil contract, which requires in the contracting parties the capacity to contract it, that slaves can not contract a regular marriage, and that the cohabitation confers no right on them or their children; (Laws of Alabama, Maryland, and North Carolina.)"[8]

Thus the right of (1) alienation, either by will or *inter vivos*, was both a cause and a consequence of the property conception. It included transfer of the whole or part of the subject's obligations, for valuable or other consideration, to other persons and places, even beyond the jurisdiction of the State.[9]

It was here that the incident of (3) separation of families, also involved in alienation, was made capable of extension until checked by law. This was finally done in 1801 by a decree of the Supreme Court of Appeals which declared that

"An equal division of slaves in number and value is not always possible and is sometimes improper when it cannot be exactly done without separating infant children from their mothers which humanity forbids and will not be

---

1 Stroud's Sketch of Slave Laws, p. 61.

2 Opinion of Daniel Dulaney, Esq., Attorney-General of Maryland. 1 Maryland Reports, pp. 561, 563.

3 Dr. Taylor's Elements of the Civil Law, p. 529.   4 Jay's Inquiry, p. 132.

5 Stroud's Sketch, p. 50.   6 Wheeler's Law of Slavery, p. 41.

7 Civil code of La., 1853.   8 Cochin: Results of Slavery, p. 392.

9 Ballagh: Slavery in Va., pp. 62-64.

countenanced in a court of equity, so that a compensation for the excess must in such cases be made and received in money." The right to separate husband and wife and larger children, however, still remained.[1]

The masters do not absolutely refuse to allow their Negroes to "marry off the place," but they discourage intercourse as much as possible between their Negroes and those of other plantations.

When a man and woman wish to live with each other they are required to ask leave of their master, and, unless there are some very obvious objections, this is always granted; a cabin is allotted to them, and presents are made of dresses and housekeeping articles. A marriage ceremony, in the same form as that used by free people, is conducted by the Negro preacher, and they are encouraged to make the occasion memorable and gratifying to all by general festivity. The master and mistress, if on the plantation, usually honor the wedding by their attendance; and, if they are favorite servants, it is held in the house and the ceremony performed by a white minister.[2]

Legal marriage is unknown among the slaves; they sometimes have a marriage form—generally, however, none at all. The pastor of the Presbyterian church in Huntsville had two families of slaves when I left there. One couple were married by a Negro preacher; the man was robbed of his wife a number of months afterwards, by her "owner." The other couple just "took up together," without any form of marriage. They are both members of churches—the man a Baptist deacon, sober and correct in his deportment. They have a large family of children—all children of concubinage—living in a minister's family.[3]

Persons who own plantations and yet live in cities, often take children from their parents as soon as they are weaned, and send them into the country; because they do not want the time of the mother taken up by attendance upon her own children, it being too valuable to the mistress. As a favor, she is, in some cases, permitted to go to see them once a year. So, on the other hand, if field slaves happen to have children of an age suitable to the convenience of the master, they are taken from their parents and brought to the city. Parents are almost never consulted as to the disposition to be made of their children; they have as little control over them as have domestic animals over the disposal of their young.[4]

One of my neighbors sold to a speculator a Negro boy about fourteen years old. It was more than his poor mother could bear. Her reason fled and she became a perfect maniac, and had to be kept in close confinement. She would occasionally get out and run off to the neighbors. On one of these occasions she came to my house. She was indeed a pitiable object. With tears rolling down her cheeks and her frame shaking with agony, she would cry out, "Don't you hear him? They are whipping him now, and he is calling for me!"[5]

Many advertisements like the following occurred:

Absconded from the subscriber, a negro man by the name of Wilson. He was born in the county of New Kent, and raised by a gentleman named Ratcliffe, and by him sold to a gentleman named Taylor, on whose farm he had a wife and several children. Mr. Taylor sold him to a Mr. Slater, who, in consequence of removing to Alabama, Wilson left; and when retaken was

---

[1] Ballagh: Slavery in Va., pp. 62-64.   [2] Olmsted: Seaboard Slave States, p. 79.

[3] Quoted from Rev. W. T. Allan, of Alabama, in Slavery as it is, p. 47.

[4] Quoted from Angelina Grimke Weld, of S, C., in Slavery as it is, pp. 56-57.

[5] Quoted from Rev. F. Hawley, of Conn., in Slavery as it is, p. 97.

sold, and afterwards purchased, by his present owner, from T. McCargo and Co., of Richmond.[1]

$20 Reward for my negro man Jim.—Jim is about 50 or 55 years of age. It is probable he will aim for Savannah, as he said he had children in that vicinity.   J. G. Owens.
Barnwell District, S. C.[2]

$100 reward will be given for my two fellows, Abram and Frank. Abram has a wife at Colonel Stewart's in Liberty county, and a sister in Savannah at Capt. Grovenstine's. Frank has a wife at Mr. Le Cont's, Liberty county; a mother at Thunderbolt, and a sister in Savannah.   Wm. Robarts.
Walthourville, 5th Jan., 1839. [3]

Runaway—My negro man, Frederick, about 20 years of age. He is no doubt near the plantation of G. W. Corprew, Esq., of Noxubbee county, Mississippi, as his wife belongs to that gentleman, and he followed her from my residence. The above reward will be paid to anyone who will confine him in jail and inform me of it at Athens, Ala.   Kerkman Lewis.
Athens, Ala. [4]

$50 Reward.—Ran away from the subscriber, a negro girl named Maria. She is of a copper color, between 13 and 14 years of age—bareheaded and barefooted. She is small for her age—very sprightly and very likely. She stated she was going to see her mother at Maysville.   Sanford Thomson. [5]

Committed to jail of Madison county, a negro woman who calls her name Fanny, and says she belongs to William Miller, of Mobile. She formerly belonged to John Givins, of this county, who now owns several of her children.   David Shropshire, Jailor. [6]

$50 Reward.—Ran away from the subscriber, his negro man Pauladore, commonly called Paul. I understand Gen. R. Y. Hayne has purchased his wife and children from H. L. Pinckney, Esq., and has them now on his plantation at Goose Creek, where, no doubt, the fellow is frequently lurking.
                                                                      T. Davis. [7]

The following is a standing advertisement in the Charleston (S. C.) papers:

120 Negroes for Sale.—The subscriber has just arrived from Petersburg, Virginia, with one hundred and twenty likely young negroes of both sexes and every description, which he offers for sale on the most reasonable terms.
The lot now on hand consist of plough boys, several likely and well-qualified house servants of both sexes, several women with children, small girls suitable for nurses, and several small boys without their mothers. Planters and traders are earnestly requested to give the subscriber a call previously to making purchases elsewhere, as he is enabled and will sell as cheap, or cheaper, than can be sold by any other person in the trade.
                                                                      Benjamin Davis. [7]

One description of a separation of a family by auction will suffice:

From these scenes I turn to another, which took place in front of the noble "Exchange Buildings" in the heart of the city [Charleston, S. C.]. On the left side of the step as you leave the main hall, immediately under the windows

---

[1] Richmond *Whig*, July 23, 1837.   [2] Savannah *Republican*, Sept. 3, 1838.
[3] Savannah *Georgian*, Jan. 17, 1839.   [4] *Southern Argus*, Oct. 31, 1837.
[5] Lexington (Ky,) *Observer and Reporter*, Sept. 28, 1838.
[6] Jackson (Tenn.) *Telegraph*, Sept. 14, 1838.
[7] All of these advertisements are quoted in American Slavery as it is, pp. 166, 167.

of that proud building, was a stage built, on which a mother with eight children were placed, and sold at auction. I watched their emotions closely, and saw their feelings were in accordance to human nature. The sale began with the eldest child, who, being struck off to the highest bidder, was taken from the stage or platform by the purchaser, and led to his wagon and stowed away, to be carried into the country; the second and third were also sold, and so on until seven of the children were torn from their mother, while her discernment told her they were to be separated probably forever, causing in that mother the most agonizing sobs and cries, in which the children seemed to share. The scene beggars description; suffice it to say, it was sufficient to cause tears from one at least "whose skin was not colored like their own," and I was not ashamed to give vent to them.[1]

The Presbyterian Synod of Kentucky said to the churches under their care, in 1835:

Brothers and sisters, parents and children, husbands and wives, are torn asunder, and permitted to see each other no more. These acts are daily occurring in the midst of us. The shrieks and agony often witnessed on such occasions proclaim, with a trumpet tongue, the iniquity of our system. There is not a neighborhood where these heart-rending scenes are not displayed. There is not a village or road that does not behold the sad procession of manacled outcasts, whose mournful countenances tell that they are exiled by force from all that their hearts hold dear.[2]

Irregularities involved not only slaves but masters. A sister of President James Madison said:

We Southern ladies are complimented with the names of wives; but we are only the mistresses of seraglios.[3]

As it relates to amalgamation, I can say, that I have been in respectable families (so-called), where I could distinguish the family resemblance in the slaves who waited upon the table. I once hired a slave who belonged to his own uncle. It is so common for the female slaves to have white children, that little or nothing is ever said about it. Very few inquiries are made as to who his father is.[4]

Amalgamation was common. There was scarce a family of slaves that had females of mature age where there were not some mulatto children.[5]

Further proof of this is found in the statistics of mulattoes; the United States Census found 405,751 mulattoes in 1850, and 588,352 in 1860. These figures were, moreover, without reasonable doubt below the truth, as "mulatto" was probably taken to mean a person, visibly at least half white. Probably one-fifth of the slaves in 1860 had distinct traces of white blood.

---

[1] Testimony of Silas Stone, of Hudson, N.Y., 1807, in American Slavery as it is, p. 167.
[2] Address, p. 12.   [3] Goodell, Slave Code, p. 111.
[4] Testimony of Rev. Francis Hawley, of Conn., resident fourteen years in Carolina; quoted in American Slavery as it is, p. 97,
[5] Testimony of Rev. Hiram White, of N. C., *Ibid.*, p. 51.

One further quotation from a Southern student of slavery will show the best possible picture of slavery and the family:

In custom the conception of the personality of the slave tended to supplant that of property, and was recognized to a far greater extent than accorded with the strict letter of the law. The slave was here viewed as a human being possessed of like emotions, desires and ambitions as free men and whites, many of which might be reasonably gratified without impairing any obligation of service due the master. Even practices in which damage was a possible or even certain result to the property element found a continuing sanction in custom. The common recognition of marital and family rights, for instance, was the outgrowth of a sentiment of humanity rather than of economic interest. That the ties so established were so accorded the full recognition they deserved is by no means true, but their existence, even when hampered, distinctly mitigated the conditions of slavery. So also slave-breeding, however unfortunate some of its applications may have been, had its origin in humanity. Its development prevented the introduction of the barbarous practice of the Spanish West Indies, where marriage was denied because it was cheaper to import slaves than to raise them. The abuse of breeding in the prostitution of females was not only lessened by heavy legal and social penalties, but met a natural check in the density of population, whose increase even the domestic trade, a necessity for the existence of slavery in the old States, was unable to prevent. The desire to procreate slaves when they were cheap was anything but economic in cause or effect. The damage to service in child-bearing and the cost of rearing the infant was viewed as involving a net loss, and as one of the burdens incident to a human slave system. It was upon this economic ground that conscientious anti-slavery slaveholders were wont to base their strongest arguments. Slave-breeding in the opprobrious use of the term probably had an extensive existence with a certain class, which was governed neither by economic nor moral considerations, but as this class is usually small in any civilized society and as historic evidence shows its limited extent in Virginia, the offense was kept within bounds by public sentiment and legal penalties.[1]

Section 4. Present Conjugal Condition. The United States Census has collected separate statistics of conjugal conditions among Negroes only in 1890 and 1900. The figures for whites and Negroes are:

---

[1] Ballagh: History of Slavery in Virginia, pp. 97, 98.

Negro Population at least 15 years of age and White Population at least 15 years of age, classified by Conjugal Condition, and per cent Distribution

CONJUGAL CONDITION	POPULATION AT LEAST 15 YEARS OF AGE				PER CENT DISTRIBUTION			
	Negro		White		Negro		White	
	1900	1890	1900	1890	1900	1890	1900	1890
Continental United States	5,323,591	4,265,271	44,291,680	35,989,102	100.0	100.0	100.0	100.0
Single	1,836,968	1,495,078	15,920,736	13,307,975	34.5	34.8	35.9	37.0
Married	2,866,703	2,362,947	24,775,625	19,917,695	53.9	55.0	55.9	55.4
Widowed	565,340	411,877	3,312,259	2,553,743	10.6	9.6	7.5	7.1
Divorced	33,059	15,900	164,498	104,954	0.6	0.4	0.4	0.3
Unknown	21,521	9,469	118,562	54,735	0.4	0.2	0.3	0.2

The conjugal condition by sex and age is as follows:

Per cent Distribution by Conjugal Condition, for the Negro Population by Sex and Age Periods: 1900 and 1890

AGE PERIOD	PER CENT OF NEGRO MALE POPULATION						PER CENT OF NEGRO FEMALE POPULATION					
	Single and unknown		Married		Widowed and divorced		Single and unknown		Married		Widowed and divorced	
	1900	1890	1900	1890	1900	1890	1900	1890	1900	1890	1900	1890
Continental United States: 15 years and over	39.8	40.0	54.0	55.5	6.2	4.5	30.1	30.2	53.7	54.6	16.2	15.2
15 to 19 years	98.2	99.1	1.7	0.9	0.1	(1)	83.3	85.0	15.7	14.4	1.0	0.6
20 to 24 years	64.9	65.8	33.8	33.4	1.3	0.8	39.9	38.3	54.6	57.3	5.5	4.4
25 to 29 years	33.4	30.3	63.3	67.3	3.3	2.4	20.8	17.7	69.4	73.7	9.8	8.6
30 to 34 years	21.4	18.7	73.7	77.7	4.9	3.6	13.1	11.8	73.1	76.4	13.8	11.8
35 to 44 years	13.5	11.5	79.1	82.9	7.4	5.6	8.2	7.5	72.3	74.7	19.5	17.8
45 to 54 years	7.4	6.5	81.4	85.1	11.2	8.4	5.3	5.0	65.3	66.3	29.4	28.7
55 to 64 years	5.5	5.2	78.6	83.2	15.9	11.6	4.4	4.4	51.9	51.6	43.7	44.0
65 years and over	5.0	5.7	69.6	74.4	25.4	19.9	4.8	4.7	28.9	29.0	66.3	66.3
Age unknown	46.7	43.8	47.4	50.8	5.9	5.4	30.1	27.7	45.6	47.7	24.3	24.6

1 Less than one-tenth of 1 per cent.

If we illustrate these percentages by a diagram we have this:

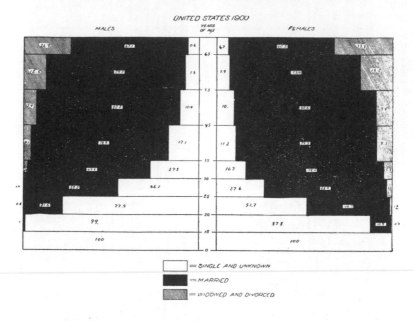

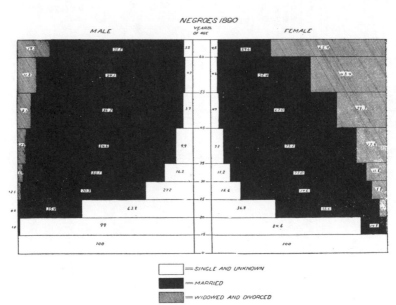

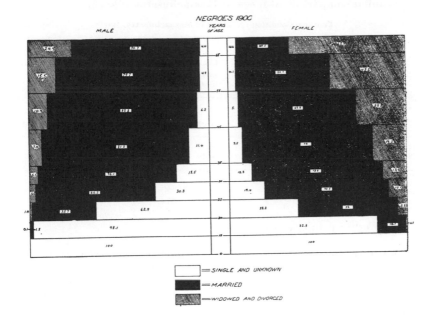

A comparison of the conjugal condition of the races in the South gives these figures:

Per cent Distribution of the Population at least 15 years of age, by Conjugal Condition, for Negro and White Races, by Sex, for the South: 1900 and 1890 [1]

CONJUGAL CONDITION	MALE				FEMALE			
	Negro		White		Negro		White	
	1900	1890	1900	1890	1900	1890	1900	1890
South Atlantic and South Central Divisions.Total	100.0	100.0	100.0	100.0	100.0	100.0	100 0	100.0
Single	38.4	39.1	39.6	40.7	29.5	29.8	30.7	31.5
Married	55.0	56.3	55.7	55 2	54.1	55 0	58.0	56.7
Widowed	5.7	4.2	4.2	3.7	15.3	14.5	10.8	11.4
Divorced	0.4	0.2	0.2	0.2	0.8	0.5	0.3	0.3
Unknown	0.5	0.2	0.3	0.2	0.3	0.2	0.2	0 1

[1] Negroes in the United States, 1904, p. 49.

A similar comparison of races in Massachusetts follows:

Conjugal Condition—Negroes of Massachusetts, 1900

MALES	Single	Married	Widowed	Divorced
Native white, native parents	52 84	41.75	4.34	0.34
Negro	57.12	38.07	3.89	0.23

FEMALES	Single	Married	Widowed	Divorced
Native white, native parents.........	50.64	37.27	11.33	0.47
Negro	50.99	35.71	12.42	0.37

34th Report, Mass. Bureau of Statistics.

Some other comparisons follow:

Conjugal Condition of the Negroes of Xenia, of Farmville, of Sandy Spring, and of the Population of the United States, by Sex

[The per cents for Xenia, for Farmville, and for Sandy Spring are computed from schedules: those for the United States are taken from the United States census reports for 1890 and 1900.]

CIVIL DIVISION	PER CENT OF MALES 20 YEARS OF AGE OR OVER				PER CENT OF FEMALES 20 YEARS OF AGE OR OVER			
	Single	Married	Widowed	Divorced	Single	Married	Widowed	Divorced
Xenia	22.06	65.28	8.50	a4.16	15.13	57.57	21.05	a6.25
Farmville	25.00	65.44	5.15	b4.41	17.30	55 03	23.90	b3.77
Sandy Spring.....	15.35	76.72	4.23	b3.70	14.36	69.31	13.86	b2.47
United States— Native whites, native parents—								
1890..............	28.54	66.08	4.74	c.64	18.75	67.88	12.79	c.58
1900..	28.3	65.4	5.4	c.9	19 6	66.9	12.7	c.8
Native whites, foreign parents—								
1890.....	48.82	48.65	2 25	c.28	34.83	58.76	6.02	c.39
1900.............	43.7	52.9	2.9	c.5	31.9	60.4	7.1	c.6
Foreign whites—								
1890.............	28.06	65.93	5 51	c.50	15 39	68.05	16 1	c.35
1900	25.6	67.3	6.5	c.6	14.7	68.0	16.9	c.4
Negroes—								
1890.........	25.01	69 02	5.40	c.57	15.71	65.02	18.41	c.86
1900....	26.4	65.5	7.0	cl.1	17.4	62.5	18.8	cl.3
Total United States								
1890.............	30.95	63.83	4.65	c.57	19.92	66.35	13 19	c.54
1900.............	30 1	63.6	5.4	c.9	20.5	65.5	13 2	c.8

a Including separated.   b Separated   c Including unknown.

Conjugal Condition of the Negroes of Xenia, of Farmville, of Sandy Spring, and of the Populations of Various Foreign Countries, by Sex [1]

[The per cents for Xenia, Farmville, and Sandy Spring, are computed from schedules; those for foreign are taken from Mayo-Smith's Statistics and Sociology. The figures for divorced are not shown for foreign countries.]

CIVIL DIVISION	PER CENT OF MALES 15 YEARS OF AGE OR OVER			PER CENT OF FEMALES 15 YEARS OF AGE OR OVER		
	Single	Married	Widowed	Single	Married	Widowed
Xenia	31.6	57.4	a7.4	25.1	51.0	b18.3
Farmville	41.9	50.7	c4 0	32.1	45.4	d19.4
Sandy Spring	32.5	61.2	e3.5	25 1	60.9	f 11.9
France	36.0	56.5	7.5	30.0	55.3	14.7
Germany	40.9	53.7	5.3	36.5	50.8	12.4
Great Britain	39.5	54.9	5.6	37.3	50.9	11.8
Hungary	31.5	63.7	4.7	22.0	62.8	15.0
Ireland	49.3	44.8	5.9	43.5	42 1	14.4
Italy	40.9	53.1	6.0	33.2	53.2	13.6

a Also 3.1 per cent separated and 0.5 per cent divorced.
b Also 4.6 per cent separated and 1 per cent divorced.
c Also 3.4 per cent separated.   d Also 3.1 per cent separated.
e Also 2.9 per cent separated.   f Also 2.1 per cent separated.

[1] The Negroes of Xenia, Ohio, p. 1018.

In these statistics we have striking evidence of the needs of the Negro American home. The broken families indicated by the abnormal number of widowed and separated, and the late age of marriage, show sexual irregularity and economic pressure. These things all go to prove not the disintegration of Negro family life but the distance which integration has gone and has yet to go. Fifty years ago "family" statistics of nine-tenths of the Negroes would have been impossible. Twenty-five years ago they would have been far worse than today, and while there is no perceptible change of moment in the statistics of 1890 and 1900, most of the tendencies are in the right direction, and a healthier home life is in prospect.

Section 5. The Size of the Family. The birth rate of the Negro American is not accurately known. It probably runs from 27 per thousand, as indicated by statistics in Massachusetts, to a birth rate of over 40 per thousand in the rural districts of the South, where the race is still massed. A table of fecundity on a sugar plantation is given as follows:

Children of each female	Females 15 to 19 years of age			Females 20 to 29 years of age			Females 30 to 39 years of age			Females 40 yrs. of age or over			Females age not reported		
	Females	Children	Children living	Females	Children	Children living	Females	Children	Children living	Females	Children	Children living	Females	Children	Children living
None..	11	....	..	7	....	....	1	....	....	1	....	....	2	....	....
1......	2	2	1	11	11	9	....	....	....	....	....	....	1	1	..
2......	4	8	5	6	12	9	1	2	2	....	....	....	2	4	2
3......	....	....	....	4	12	6	....	....	....	....	....	....	2	6	3
4......	....	....	....	2	8	6	....	....	....	....	....	....	2	8	5
5......	....	....	....	1	5	2	....	....	....	1	5	5	3	15	6
6......	....	....	....	1	6	6	1	6	3	....	....	....	....	....	....
7......	....	....	....	....	....	....	....	....	....	....	....	....	1	7	5
8......	....	....	....	....	....	....	....	....	....	1	8	3	1	8	7
9......	....	....	....	....	....	....	1	9	5	....	....	....	....	....	....
10.....	....	....	....	....	....	....	....	....	....	....	....	....	3	30	15
11.....	....	....	....	....	....	....	....	....	....	1	11	10	....	....	....
12.....	....	....	....	....	....	....	....	....	....	1	12	10	1	12	1
13.....	....	....	....	....	....	....	....	....	....	....	....	....	1	13	5
14.....	....	....	....	....	....	....	....	....	....	....	....	....	....	....	....
15.....	....	....	....	....	....	....	....	....	....	1	15	6	....	....	....
16.....	....	....	....	....	....	....	....	....	....	2	32	17	....	....	....

Of these 80 women 58 have had children. These 58 have had 268 children, or an average of 4.62 per woman, of which 154, or 57.5 per cent are still living. In 34 cases out of the 58 the first child was still living.[1]

[1] U. S. Bulletin of the Bureau of Labor 38:103.

Comparing the number of women of child-bearing age we may get some measure of fecundity, although a distorted one on account of the large infant mortality among Negroes:

Number of children under 5 years of age to 1,000 females 15 to 44 years of age for the Continental United States:[2]

	Total	White	[3] Colored	Excess of Colored
1900............	474	465	543	78
1890............	485	473	574	101
1880............	559	537	706	169
1870............	572	562	641	79
1860............	634	627	675	48
1850............	626	613	694	81
1840[1]........	....	744	....	....
1830[1]........	....	781	....	....

[1] Women 15 to 49 years of age.
[2] Twelfth Census, Bulletin No. 22.
[3] Negro, Indian and Mongolian.

Number and per cent of children under 10 and 5 years of age, respectively, in the Negro, Indian and Mongolian population, and decrease in per cent during the preceding ten years, 1890-1900[1]

CENSUS	Per cent of Negro, Indian and Mongolian population		DECREASE IN PER CENT			
			Under 10 years of age during—		Under 5 years of age during—	
	Under 10 yrs. of age	*Under 5 years of age*	*Preceding 10 years*	*Preceding 20 years*	*Preceding 10 years*	*Preceding 20 years*
Continental United States.						
1900	27.1	13.6	1.1	4.8	0.2	2.9
1890	.28.2	13.8	3.7	2 3.8	2.7	2 0.5
1880	31.9	16.5	2 7.5	2 1.6	2 3.2	2 0.5
1870	24.4	13.3	5.9	6 9	2.7	2.2
1860	30.3	16.0	1.0	2.9	0.5	
1850	31.3	16.5	1.9	2.9		
1840	33.2		1.0			
1830	34.2					

[1] Twelfth Census, Bulletin No. 22.
[2] Increase.

Number and per cent of children under 10 and 5 years of age, respectively, in the white population, and decrease in per cent during 10 years: 1800 to 1900 [1]

CENSUS	Per cent of white population		DECREASE IN PER CENT			
			Under 10 years of age during—		Under 5 years of age during—	
	Under 10 yrs. of age	*Under 5 years of age*	*Preceding 10 years*	*Preceding 20 years*	*Preceding 10 years*	*Preceding 20 years*
Continental United States.						
1900	23.3	11.9	0.4	2.6	0.1	1.5
1890	23.7	12.0	2.2	2.7	1.4	2.1
1880	25.9	13.4	0.5	2.5	0.7	1.9
1870	26.4	14.1	2.0	2.2	1.2	0.7
1860	28.4	15.3	0.2	3.2	0.5	2.1
1850	28.6	14 8	3.0	3.9	2.6	3.2
1840	31.6	17.4	0.9	1.8	0.6	
1830	32.5	18.0	0.9	1.9		
1820	33.4		1.0	1.0		
1810	34 4					
1800	34.4					

Number of children under 5 years of age to 1,000 females 15 to 44 years of age in cities having at least 25,000 inhabitants and in smaller cities or country districts by main geographic divisions, and the ratio of those numbers to the number for the whole division taken as 100: 1900 [1]

DIVISION OR RACE	Number of children under 5 years of age to 1,000 females 15-44 years of age: 1900			Ratio to No. in whole division taken as 100.		Differ-ence in ratio
	Total	In cities hav-ing at least 25,000 inhab-itants	In smaller cities or country dis-tricts	In cities hav-ing at least 25,000 inhab-itants	In smaller cities or country dis-tricts	
Total population:						
Continental United States........	518	390	572	75.3	110 4	35.1
White population:						
Continental United States........	508	399	559	78.5	110.0	31.5
Negro, Indian and Mongolian popu-lations:						
Continental United States........	585	260	651	44.4	111.3	66.9

1 Twelfth Census, Bulletin No. 22.

From this we may conclude:

1. The Negro birth rate exceeds and has always exceeded the white birth rate.

2. The Negro birth rate probably decreased largely until 1870; then it possibly increased somewhat and afterward rapidly decreased.

3. The Negro birth rate in the country districts is high. In the city it is low because of the immigrant character of the population.

Infant mortality among Negroes is very large but decreasing:

Death rate of children under 1 year of age

COLOR		REGISTRATION RECORD					
		Total	Regis-tra-tion cities	Registration States			Registra-tion cities in other States
				Total	Cities	Rural	
White	1890..	249.38	278.19	241.40	257.22	137.63	260.67
	1900..	158.0	171.1	156.0	180.4	116.0	161.4
Colored...	1890..	494.27	525.13	457.83	579.77	204.49	509.61
	1900..	371.5	387.0	343.8	397.2	218.9	383.8

These records are but partial, and refer to city Negroes chiefly. The Atlanta University study of 1897 found 1137 city families containing 4742 individuals, composed as follows:

Heads of families	1,974	41.63%
Children	2,167	45.70%
Grandparents	100	2 11%
Uncles and aunts ....,........	138	2.91%
Grandchildren	113	2 38%
Nephews and nieces............................. ..	70	1.47%
Other relatives......................................	37	.78%
Boarders and lodgers.................	143	3.02%
	4,742	100.00%

The size of the Negro family is unknown. There were; in 1900, 1,833,854 private Negro families in the United States. Such private families represent 98 per cent of the total population. Assuming that they represent 98 per cent of the Negro population—and this is pure assumption—they would contain 8,663,973 or 4.6 persons to a family, a figure probably lower than the truth. Some data bearing upon the size of the family may be found in the bulletins of the United States Bureau of Labor; by combining four tables there we have this:

Negro Families by Size in Four Towns

Members	INCLUDING ALL CHILDREN BORN		INCLUDING ALL CHILDREN LIVING		INCLUDING THE PRESENT CENSUS-FAMILY GROUP	
	No. of Families	No. of Persons	Families	Persons	Families	Persons
1	22	22	54	54	78	78
2	108	216	209	418	191	382
3	109	327	189	567	194	582
4	109	436	152	608	154	616
5	76	380	110	550	125	625
6	59	354	90	540	91	546
7	49	343	75	525	56	392
8	58	464	70	560	45	360
9	37	333	32	288	36	324
10	45	450	24	240	19	190
11	37	407	19	209	14	154
12	24	288	10	120	2	24
13	27	351	8	104	2	26
14	26	364	2	28	2	28
15	13	195	2	30	1	15
16	7	112	....	....		
17	6	102	1	17		
18	3	54				
19	1	19				
20	1	20				
21	1	21				
22	1	22				
24	1	24				
25	1	25				
Total.. 821		5,329	1,047	4,858	1,010	4,342
Average		6.49		4.64		4.3

A table of Negro families by size in four small towns, a district in the black belt, and for all races in the United States, 1890 and 1900, follows in percentages:

Members in family	Georgia Country district Negroes	Ohio Town Negroes	Maryland Town Negroes	Virginia Town Negroes	United States Total families	
					1890	1900
1	9.09	10 18	5.45	4.96	3.63	5.00
2–6	73.95	80.84	63.64	72.90	73.33	74.70
7–10	15.33	8.18	26.06	19.47	20.97	18.10
11 and over	1.63	.80	4.85	2.67	2.07	2.20
Total.....	100.00%	100.00%	100.00%	100.00%	100.0.%	100.00%

The sources of error in these statistics are: the broken families among Negroes, which for economic and social reasons increase the apparent families of one and two, and the absence of large hotel and institution families in the Negro group.

The economic condition of the Negro is influencing the sex morals of the race in two ways: First, present low wages and a rising economic standard is postponing marriage to an age dangerously late for a folk in the Negro's present moral development.   Secondly, present economic demand draws the Negro women to the city and keeps the men in the country, causing a dangerous disproportion of the sexes, as Mr. Kelly Miller has pointed out. [1]

The enormous preponderance of colored females over males, especially in our large cities, is a persistent and aggravating factor which has almost wholly escaped the attention of our sociological philosophers.   The census of 1900 gives 4,447,568 Negro females against 4,393,221 Negro males, leaving an excess of 54,347 of the gentler sex in the United States.   This gives a residue of thirteen left-over women to each thousand of the male population.   But this is utterly insignificant when compared with the excesses revealed by the statistics of the large cities.   The predominance of the female element is perhaps the most striking phenomenon of the urban Negro population.

The subjoined figures will show this excess in fifteen cities of more than 20,000 Negroes.

Excess of Colored Females, 1900

CITY	Females	Males	Excess of females	No. females to each 100 males
Washington........	48,354	38,348	10,006	126
Baltimore	44,195	35,063	9,132	126
New Orleans.......	42,585	35,129	7,456	121
Philadelphia	33,673	28,940	4,733	116
New York..........	33,534	27,132	6,402	124
Memphis..	25,359	24,551	808	103
Louisville	20,297	18,842	1,455	108
Atlanta	20,921	14,806	6,115	143
St. Louis	18,020	17,496	524	103
Richmond	17,878	14,354	3,524	123
Charleston	17,552	13,970	3,582	125
Nashville	16,775	13,269	3,506	125
Chicago	14,077	16,073	*1,996	88
Savannah	15,344	12,746	2,598	120
Norfolk	10,738	9,492	1,246	113
Total	379,312	320,221	59,091	118

* Surplus Males.

These cities, with an aggregate Negro population of 699,533, show a female excess of 59,091.   Chicago is the only city where the females are not in the majority, which is doubtless due to the fact that a new city is always first settled by the men, who pave the way for a subsequent female influx.   If every Negro male in these cities should be assigned a helpmeet there would still remain eighteen left-over females for every one hundred couples.   In Atlanta this unfortunate residue reaches the startling proportion of 43 out of a hundred.   Washington and Baltimore have respectively 10,006 and 9,132 hopeless females, for whom there are neither present nor prospective husbands.   No such astounding disproportion prevails anywhere among the white race.   The surplus women who give Mrs. Gilman such anxious solicitude scarcely exceed one in a hundred even in such man-forsaken cities as New York and Boston.   If then the evil be a threatening one among the white race with such an insignificant surplus, what must be said of its multiplied enormity when we turn to the situation of the black race, where the excess is more than one-sixth of the male sex?   Preponderance of one sex

[1] Miller: Race Adjustment, pp. 169-170.

over the other forebodes nothing but evil to society. The maladjustment of economic and social conditions upsets the scale where nature intended a balance. The argument of Mrs. Gilman is as correct as it is courageous: "Where women preponderate in large numbers," she says, "there is a proportionate increase in immorality, because women are cheap; where men preponderate in large numbers there is also immorality because women are dear."

Section 6. Sexual Morals. Without doubt the point where the Negro American is furthest behind modern civilization is in his sexual *mores* This does not mean that he is more criminal in this respect than his neighbors. Probably he is not. It does mean that he is more primitive, less civilized, in this respect than his surroundings demand, and that thus his family life is less efficient for its onerous social duties, his womanhood less protected, his children more poorly trained. All this, however, is to be expected. This is what slavery meant, and no amount of kindliness in individual owners could save the system from its deadly work of disintegrating the ancient Negro home and putting but a poor substitute in its place. The point is however, now, what has been the effect of emancipation on the *mores* of the Negro family.

The great and most patent fact has been differentiation: the emergence from the mass, of successive classes with higher and higher sexual morals. Of this, unfortunately, there is no adequate measurement. Subjoined are the figures of total and illegitimate births in Washington, D. C.:

Washington, D. C.

Year	Total Negro Births Reported	Percentage of Illegitimate Births Reported	Negro Population
1870			43,404
1879	1,659	18.8	
1880	1,793	18.1	59,596
1881	1,536	18.6	
1882	1,592	19.7	
1883	1,397	21.1	
1884	1,482	20.2	
1885	1,500	22.2	
1886	1,584	22.9	
1887	1,761	19.5	
1888	1,756	22.3	
1889	1,804	26.2	
1890	1,848	26.4	75,572
1891	1,891	25.0	
1892	1,910	27.1	
1893	1,963	26.7	
1894	2,001	25.7	
1895	1,942	26.8	
1896	1,842	27.0	
1897	1,875	25.9	
1898	2,043	25.1	
1899	1,737	27.6	
1900	1,867	25.5	86,702
1901	1,735	24.3	
1902	1,846	24.7	
1903	1,817	22.7	
1904	2,224	24.6	
1905	2,275	24.7	
1906	2,199	22.1	
1907	2,322	21.4	

These figures are very imperfect. The total Negro births in Washington are quite unknown, being only partially reported; the illegitimate birth reports come from hospitals and city physicians, and it is impossible to say whether they are as far below the truth as the total birth reports, or not. Comparing this reported illegitimacy with other localities, we have:

Massachusetts, 1856-91........................ . 13   per 1,000
Belgium, 1900...... ... . 74.5 "   "
Austria, 1881-95............................ ,... 147.7 "   "
Negroes in Washington, 1907................ 214   "   "
Large cities of Bavaria...... 268   "   "
Salzburg (Province, Austria)................ 272   "   "
Kaernthen (Province, Austria) 435   "   "
Jamaica, 1897.......... 611   "   "

Compared with the population the apparent illegitimate birth-rate of Washington Negroes was:

1880 .... 5.4 per 1,000 births.
1890 .... 6.4 "   "   "
1900 .... 5.5 "   "   "

While these figures are a very doubtful basis of exact judgment, they point without doubt to wide-spread sexual irregularity. But this irregularity belongs to the undifferentiated mass: some of them decent people, but behind civilization by training and instinct. Above these and out of these are continually rising, however, classes who must not be confounded with them. Of the raising of the sex *mores* of the Negro by these classes the fact is clear and unequivocal: they have raised them and are raising them. There is more female purity, more male continence, and a healthier home life today than ever before among Negroes in America. The testimony supporting this is overwhelming.

A Baltimore slum-worker says:

My work in a large city has covered a period of nearly fourteen years. Thousands of girls have passed under my observation; many of them have already begun their careers, several are teachers in the Baltimore city school system, and are doing their part in life. The home life of all these individuals was not of the best kind, but with this much to be deplored in their condition I believe the per cent of immorality to be low.

At this writing, my work is in a veritable slum. Degradation of every kind is rampant. In the next block above us houses of ill fame line both sides of the street. The occupants of these places are white. In a street parallel to this are houses occupied by both white and colored. Many of our children come from these places. The greatest per cent of degradation I have ever witnessed exists here. What the harvest shall be only Providence knows; but, taken all in all, I believe that 8 per cent would cover the mathematical reckoning as far as figures may be taken indicative of conditions of society.

The principal of Hampton writes:

I have had an experience of twenty-one years with colored people, during which time I have been intimately acquainted with a large number of them at Hampton Institute. I have gone into their homes and have had perhaps as much opportunity as most any white man for knowing intimately their life.

I am glad to bear witness to my knowledge of the clean, pure lives of a large number whom I have known. I have often said, what I believe to be true, that it would be hard to find in any white institution in the North the freedom from low talk and impure life as is to be found at Hampton, where 1,000 young people of two races are brought together. The colored race is not degraded. Many of the young people who came to me years ago had no conception of the wrong of certain lines of conduct and who, since they have gained that knowledge, have lived up to what they know. I have seen young people coming from one-room cabins, where morality seems well nigh impossible, who sloughed that old life, and have made good use of the cleared knowledge which they have gained at Hampton.

I have often said that my own boy would be less likely to hear low talk here than in most Northern institutions for the whites. My own judgment in the matter is confirmed in the experience of others. For a number of weeks an English gentleman, who is making a most careful study of the race, has been staying at the school. He has mingled with the boys in their play, in their workshops and in their dormitories, and he confirms my impression and that of my disciplinarian, who himself is a colored man, living in close contact with the young people of the school.

A Southern white woman of Virginia says:

It was the most sorrowful part of slavery that there could be no legal marriage for the slaves, no protection for the virtue of women. Even now there are no laws to protect the colored girl, such as have always existed for her white sisters. In discussing any question that relates to the Negroes, regard should be given to the rapid formation of classes among them. There is a respectable class, and this class is increasing, where married parents live virtuous lives, guard the sanctity of their homes, and strive to bring up their children in the path of virtue.

The principal of a large Negro girls' school writes:

When a Southern white man told my predecessor that all Negro women were impure his reply was, "I suppose you know, I don't." I have seen Negro women who I have good reason to believe are living virtuous lives under conditions of trial such as our virtuous white women as a class know nothing about. Through my sainted wife I know of examples of colored women whose firmness in resisting temptation makes them worthy to represent any race.

Of those same women I can speak without reserve on all these points. Their modesty and genuine worth are conceded by white, as well as colored; their marital fidelity is above question. Many of them have passed through the stage of courtship and entered married life under my own personal observation, and even the most fastidious could find nothing but what was proper and pure. We have Negro women around us here who are for duty's sake remaining single, though sought by the very best of our young men.

One of the most touching things to come under my notice has been the many mothers who come to beg us to take their girls, saying, "I know I am not what I ought to be, but I don't want her to be like me." We could fill Scotia over and over again every year with girls whose parents want them in a safe place, so that they may grow into good women. In these nearly fifteen years we have not had the basis of a scandal involving a member of this school inside of our grounds, and we believe that our record as a school, both for honesty and purity, will bear comparison with the female schools generally.

It would not be wise however in our zeal to refute the false assertions in Mr. Thomas's book to overlook the fact that many of them are in a measure true. We cannot do our duty to the Negro while we keep ourselves ignorant of his true condition, and no Thomas or any other man can overdraw the picture of the morals of the uncared-for masses of the Negro in the South, not because they are Negroes, but because they are uncared for.

From the black belt of Alabama a white woman writes:

I have been for thirteen years working among, for and with, Negroes. The first four years' work and life were at Hampton, and I will say nothing much about that, for the Hampton teachers have a better and larger knowledge of students and graduates than I have. I would say, however, that it was because I saw such positive proof of high-mindedness and beauty of character among the Negroes and because we saw, year after year, the coming in of earnest, self-respecting boys and girls, that Miss Dillingham and I felt we must go out and show the way of light to some who lived in dark places and had never had a chance to know what really was the right in any part of life.

It was because we had firm belief in the Negro that we came, and each year but carries deeper conviction that we were then right. We came here (Calhoun) in 1892. During the nine years since I have been constantly filled with admiration of the people who, with but little to work for and with constant and deep temptations, are able to withstand the temptation and struggle on to get a precarious living, in the strength of high convictions and deep and ever-increasing self-respect. When we came we felt that the free living represented sin, but in a very few months we believed it represented the natural life of a group of people who had never been shown or taught life on a higher plane. After a few months of life among them they took hold of what little we could do and began to reconstruct their lives. Of course we found many whom we then believed, and still feel, were leading pure, good lives, merely from inborn instincts.

In regard to the morality of our girls at school, I do not want to omit a statement which, knowing the community, seems to be almost miraculous. In the last twelve years only two girls who have ever been in our school have been known to go wrong. One was of mixed Indian, Negro and white blood. She has been brought up in a house of vice and brutality, has heard bad language and low talk and seen low life and brutal living ever since babyhood; has been brutally beaten and knocked about, and it was small wonder that she died last week in sin of every sort. The other, a girl of sixteen, is feeble-minded, so that after trying to teach her for four years we found she knew but little more than when she started in school. These two cases had not been in school for several years, and are the only ones out of many hundreds who have attended who have gone astray.

Our boys and young men from sixteen to twenty-five years of age are upright and self-respecting in the majority of cases. Of course, in this community, one of the worst in the whole South, when we came here we found all kinds, good and bad, but there is daily evidence of desire and strivings for high standards of living, and victories over self that are marvelous.

From the black belt of Mississippi a teacher writes:

The trend and tendency are very decidedly towards better things in the moral life, and it has been in existence long enough to have molded a very considerable portion of the Negro people to a nobler life than Thomas seems to know about. The more I study the matter the more I am convinced that with all the evils resultant from slavery and from the sudden freedom, the indictments brought against the race now have never been fully true, and it is less true now than formerly.

I have had fourteen years of experience and observation in teaching in the heart of the black belt of Mississippi.

There is an increasing number of men who have a high regard for chaste womanhood, who are earnest in the desire to protect women from impurity of every kind. They welcome and forward such agencies; for the promotion of purity is the White Cross with its pledge of reverence for women.

The number of girls who would resent solicitations to evil is not a small one and among those who have been carefully reared, who have had something of moral training, the percentage of those who go astray is a small one. The number of homes where the pure ideal of family life exists has increased constantly since I have been in the South. There are some pure homes among the poor and illiterate. Among those who are educated the dishonored homes are few.

A colored Y. M. C. A. secretary of wide travel and experience says:

After fourteen years of constant laboring among my people throughout the South, especially among young men in the cities and students in the boarding schools of all grades, I am firmly convinced that a heroic and successful fight is being waged against immoral tendencies inherited from centuries of debasing slavery. Of course there is much dross yet to be burned away before we can have only pure gold remaining.

I confess with great sorrow of heart that there are some members of my race, and possibly a large proportion, who could be put down as fitting one or more of the foul characteristics of Mr. Thomas, nor do I seek to cover this acknowledgment with the fact that in every other race on the earth, individuals can be found equally low in life and character. But there are various classes among the freedmen as among other people.

Born and reared in Canada, and having spent three years just prior to my coming South in 1888 as a civil servant at Ottawa, where I mingled freely in church and social life with some of the best of white Canadians, I find myself greatly encouraged as I compare my experience of the past fourteen years with those of my earlier life, and especially the three years referred to above. I have met in all sections of the country hundreds of colored women whose bearing has been as suggestive of good as that of the women of the fairer race in the North. I have also come into close contact with thousands of young men whom I know to be struggling against unfortunate inherited tendencies and unfavorable environment.

It is true that only a few of the Negro race have yet attained to the degree of perfection possible among men, but between those few and the submerged masses is a promising and inspiring host of men and women in various stages of moral, intellectual and industrial evolution.

While, then, the tendencies are hopeful, still the truth remains: sexual immorality is probably the greatest single plague spot among Negro Americans, and its greatest cause is slavery and the present utter disregard of a black woman's virtue and self-respect, both in law court and custom in the South.

One thing further may be said, with diffidence but hearty conviction. The marriage *mores* of modern European culture nations, while in many respects superior to those of other peoples, are far from satis-

factory, as Prostitution, Divorce and Childlessness prove only too con-
clusively. Much has been written as to remedies and improvements,
chiefly in the line of punishing prostitution, denying divorce and
stressing child-bearing as a duty. It seems to the writer that here
the Negro race may teach the world something. Just as Olivier has
pointed out that what is termed Negro "laziness" may be a means of
making modern workingmen demand more rational rest and enjoyment rather than permitting themselves to be made machines, so too
the Negro woman, with her strong desire for motherhood, may teach
modern civilization that virginity, save as a means of healthy motherhood, is an evil and not a divine attribute. That while the sexual
appetite is the most easily abused of all human appetites and most
deadly when perverted, that nevertheless it is a legitimate, beneficent
appetite when normal, and that no civilization can long survive which
stigmatizes it as essentially nasty and only to be discussed in shamefaced whispers. The Negro attitude in these matters is in many respects healthier and more reasonable. Their sexual passions are strong
and frank, but they are, despite example and temptation, only to a
limited degree perverted or merely commercial. The Negro mother-
love and family instinct is strong, and it regards the family as a
means, not an end, and although the end in the present Negro mind
is usually personal happiness rather than social order, yet even here
radical reformers of divorce courts have something to learn.

Part 2. The Home [1]

Section 7. Africa. The general description of African homes given
in Ratzel[2] presents a good picture of the present Negro home on that
continent:

The domiciles of the Negroes, in the widespread tendency to grouping
round a central point, and to fencing, as well as in the prevalent light construction with grass, reeds, stalks or boughs, show a principal due to no-
madism. Genuine nomads build temporary huts of brushwood, which they
protect by laying mats or skins over them; a construction which extends
from the fish-eaters of the Red Sea even to the Hottentots. The only firm
part of these huts is some kind of stone wall carried round them to prevent
the rain from washing away the sand, and the water from pouring into the
house. [2]

Among the pastoral races the individual huts are usually placed in a circle
round an open space, into which the herds are driven and at night. Larger
villages often contain several enclosures, hedged or palisaded, for herds and
flocks; and the whole settlement is finally once more surrounded by a large
hedge. This main hedge is further strengthened with a stockade, and in the
agricultural villages a ditch is added. All the Babemba villages are thus
fortified. But a chief point in laying out an African village is to make the
approach difficult. This is defended, as for instance by the Fans, with poi-

---

[1] Considerable parts of sections 7-11 were first published by the editor in the *Southern Workman*, vols. 30 and 31, and are here reproduced by permission.

[2] Ratzel: History of Mankind, II; pp. 398-402.

soned splinters of reed stuck in the ground just after the Borneo fashion; or, in extreme cases, is placed in a forest stream, in the sand of which tell-tale footprints are quickly washed out.[1]

The conical style of hut-building prevails among nearly all the Negroes of Africa. The plan is circular or oval, the elevation conical or bee-hive shaped, with the entrance low; the height being that of a man, and the diameter twice as much. The bee-hive shape is the most frequent. Even the large handsome palaces of the Waganda and Wanyoro, or the regular huts of the tribes on the Upper Nile, are nothing else. Around this type are grouped the huts from the Niger to the Nile, and from Suakop to Sobat. Roomier and more comfortable huts are found especially in the Upper Nile district: as among the Bongos, whose huts run to 24 feet in height, or the Jurs; but however commodious the internal dimensions may be, the door is always low and, as a rule, there are no windows.

While the round or scattered arrangement of the village harmonises with the circular plan of this style of architecture, rectangular huts result in its being laid out in streets. A band of rectangular hut-building passes from the Manyema country through the northern Congo basin to the Cameroons. Here two rows of dwelling-huts form a street or row, closed at the two ends by council-houses, or similar "public buildings." The ingress and egress are in the longitudinal sides. The houses of one side often lie under one common roof, so as to produce two "long houses" lying opposite to each other. In this we may perhaps recognise the early state of things out of which the rectangular single premises have grown. We are still more reminded of the American or Polynesian "long houses" by the sleeping quarters for unmarried men which are found, from the Madi country westwards, through the whole region of rectangular building. In West Africa the little round huts of the restless Babongo are found intermingled with the rectangular Fan huts.

From the Fish river to Uganda and Liberia, Africa, devoid of cities, shows only slight variations in style of building and arrangement; and these are due partly to the material, partly to transmitted customs. South of the Zambesi the building is not so good because material is less abundant, and quite the best building is in the northeast; but the work is everywhere transitory, because straw, reeds, and mud are used by preference.[2]

Larger buildings, used as palaces and assembly houses, are executed in both styles. The palace huts of the Wahuma chiefs, which are over 30 feet high, and have an arched entrance 12 or more feet high; the palace-hall of the Monbuttu king, described by Schweinfurth, 50 feet high, 65 feet wide, 165 feet long, are mighty edifices for the circumstances of Central Africa. The "palaver huts" of West Africa do not fall far short of these. Cholet found the hall of a small chief in the trading village of Kosso to be 13 feet long and 65 wide. Buildings of this kind are decorated with colors, usually black, white and red, and with wood-carvings. Here, again, South Africa is behind the northern equatorial region.[3]

In East Africa we find the mud-huts, often half under ground, surrounding a large rectangular court, known as tembe, and in transition-regions like Darfour, we see stone and mud-houses mixed with the conical huts; but, wherever Moorish and Arab influences in Africa has not led to stone building, and so to the ornamental style, the village-premises in Africa are of little compactness, and correspondingly small and perishable.[4]

---

[1] Ratzel: History of Mankind, Vol. II, p. 398.

[2] Ibid, pp. 399-400.   [3] Ibid, p. 400.   [4] Ibid, p. 401.

Some villages on the west coast are described as composed of low, square, gable- roofed huts, ranging on both sides of one or more broad streets, and built always on the banks of streams—the natural highways of the land. In the rear of each house is a small kitchen garden, but the plantations, worked by the women, are a mile or so distant in the forest. [1] Further east, on the banks of the Congo, villages may be found consisting of a number of low conical grass huts, ranged round a circular common. In the center are several large shady fig trees. The doorways to the huts are very low—scarcely thirty inches in height. [2] Further down the Congo appear the long-house villages, much like similar types among the North American Indians. The long rows of houses are all connected together in blocks of from fifty to three hundred yards in length. The doorways are square apertures in the walls, two feet square and about a foot and a half above the ground. Within, the long block is divided into several apartments for the respective families forming the clan. The roof glistens with a coating of tar, and there are shelves for fuel and netting for swinging the crockery. [3] The town of Ikondu in the northern part of the Congo Free State has for homes double cages tastefully built of grass-cane, 7 feet long by 5 feet wide and 6 feet high. These cages are separate but connected by a common roof, so that the central apartments are common to both cages, and in these the families meet, perform their household duties, receive friends, and chat. "These cane cages are as cozy, comfortable and dry as ships' cabins," and are surrounded by banana trees, gardens and great tracts of waving sugar-cane. [4]

Of the homes themselves we learn that they usually consist of one and two rooms, kept in a neat and orderly manner, for the most part, and not crowded with inmates. The hut was designed primarily for sleeping and shelter in time of storm, and most of the lives of inmates were passed out of doors. A hut on the west coast is described as consisting of two rooms, one used as a kitchen and sitting-room, the other as a sleeping apartment. In the middle of the kitchen, elevated above the clay floor, was the fire-place, the smoke of which must escape by the low door. Here, from morning to night, some sort of cooking is carried on by the women—steaming cassava, boiling or roasting plantains, stewing fish or wild meat. The children have some little mess of their own to cook—an ear of maize, or some little fish. [5]

At night, when the evening meal was served, all this village seated themselves together but grouped by families, in the open air, either on low stools or on the ground, around the basin of vegetables and the little iron pot with fish and nut gravy. Plantain leaves were used as plates, and torches of the gum trees flared and lighted the night. After the meal, all drank from jugs of water, carefully cleaned mouth and teeth with their fingers, and threw away the plates on the waste heap at the end of the street. [6]

1 Nassau: Mawedo, p. 31.   2 Stanley: Through the Dark Continent, II, p. 72.
3 Stanley: Through the Dark Continent, II, pp. 133-135.
4 Stanley: Ibid, II, pp. 169-170.   5 Nassau: Mawedo, p. 52.   6 Nassau: Ibid, p. 31.

Such homes and customs vary infinitely in different parts of Africa. Among the Zulus of South Africa the huts are built in circular kraals and are made of long poles, the ends of which are fastened in the ground and the tops bent together and lashed about with a tough native vine. Thus a strong, basket-like roof is made, resting on upright posts and covered tightly with long grass. Such huts are very strong, are impervious to rain, and within, the dirt floors are often polished like a mirror. [1] At the other extreme of Africa, about the headwaters of the Nile, Schweinfurth found dwellings 30 x 20 feet, with projecting roofs, covered with grass and skins. The walls were 5 to 6 feet high, and bound together with split Spanish reed. Such huts are astonishingly strong. The doorway is large and closed by a door made of one piece. The hut is divided into two apartments. The huts of the Dinka, still further down the Nile, are conical and often 40 feet in diameter. Their foundations are of clay and chopped straw, and the supports of hard wood. Such buildings last eight or ten years. [2]

This casual glance at some of the homes of the African barbarians of today will serve to give us, perhaps, a fairly correct idea of the homes of our Negro ancestors. The slaves came from all parts of Africa, from all stages of barbaric culture, and from homes like those we have noted, as well as, probably, from others worse and better.

Section 8. Slavery. Once landed in the West Indies and "seasoned" to the new climate and surroundings, the slaves built houses not unlike those they had left at home. Nothing was provided for them save some rough building material. From this the slaves constructed their homes, driving four posts into the ground and weaving the walls of wattles so as to make a room 10 x 15 feet and 5 or 6 feet high, or possibly two rooms. There was no floor, window, or fireplace, and the roof was thatched with palms. Furniture was scanty; a rough platform raised the sleepers from the earth, and this sometimes had a mat or blanket; then there was perhaps a table, some low stools, an earthen jar for water, an iron pot for cooking and calabashes for eating. The cooking was done out of doors usually, and if the fire was made indoors there was no place for smoke to escape save through the doorway.

When slaves were few and land plentiful these rude homes were not unpleasant. They often had two rooms, could be kept clean and shady; and something like the old African life, with quasi-chief, medicine-man and polygamy appeared. Such tendencies, however, quickly passed, and the cold brutality of slavery appeared, where life was nothing and sugar was all. The homes of the slaves became dirty one-room lodges where, crowded like cattle, men slept in dreamless stupor after endless hours of forced and driven toil. All pretense at marriage and the protection of black women was virtually swept away, and

1 Tyler: Forty Years Among the Zulus, pp. 41-43.
2 Schweinfurth: Heart of Africa, II, pp. 118, 119, 160.

herded and whipped like cattle, the black men existed until like beasts
they fell in their tracks and died, and fresh loads of half putrid new-
comers were emptied on the shores by the thrift of British noblemen
and New England deacons.

When slaves were brought to the mainland of America, different
building materials and colder climate substituted the square log hut
for the older forms. At first the slaves were housed in rough cabins
near the master, and the accommodations of the two differed chiefly
in size and furniture. Thus arose the first type of slave home in
America—the "Patriarchal Group." The central idea of this arrangement was distinctly mediæval and feudal, and consequently familiar
to its white founders. First there was the house of the master—a large
log house of two or four rooms; near it were grouped the one-room log
cabins. With the light building material of the Indies it cost little
more trouble to build two rooms than to build one. But with the heavy
logs of Carolina pine, one room was as much as could be afforded. The
room was ten to fourteen feet square, and six or more feet high; it had
still the dirt floor. A cooler climate, however, made some other provisions necessary; a rough fire-place of stones was made, sometimes
with a hole in the roof for the smoke and sometimes with a chimney
of clay and wood. A hole in the wall, closed by a wooden shutter,
served with the door for light and ventilation. The slave cabin was
thus a smaller and meaner edition of the Big House; there the chimney was stone or brick, the house of logs, with board floor, and parti-
tioned into two or four rooms and a hall. Here the group lived as
master and men. At first the bond between them was almost purely
legal and economic. The slaves were white and black, and the social
station of the master not usually high. The condition of the bondsmen
therefore depended largely on accident and whim. Here they were
squalid, dirty, and driven with the lash; there a lazy, dawdling crowd,
or again, simply thrifty farm-hands. Out of this chaos evolved the
Virginia ideal. The white bond-servants became gradually free and
migrated southward; a rigid slave-code carefully fixed the status of
the black slave; he was no longer allowed to intermarry with white
servants or to become a full-fledged freeman; on the other hand, exces-
sive and wanton cruelty toward him was in some degree restrained.
The slave had learned the English language and had assumed Chris-
tianity. Bonds of friendship and intimacy grew up between black
and white; the physical group of Big House and cabins differentiated;
some came nearer, others receded, but all formed a great feudal family
of lord and retainers.

But the curse of such families, with slaves at the bottom and a privileged aristocracy at the top, ever was and ever will be, sexual debauchery. The morals of black women and white men are found to be ruined
under such an arrangement, unless long-revered custom and self-
respect enter to check license. But the African home with its customs had long ago been swept away, and slavery is simply a system
for crushing self-respect. Nevertheless time was slowly beginning to

provide remedies. White fathers could not see their black children utterly neglected, and white mothers saw the danger of surrounding their sons with vice and ignorance. Thus, gradually, the better class of slaves were brought closer into the bosom of the family as house-servants. Religion and marriage rites received more attention and the Negro monogamic family rose as a dependent off-shoot of the feudal slave regime. The first sign of this was the improvement in the Negro home; the house of the house-servants became larger, sometimes with two rooms; a more careful regard for outward decency was manifest, and the direct intercourse between the cabin and Big House brought better manners and ways of living.

One can easily imagine in this development how slavery might have worked itself out for the good of black and white. And usually those persons North and South who dwell on the advantages and training of slavery have this phase of development in mind.

The cotton-gin doomed the patriarchal slave group. Commercial slavery, which looked upon the slave primarily as an investment, meant death to the Negro home. One of the first signs of the changed condition of things was, perhaps, the "Detached Group" as I shall designate the second type of slave homes. The "Detached Group" was the group of slave cabins without a Big House—i. e., removed from the direct eye of the master, either to a far part of the same plantation or to a different plantation. The Big House has turned to brick, with imposing proportions, surrounded by trees and gardens and a certain state and elegance with which the old South was flavored. The house-servants are now either lodged in the Big House or in trim cabins near. The mass of the slaves are down at the "quarters" by themselves, under the direct eye of the overseer. This change was slight in appearance but of great importance; it widened the distance between the top and bottom of the social ladder, it placed a third party between master and slave, and it removed the worst side of the slave hierarchy far from the eyes of its better self.

From the "Detached Group" to "Absentee Landlordism" was but a step. The rich lands to the southwest, the high price of cotton, and the rapidly increasing internal slave trade, was the beginning of a system of commercial slavery in the gulf states which will ever remain a disgraceful chapter in American history. In its worst phase there was no Big House and cultivated master, only an unscrupulous, paid overseer, lawless and almost irresponsible if he only made crops large enough. The homes of the field hands were filthy hovels where they slept. There was no family life, no meals, no marriages, no decency, only an endless round of toil and a wild debauch at Christmas time. In the forests of Louisiana, the bottoms of Mississippi, and the Sea Islands of Georgia, where the Negro slave sank lowest in oppression and helplessness, the Negro home practically disappeared, and the house was simply rude, inadequate shelter.

But whither went the Big House, when so entirely separated from the slave quarters? It moved to town and with it moved the house-servants. These privileged slaves were trained and refined from contact with the masters; they were often allowed to accumulate a *peculium;* they were in some cases freed and gained considerable property, holding it in some friendly white man's name. Their home life improved, and although it was far from ideal, yet it was probably as good as that of the Northern workingman, with some manifest differences; sexual looseness was the weakest point, arising from subordination to the whites and the lessons learned therefrom by the servants themselves. They lived often in small one or two-room homes behind the masters' mansions, reached by alleys—a method which has since left the peculiar alley problem in Southern cities. Some of the slaves and the freedmen lived in a Negro quarter by themselves, although the distinctive Negro quarter of towns is largely post-bellum.

Thus we have in slavery times, among other tendencies and many exceptions, three fairly distinct types of Negro homes: the patriarchal type, found at its best in Virginia, where the housing of the slaves might be compared with that of the poorest of the Northern workingmen; the separate group and absentee type where the slaves had practically no homes and no family life; and the town group where the few house-servants were fairly well housed. In discussing slavery and incidents connected with it, these varying circumstances are continually lost sight of.

The house of the slave, which I have sought to show in its various relationships and degrees of squalor, had certain general characteristics which we must notice carefully. First, there was the lack of comfort; the Negro knew nothing of the little niceties and comforts of the civilized home—everything of beauty and taste had disappeared with the uprooting of the African home, and little had been learned to replace them. Thus, even to this day, there is a curious bareness and roughness in the country Negro home, the remains of an uncouthness which in slavery times made the home anything but a pleasant, lovable place. There were, for instance, few chairs with backs, no sheets on the beds, no books, no newspapers, no closets or out-houses, no bedrooms, no tablecloths and very few dishes, no carpets and usually no floors, no windows, no pictures, no clocks, no lights at night save that of the fire-place, little or nothing save bare rough shelter.

Secondly, and closely connected with the first, was the lack of hygienic customs: every nation has its habits and customs handed down from elders, which have enabled the race to survive. But the continuity of Negro family tradition had been broken and the traditions of the white environment never learned; then, too, the rules and exactions of the plantation favored unhealthy habits; there ensued a disgusting lack of personal cleanliness, bad habits of eating and sleeping, habits of breathing bad air, of wearing inadequate clothing—all such changes and abuses in everyday life for which the world's grandchildren must eventually pay.

Thirdly, there was in the slave home necessarily almost an entire lack of thrift, or the ordinary incentives to thrift. The food and fuel were certain, and extra faithfulness or saving could make little or no difference. On the other hand, cunning and thieving could secure many a forbidden knick-knack, far more than honest cultivation of the little garden spot which each family often had. The thriftiest slave could only look forward to slavery for himself and children.

Fourthly, there was the absence of the father—that is, the lack of authority in the slave father to govern or protect his family. His wife could be made his master's concubine, his daughter could be outraged, his son whipped, or he himself sold away without his being able to protest or lift a preventing finger. Naturally, his authority in his own house was simply such as could rest upon brute force alone, and he easily sank to a position of male guest in the house, without respect or responsibility.

Fifthly, and correlated to the last, was the absence of the mother. The slave mother could spend little or no time at home. She was either a field-hand or a house-servant, and her children had little care or attention. She was often the concubine of the master or his sons, or, if unmolested in this quarter, was married to a husband who could not protect her, and from whom she could at any time be parted by her master's command or by his death or debts. Such a family was not an organism at best; and, in its worst aspect, it was a fortuitous agglomeration of atoms.

From the following pictures of slave homes one gets varying degrees, ranging from the worst to the best:

The dwellings of the slaves were palmetto huts, built by themselves of stakes and poles, thatched with the palmetto leaf. The door, when they had any, was generally of the same materials, sometimes boards found on the beach. They had no floors, no separate apartments, except the Guinea Negroes had sometimes a small enclosure for their "god house." These huts the slaves built themselves after task and on Sundays.—Florida, 1830.

The houses for the field-slaves were about fourteen feet square, built in the coarsest manner, with one room, without any chimney or flooring, with a hole in the roof to let the smoke out.—South Carolina, 1819.

The huts of the slaves are mostly of the poorest kind. They are not as good as those temporary shanties which are thrown up beside railroads. They are erected with posts and crotches, with but little or no frame work about them. They have no stoves or chimneys; some of them have something like a fireplace at one end, and a board or two off at that side, or on the roof, to let off the smoke. Others have nothing like a fireplace in them; in these the fire is sometimes made in the middle of the hut. These buildings have but one apartment in them; the places where they pass in and out serve both for doors and windows; the sides and roof are covered with coarse, and in many instances with refused, boards.—1840.

On old plantations the Negro quarters are of frame and clapboards, seldom affording a comfortable shelter from wind or rain; their size varies from 8 by 10 to 10 by 12 feet, and six or eight feet high; sometimes there is a hole cut for a window, but I never saw a sash or glass in any. In the new country and in the woods, the quarters are generally built of logs, of similar dimensions.—1840.

Amongst all the Negro cabins which I saw in Virginia I cannot call to mind one in which there was any other floor than the earth; anything that a Northern laborer or mechanic, white or colored, would call a bed; nor a solitary partition to separate the sexes.—Virginia, 1840.

The slaves live generally in miserable huts, which are without floors and have single apartment only, where both sexes are herded promiscuously together.—Missouri, 1837.

The dwellings of the slaves are log huts, from 10 by 12 feet square; often without windows, doors, or floors, they have neither chairs, table or bedstead.—Alabama, 1837. [1]

On a very large plantation there were many exceptionally small Negro cabins, not more than twelve feet square interiorly. They stood in two rows with a wide street between them. They were built of logs with no windows —no opening at all except the doorway, with a chimney of sticks and mud; with no trees about them, no porches or shade of any kind. Except for the chimney—the purpose of which I should not readily have guessed—if I had seen one of them in New England I should have conjectured that it had been built for a powder-house, or perhaps an ice-house; never for an animal to sleep in.—South Carolina, 1859. [2]

There was a street or common two hundred feet wide, on which the cabins of the Negroes fronted. Each cabin was a frame building, the walls boarded and whitewashed on the outside, lathed and plastered within, the roof shingled; forty-two feet long, twenty-one feet wide, divided into two family tenements, each twenty-one by twenty-one; each tenement divided into three rooms—one the common household apartment, twenty-one by ten; each of the others (bedrooms), ten by ten. There was a brick fireplace in the middle of the long side of each living-room, the chimneys rising in one, in the middle of the roof. Besides these rooms, each tenement had a cock-loft, entered by steps from the household room. Each tenement is occupied, on an average, by five persons. There were in them closets, with locks and keys and a varying quantity of rude furniture. Each cabin stood two hundred feet from the next, and the street in front of them being two hundred feet wide, they were just that distance apart each way. Each cabin has a front and back door, and each room a window closed by a wooden shutter, swinging outward on hinges. Between each tenement and the next house is a small piece of ground enclosed with palings, in which are coops of fowl, with chicken hovels for nests and for sows with pig. In the rear of the yards were gardens, a half acre to each family. Internally the cabins appeared dirty and disordered, which was a pleasant indication that their home life was not much interfered with, though I found certain police regulations were enforced.—South Carolina, 1859. [3]

Section 9. The Country Home. There were reported in 1900, 1,832,818 private Negro homes in the United States Assuming that these homes are distributed approximately in the same proportion as the population, and we may conclude that 74% of these homes, or 1,350,000, are in the country districts of the South.

Here, as we would expect, the Negro home is for the most part either the actual slave home or its lineal descendant. Emancipation brought

---

[1] The above quotations are from Weld's Slavery as It Is.
[2] Olmsted: Seaboard Slave States, p. 11.   [3] Ibid, II, pp. 49-50.

at first no violent or far-reaching change in Negro country-home life. In the back districts there was no change at all. Big House and slave quarters remained and toil, though nominally on a wage basis, was really the old forced labor with a Christmas donation. Gradually, in towns and other regions, emancipation gave rise to an attempt to substitute a sort of State slavery for individual bondage. The machinery of the State judiciary, was, in many cases, after the withdrawal of the Freedmen's Bureau, used to place Negroes under the control of the State. "Vagrancy," theft, loitering, "impudence" and assault were the easily proven charges which forced large numbers of Negroes into penal servitude. The next step was to hire the labor of these persons to private contractors; thus was born the Convict Lease System. Many large planters conducted their plantations with such labor, and erected for them "barracks" and "stockades"—i. e., large enclosed quarters, guarded by high fences and crowded with inmates. These quarters were wretched, insanitary and small, and the death rate of convicts was enormous. The Convict Lease System was, however, found to be better suited to certain large operations such as brickmaking, road-building and mining, than to ordinary farming, and its use on the regular plantations was therefore limited, although not entirely discarded even to-day.

The share and rent systems of farming gradually came to replace the slave system in most cases. The best class of masters entered into contracts with their freed slaves, and the latter worked on as hired laborers. There were, however, difficulties in the carrying out of this plan. The Negroes naturally felt like seeing something of the world after freedom came. To stay on the old plantation and pursue the same dull round of toil had little attraction to a people fired with new thoughts and new ambitions. It was therefore very difficult to stop the roving instinct of the new laborers. To some extent this was accomplished by offering better wages and better houses. Frame cabins and board floors came gradually to replace the worst of the slave quarters. Still this change was but gradual and was checked by the crop-lien system or Slavery of Debt, which was soon powerful enough to keep the tenant from moving by legal process, despite his likes or dislikes. Consequently the living conditions of such freedmen were but a degree above those of former times. In the course of decades, however, a change was noticeable. The dirt-floor has practically disappeared, and fully half the log-cabins have been replaced by frame buildings, and glass windows have appeared here and there.

The great impulse toward better housing came however from the new land owners. Immediately after emancipation the Negroes began to buy land, aided somewhat by the Freedmen's Bureau, somewhat by army bounties, but mostly by the general bankruptcy. The peasant proprietors who thus arose, gradually demanded better houses. But here the anomalous situation of Southern industry showed itself: there was no ideal home-making to which the better class of freedmen could look. There were no white, green-blinded New England cottages scattered here and there, no middle class dwellings—only the Big House and the slave-pen, and nothing between. The black landholder could not think of building a mansion and he therefore built a slave cabin with some few improvements. He put a porch on the front, perhaps, cut one or two windows, and at last added a lean-to on the back for a kitchen. He beautified the yard and his wife made some tasty arrangements indoors. If he went further than this in the number of rooms or the furniture, the chances are that he got his new ideas from his friends who had moved to town.

The attraction of town life was very great to the freed slave. His few holidays and stolen pleasures in the past had centered there, and the whole aspect of concentrated life there pictured to him a long-cherished ideal of liberty. Many therefore at the first chance migrated to town, worked as mechanics or laborers and built them homes. They found in town new ideas of small comfortable dwelling places and some of them built little two, three and four-room houses such as were never seen in the country. From these patterns the country Negro learned, and two and three-room homes appeared here and there in the country. Still the reign of the one-room cabin was not seriously disputed, and an investigation in a typical black-belt county shows 40% of the families in one room, 43% in two rooms, 10% in three rooms and 7% in four or more rooms. If these figures are true for the South, 440,000 Negro rural families still live in one room.

Let us now notice more particularly what a one-room home is and means. Of course it has no peculiarly intimate connection with the Negro or the South. It is the primitive and natural method of dwelling of all men and races at some time. The cave-dwellers, the American Indians, the French peasants, the American pioneers, all lived in the one-room homes. Under certain conditions of life such homes may be fairly comfortable. Given a man and wife, the necessity of economy of heat, an active outdoor life, and a scarcity of the finer sort of building material, there can be no better home than the old roomy log hut with its great fireplace. An increase in the number of inmates, however, or a decrease in the size of the house, or a change in the manner of life, can easily transform this kind of home into a veritable pest house. This was exactly the history of the Negro's one-room cabin. Large families of children grew to maturity in it under poor moral restraint at best. There was not available building material to provide large houses, so that the original houses were built smaller and then cut in halves, with a family in either part, and then jammed closely together so as to cut off light and air. The improvements since the war have tended toward the addition of one room, more rarely two, and the changing of the building material from logs to sawn lumber. The great defects of the Negro country home, however, are still plain. They may be classed under eight chief heads:

(a) *Poor Light*. Glass windows in the country Negro homes are the exception. The light enters therefore only in pleasant weather, and then chiefly from the open door or one or two small apertures in the wall, usually of two or three square feet.

(b) *Bad Air.* A natural consequence of this is bad air and almost no ventilation. There are plenty of corners never reached by sunlight or fresh air, and as cooking, washing and sleeping go on in the same room an accumulation of stale sickly odors are manifest to every visitor. At night, when the air holes in the walls and the doors are tightly closed, from two to a dozen people sleep in a condition of air which is fatal to health. In the older log-hut the chinks in the walls admitted some fresh air. In the new board homes even this source is shut off. One of the most fruitful sources of lung disease among post-bellum Negroes is this wretched ventilation in their homes.

(c) *Lack of Sanitary Appliances.* A room so largely in use is with difficulty kept clean. The dish-water forms a pool beside the door; animals stray into the house; there are either no privies or bad ones; facilities for bathing even the face and hands are poor, and there is almost no provision for washing other parts of the body; the beds are filled with vermin. To be neat and tidy in such homes is almost impossible. Now and then one does find a tiny cabin shining and clean, but this is not the rule.

(d) *Poor Protection Against the Weather.* The average country home leaks in the roof and is poorly protected against changes in the weather. A hard storm means the shutting out of all air and light; cold weather leads to everheating, draughts, or poor ventilation; hot weather breeds diseases. The conditions are aggravated in cases where the huge old-fashioned fireplace has been replaced by a poor smoky stove.

(e) *Crowding.* So far as actual sleeping space goes, the crowding of human beings together in the Black Belt is greater than in the tenement district of large cities like New York. In one black-belt county, out of 1474 Negro families living in the country district, 761 lived in one room, 560 in two rooms, 93 in three rooms and 60 in four or more rooms. In this county there were 25 persons for every ten rooms of house accommodation, while in the worst tenement districts of New York there are not above 22.

From the single couple in one room it was an easy transition to large families with grown children occupying diminutive single-room dwellings. Sometimes married sons or daughters continue to live at home, thus introducing a second or third family. Finally the migration of young men in search of work at different seasons and in different years brings in a class of male lodgers. As a result many families entirely outgrow the physical home and use it only for sleeping and huddling in time of storm. Of real group family life there is, in such cases, little, and in this absence of group training and presence of discomfort and temptation there develop untold evils.

(f) *Poor Food.* In such homes the matter of storing and preparing food and drink is a serious problem. The well water is often tainted, or the spring so far away as to make water scarce. The cupboards for keeping food are dark, dirty and ill-ventilated. The method of preparing the meals before the fireplace or over the rickety stove is wasteful and unhygienic, filling the room with odors and making the food difficult to digest.

(g) *Lack of Privacy.* Above all, the moral and educational effect of living in one room is very bad. Of course one must not suppose that all modesty and home training disappear under such circumstances. Often there is peculiar ingenuity in guarding the children and inculcating good habits. Still, the lack of any considerable degree of privacy, the difficulty of cleanliness in a room so much used, the crowding and hurry and vulgarity of life, is bound to leave its impress on the children and to send them into the world sadly lacking in that finer sense of propriety and decency which it is the peculiar province of the home to impart.

(h) *Lack of Beauty.* Finally, it is manifest that the sense of harmony and beauty receives its first training at home. At best, the ordinary Negro country home is bare and lonely, and at worst, ugly and repelling. Out of it are bound to come minds without a sense of color contrast, appropriateness in dress, or adequate appreciation of the beautiful world in which they live. Pictures in these homes are usually confined to handbills and circus posters; the furniture is rude, tables are not set for meals, beds are not properly made. When there is an attempt at decoration it usually lacks taste and is overdone.

Such is a picture of the poorer homes of the Negro in the country districts of the South. It varies, of course, in time and place. There are sections with much more of squalor and indecency than I have pictured. There are other sections where the homes are larger and the conditions greatly improved. On the whole, however, the one and two-room cabins still prevail and the consequences are bad health, bad morals, and dissatisfaction with country life.

Section 10.   The Village Home. Migration to town was one of the first results of imagination. In 1900 17.2% of the Negroes of the South lived in cities of at least 2500 inhabitants and probably one-fifth in places of at least 1000 inhabitants.

There is considerable difference in the condition of this population in the villages and in the larger cities; and as the course of urban migration is usually from the country to the village, then to the town and thence to the city, it is important that we devote some attention to the freedman's home in the villages of the South.

The village community varies in size and kind. The most primitive is a cluster of farm houses with outlying fields, something like the German *dorf.* This kind of community is not well developed in the South, the constituent homes seldom being near enough together to form farm villages like those of the old world. Nevertheless, the partial clustering of a few score of people make a community life which differs considerably from the country life proper. Two communities in DeKalb county, Georgia, will illustrate this phase of life. Doraville and a neighboring unnamed village contain in all eleven families, with an average of twelve to a family. Five of these families own their homes, while the rest rent on shares. The farms, being within twenty miles of Atlanta, are small—from one to eleven acres. Most of the houses are rudely constructed of logs or boards, with one large and one small room. There is usually no glass in the openings which serve as windows, and they are closed by wooden shutters. The large room always contains several beds, and some home-made furniture, consisting of tables, chairs and chests. A few homes have three rooms each, and one has five. Most of the homes are poverty-stricken and dirty, but a few are well-kept and neat.

Another village group is found in Israelville, Prince Edward county, Virginia. Here are 123 inhabitants, strung along in a straggling community and forming a sort of suburb to Farmville, two miles distant. Twenty-two of the 25 families own their homes, and the other three rent from colored landlords. Seven families live in one-room log cabins; nine live in two-room log cabins; i. e., in cabins with a lower room and a loft for sleeping purposes. Three families live in three-room frame houses, and six in houses of four or more rooms. The average size of the family is five, and there are, on an average, two persons to a room, or $2\frac{1}{2}$ rooms to a family. These homes are distinctly of two kinds—old dirty log huts, and new neat frame houses. The Atlanta Conference of 1897 gave us a glimpse of conditions in several villages. As an example of bad conditions let us take a group of fourteen families in Tuskegee, Alabama. There were 79 persons in these families—36 males and 43 females—inhabiting 35 rooms, making an average of $2\frac{1}{4}$ persons to a room, and nearly 3 persons to each sleeping-room. Only two of these families owned their homes, the other twelve paying on an average $3.40 a month in rent. Three other groups—one in Tuskegee, one in Macon, Mississippi, and one in Sanford, Florida, present a better picture. Here 48 families of 220 persons occupy 203 rooms, 118 of which are sleeping-rooms. Thirty-five own their homes and 12 rent at an average of $3.27 a month.

Perhaps we can find in Farmville, Virginia, as good a picture as is needed of the small-town life. Farmville is near the geographic center of an old slave State and had 2471 inhabitants in 1900, of whom half or more were Negroes. Two hundred and sixty-two Negro families in 1890 occupied homes as follows:

SIZE OF FAMILY	FAMILIES OCCUPYING DWELLINGS OF				
	One room	Two rooms	Three rooms	Four rooms and over	Total
1 member	1	9	1	2	13
2–3 members	12	43	13	18	86
4–6 members	4	59	19	23	105
7–10 members	..	22	11	18	51
11 or more members	..	1	1	5	7
Total families	17	134	45	66	262
Total rooms	17	268	135	330	750

The one-room cabins are rapidly disappearing from the town. Nearly all of the 17 are old log cabins. They have one or two glass windows a door, and a stone fireplace. They are 15 or 20 feet square. The 134 two-room homes are mostly tenements: a large, cheaply-built frame house is constructed so as to contain two such tenements. The upper room is often used as the kitchen, and the lower as living and sleeping-room. The rooms are 15 and 18 feet square and have two windows. Three-room houses are generally owned by their occupants, and are neater than the tenements. They are usually tiny new frame structures, with two rooms, one above the other in front, and a small one-story addi-tion at the back for a kitchen. To this a small veranda is often added. Four-room houses have either a room above the kitchen or are like the double tenements. Few of the houses have cellars and many are poorly built. The locations, however, are usually healthful and the water good. Gardens are generally attached. Six and a half per cent of the families live in one room, 51.1 per cent in two rooms, 17.2 per cent in three rooms; there are 1.6 persons to a room, and nearly three rooms to a family. Forty-three and a half per cent own their homes, mostly from two to five rooms. Of the 148 tenants, 15 rent from Negro land-lords.

To the above may be added, by way of comparison, a short account of Covington, Ga., the county seat of Newton county. This is a town of 2000 inhabitants, about evenly divided between the races. In the surrounding country there are many small communities composed entirely of Negroes, which form clans of blood relatives. A few of these settlements are neat and thrifty, but most of them have a dirty, shiftless air, with one-room cabins and numbers of filthy children. Such communities furnish the emigrants for the towns. In Covington there are a few one-room cabins, but the average family occupies two or three rooms. The houses are all one-story, and a common type is that of two rooms with a hall between, and sometimes a kitchen at-tached to the back end of the hall. Often there is also a front porch. There are detailed statistics available for fifty of the better-class fami-lies. Forty-one of these own their homes and nine rent. The homes consist of

Two rooms, ... 9
Three rooms, ... 14
Four rooms, ... 14
Five rooms or more, ... 13

In all, 188 individuals occupy 184 rooms. There is also a lower element in the town and a great deal of idleness and loafing, arising in part from the irregularity of work at certain seasons of the year. On the outskirts of the town are many dives and gambling-dens where liquor is sold. On Saturday nights there is much disorder here. The more thrifty Negroes buy homes on installments, putting up, often, one room at a time until they get a two or three-room home.

In Xenia, Ohio, we have these homes: [1]

Xenia, O., Families by Size of Family and Number of Rooms to a Dwelling

SIZE OF FAMILY	FAMILIES OCCUPYING DWELLINGS OF												
	One Room	Two Rooms	Three Rooms	Four Rooms	Five Rooms	Six Rooms	Seven Rooms	Eight Rooms	Nine Rooms	Ten Rooms	Eleven Rooms	Twelve Rooms	Total Families
1 member	8	12	13	12	3	3	..	..	..	..	..	..	51
2 members	1	18	34	20	15	12	10	2	..	..	..	..	112
3 members	6	11	32	31	17	12	11	2	2	1	..	..	125
4 members	..	8	16	20	11	10	2	2	1	1	1	..	72
5 members	..	3	13	17	20	4	3	1	..	1	1	1	64
6 members	1	..	10	6	9	2	1	1	2	..	..	..	32
7 members	..	1	5	2	1	2	1	2	..	..	1	..	15
8 members	..	1	2	6	2	1	1	..	..	..	..	..	13
9 members	..	3	1	2	..	..	1	..	..	..	..	..	7
10 members	..	..	3	..	1	..	..	..	..	..	1	..	6
11 members	..	..	..	1	..	..	..	..	..	..	..	..	1
12 members	..	..	1	..	..	..	..	..	..	..	..	..	1
13 members	..	..	..	..	..	1	..	..	..	..	..	..	1
14 members	..	..	..	..	..	1	..	..	..	..	..	..	1
Total Families	16	57	130	117	79	48	30	11	5	3	4	1	501
Total Rooms	16	114	390	468	395	288	210	88	45	30	44	12	2100

In Negro village life is the growing differentiation of conditions. Upon the country Negro just emerging from the backwoods, the village life acts as a stimulus. Left to themselves, to chance surroundings and chance acquaintances, and above all to chance openings for work, the new-comers rise or fall. The successful ones give the first evidence of awakening in improved housing—more rooms, larger windows, neater furniture, the differentiation of sleeping-room, kitchen and parlor, and general improvement in tidiness and taste. The worst immigrants sink into village slums, where vice by concentration and example assumes dangerous forms. The fact is often noted that there is more vice among village Negroes than in the country. This is true, but needs to be supported by the additional fact that the village also shows more civilized classes of Negroes.

---

[1] Bulletin of the United States Bureau of Labor, No. 48.

Between these extreme classes the mass of Negroes waver in their struggle for existence. In some towns the majority are home-owners and on the rise; in others the balance is toward the bad. If, however, the chances are against the Negro in the village, one thing is certain: he seldom returns to the farm. Quickened by the village life he passes on to the town and city to try again. Or he may have some success in the village and be fired with ambition for larger fields. Finally the taste for vice in the village slum may send criminals and degenerates to complicate the city problem, North and South. The village, then, is a clearing-house. It stimulates and differentiates; it passes no material—good, bad and indifferent—to larger centers, and unfortunately sends few back to country life to stimulate the people there. In a peculiar sense, then, the village home—the problem of housing the Negro in the smaller towns of the South—is peculiar. Good homes at this point would send out children healthy in body and soul to the city on the one hand and, with little additional effort, to the country on the other. You can with difficulty send the city boy to the country, for it is an unknown land; but the village boy knows the country partially, and properly-directed effort might be the inspiraton of neat village homes in the weird and arid waste of log cabins along the country side.

Section 11. The City Home. (a) *The Slums of Atlanta.* Atlanta is a typical post-bellum city and had, in 1900, 37,727 Negroes. This growing city is built on the foot of the Alleghanies, a series of great round-topped mounds, which presents many difficulties in drainage and grading. The city is circular in form and over half of the Negro population is crowded into two wards, one on the east and the other on the west side of the city.

The nucleus of Negro population in Southern cities is the alley. It is seen at its worst in the slums of Charleston, Savannah, Washington, and such cities. It represents essentially a crowding—a congestion of population—an attempt to utilize for dwellings spaces inadequate and unsuited to the purpose, and forms the most crushing indictment of the modern landlord system. Attention has lately been directed to the tenement-house abominations, but little has been said of the equally pestilential and dangerous alley. The typical alley is a development of the backyard space of two usually decent houses. In the back yard spaces have been crowded little two-room dwellings, cheaply constructed, badly lighted and ventilated, and with inadequate sanitary arrangements. In Atlanta the badly drained and dark hollows of the city are threaded with these alleys, usually unpaved and muddy, and furnishing inviting nests for questionable characters. The worst type of these homes is the one-room cabin with sidings of unfinished boards running up and down; no ceiling or plastering, no windows, no paint, an open fireplace, and the whole of this cheerless box set directly on the ground, without cellar or foundation. Next to these come two-room houses, built in the same way, but with one or two windows and still without porch, blinds, or fence. Such cabins are so crowded together that they nearly touch each other, and the sun must get high before it can be seen from these alleys. Sometimes such rooms are papered inside by the inmates. They are 14 or 15 feet square and 8 or 10 feet high. The furniture is scarce—a bed or two, a few chairs, a table, a stove or fireplace, a trunk or chest. The floor is bare, and there are no pictures. Sometimes six or eight persons live in two such rooms and pay $1.50 a month or more for rent; sometimes as much as $4.00. These houses have water outside in a well or street hydrant; the out-houses are used in common by several tenants. Probably twenty per cent of the Negro homes in Atlanta fall into this class.

The surroundings of these homes are as bad as the homes. In the third ward most of the streets are in very bad condition, the longest of them having paved sidewalks only about half their length, while the shorter ones are not paved at all. The streets are of soft red clay, with-out gravel or cobble stones.

In the first ward, out of 25 typical homes,

> 4 had no water on the premises,
> 12 had wells (which are dangerous in Atlanta
>   and apt to be infected by sewage),
> 9 used hydrants in the yards or on the streets.

Only four had direct sewer connections. Conditions as to light and air vary, but in general there is less to complain of here, save that the careless construction of the houses makes the sudden changes of tem-perature in the winter peculiarly trying. This lack of protection in winter is made worse by the conditions of the foundations. Most of the houses are perched on wooden or brick pillars, allowing unchecked circulation of air beneath—a boon in summer, a danger in winter. The poor drainage of many of the hollows between the hills where these alleys lie gives rise to much stagnant water, pools and the like, and the unfinished sewer system often leaves masses of filthy sediment near these homes.

In the fifth ward, one of the poorer sections, an Atlanta University senior made the following estimates:

> 30 per cent of the families live in 1 room.
> 40 " " " " 2 rooms.
> 15 " " " " 3 rooms.

Of the houses,

> 60 per cent were plastered inside.
> 50 per cent were painted outside.

About half the population dwelt in districts which may be designated as "slums," although many of these were respectable people. Only 35 per cent of the homes looked clean and neat. There were five per-sons to every two rooms in the district, and three persons to every two beds. Sixty per cent of the homes had practically no yards, and 95 per cent of the homes were rented.

In the whole city of Atlanta the Negroes lived as follows in 1900:

In 1 room, ... 622 families.
In 2 rooms, ... 1654 families.
In 3 rooms, ... 1357 families.
In 4 rooms, ... 1039 families.
In 5 or more rooms, ... 1902 families.

The great majority of the one and two-room homes and some of the others are thoroughly bad as places of shelter. In other words, a third of the black population is poorly housed and, as stated before, a fifth very poorly.

The result of all this crowding is bad health, poor family life, and crime. The actual physical crowding is often great, as for example:

42 families of 6, in 1 room.
15 families of 7, in 1 room.
12 families of 8 or more, in 1 room.
21 families of 10 or more, in 2 rooms.
6 families of 12 or more, in 3 rooms.

This crowding, however, is not nearly so bad or so dangerous as the close contact of the good, bad and indifferent in the slum districts. Vice and crime spread with amazing rapidity in this way, and its spread is facilitated by the prevalent vice of Southern police systems, which make little distinction of guilt or desert among the young and old, the criminal and the careless, the confirmed rascal and the first offender, so long as they are all black. The most pitiable thing of all is the breaking up of family life, even when the mothers and fathers strive hard to protect the home. The high death-rate of the Negro is directly traceable to these slum districts. In the country the Negro death-rate is probably low. In the healthy wards of Northern cities the Negro death-rate is low; but in the alleys of Charleston, which are probably the vilest human habitations in a civilized land, the wretched inmates die in droves, while the country complacently calculates, on that abnormal basis, the probable extinction of black folk in America.

(b) *St. Louis.*[1] At present, then, almost half of the Negroes live in six wards, in which they form from 14.71 to 22.70 per cent of the population of the ward. These wards, ranked according to the proportion of Negroes, are the fourteenth, fifteenth, fifth, fourth, twenty-second, and twenty-third. Wards 4, 5, 14 and 15 form an irregular rectangle extending west from the river. Ward 4 is the mercantile section of the town and 5 contains many factories. The partial tenement-house investigation made by the Board of Health in 1897 showed that Ward 4 contained the highest number of tenement houses. Ward 14 consists of the Union Station and streets that may be considered its inevitable environment, and is no better than such sections are apt to be in an American city. Ward 15 consists partly of fine old residences that have degenerated into second and third-rate boarding houses, and partly of poor tenements and shanties that have never been anything else. . . .

In Wards 4 and 5 the dwellings are crowded in behind factories and warehouses. The white population is chiefly Italians and other south-eastern

---

[1] Brandt in Publications of the American Statistical Association, Vol. 8.

Europeans, and these districts are considered to be about the worst slums in the city. The fourteenth and fifteenth wards are not quite so bad, but the streets where the Negroes live consist of houses that are dirty and out of repair, if not actually in a tumble-down condition. Wards 22 and 23 lie west of 14 and 15, and are of a distinctly better character. They contain a better class of Negroes, the professional and successful business men. The houses in the Negro streets are comfortable and in fairly good condition, on the average, and many are owned by the occupant. This is a comparatively old section of the town, and the houses now occupied by Negroes were built by well-to-do white residents who have since moved farther west. Ward 23 includes also a poor quarter lying along the railroad tracks in low land which was once marshes. There is a considerable number of Negroes also in wards 25 and 26, which are very desirable residence sections. This number represents chiefly domestic servants, but there are also two or three settlements of well-to-do Negroes on certain streets. The 865 in Ward 18 are nearly all servants.

In general, it is true that the Negroes are almost absent from the sections of the city where there is a large foreign population, and that, with notable exceptions, they are concentrated in the worst houses of the worst sections, wherever the natural lay of the land or the unpleasant accessories of civilization, such as railroads and factories, make residence undesirable. The overcrowding of rooms is a fact for which no statistics are available, but it is none the less a fact. . . .

The hospitality of the Negroes, and their willingness to take in any friend who finds himself without a home, receives no check from the law. There are no State regulations concerning tenement houses, and the city ordinances go only so far as to class them under "nuisances" when they do not have "adequate" sewerage, drainage, ventilation, chimneys, halls, staircases, and "all reasonable precautions and provisions in every other particular, and adequate space for all occupants, so that the occupancy of said building or any apartment shall not be dangerous to life or health." Under such provisions it is not surprising that the agent of the Provident Association should find recently fourteen Negroes living in one room.

The Negroes are kept in these undesirable localities not wholly by their own faults and incompetence, but partly by the obstacles which they encounter when they try to go into a better neighborhood. No landlord wishes to have Negro tenants come into his houses, because it means a depreciation of the property sooner or later. When a Negro family moves into a street it generally happens that the white residents give place either to more Negroes or to a much inferior class of whites. To keep up the character of the street, therefore, or to reimburse himself in advance for the depreciation which he foresees, the landlord resorts to discriminating rents. A Negro going into a house previously occupied by a white family is obliged to pay from 20 per cent to 50 per cent more than his predecessor. A certain house in Ward 25, for instance, rented for $25 per month to white tenants, but a Negro was asked $40. This is true even in the poorer districts. There are some comfortless three-room flats in Ward 14 which were occupied until recently by white people paying $8.00 per month; the Negroes living there now are charged $13. Sometimes when a Negro family moves into a "white" street the residents themselves undertake to deal with the question. . . .

In the last ten years the condition of the Negroes in St. Louis has improved considerably, and general observation shows that one accompaniment of this improvement has been the acquisition of property, both for business purposes and for homes. The discriminating rents already referred to have had some influence in this discretion, for the more intelligent and more able Negroes have seen that it would be cheaper in the long run to buy their houses than to rent them.

(c) *Washington.* [1] The National Capital was evidently intended to be a city of homes. The original lots are of generous dimensions and front upon broad streets and avenues. These lots provided ample room for separate houses, with space for yards in the front and rear, and the squares were laid out in such a manner as to give access, by alleys, to the rear of each lot. This plan probably had in view the location of stables on the alleys, in the rear of each house. As the city grew the original lots were subdivided, and as land became more valuable a majority of the residences were built in blocks, with party walls, instead of being detached villas with light on all sides. Naturally, in portions of the city devoted to business, this was the usual method of building from the outset, and these dwellings and stores were, as a rule, brought to the very front of the lot, thus leaving a considerable space in the rear, as the original lots were generally from 100 to 200 feet in depth. The owners of property, as land values increased, sometimes sold off rear portions of their lots, and sometimes built small houses, facing the alleys, which they were able to let at rentals which gave them a high rate of interest on their money. These houses were often cheap frame structures, which paid for themselves within a few years. In other cases they were of brick. As a general rule, the rooms were small and the first floor was on a level with the ground, without any ventilation under it. As a result of this, the sills soon became rotten, and dampness from the ground came through the floors. As a rule, also, there was no water in the house and no sewer connections. Water was often obtained by all of the residents of an alley from a single hydrant at the corner, and box privies were in general use. Many cheap frame and brick houses were also built upon the streets and avenues of the city prior to the adoption of proper building regulations, and these exist today, in a more or less dilapidated condition, often in proximity to handsome new dwellings. Many of these old houses are on valuable ground, and they serve to pay taxes until such time as the owner can sell his ground at a figure which he considers satisfactory. . . .

The civil war brought a large influx of Negroes:

It is estimated that from 30,000 to 40,000 Negroes from neighboring States came to this city at that time. These unfortunate and ignorant people were obliged to avail themselves of any kind of shelter they could find. In many cases rough board shacks with leaky roofs were occupied for years by growing families, and rents were paid out of all proportion to the value of the property or the means of the tenant. Industrious colored men, whose labor would only command from a dollar to a dollar and a half a day, and hardworking colored women, whose lives had been spent over the washtub, have been obliged to pay, year after year, for shelter of the most indifferent kind, an amount which has yielded the landlord twenty per cent, or more, on his investment.

The following extracts from the report of the health officer will show the conditions existing ten years after the Civil War:

Leaky roofs, broken and filthy ceilings, dilapidated floors, overcrowded,

---

[1] Sternberg: Report of Committee on Building Model Homes.

below grade, having stagnant water underneath, no drainage, no pure water supply, no fire protection, having filthy yards, dilapidated, filthy privy and leaky privy box, in bad sanitary condition generally, and unfit for human habitation, described, with few exceptions, the conditions of these hovels where the poorest class of our population stay out their miserable existence, and for which they pay rents varying from $2.50 to $10.00 per month. . . .

As specific examples of overcrowding, at a later date, I quote from the report of Miss DeGraffenried, published in 1896:

One conclusion at least is evident, that rents in these alleys are dear, considering the accommodations and environment. Moreover, the moral consequences of such narrow quarters are often disastrous. Crowded sleeping rooms contribute to vice and indecency. Indeed, crowding goes on to an extent not acknowledged to the canvasser by the tenants. At night these poor roofs shelter many more people than are here reported.

I have no doubt that lodgers are harbored in these alleys whose presence, for many reasons not creditable to the occupants, is always concealed. The confessed facts are startling enough. We have here accounts of seven persons living in two rooms—the mother and her sons 21, 17 and 7 years of age, occupying one bed-chamber. Again, nine individuals live in two rooms; eleven people in four rooms. Five, almost all adults, sleep in one room—the mother 43, a son 21, and daughters 19, 17 and 14; and four persons use another room—a mother 45, an aunt 70, a son 22, and a baby 9 months old. . . .

Deanwood, East Deanwood and Burrville are scattered villages, merging into each other, and situated along the Chesapeake Beach Railway; here dwell colored people almost entirely. The villages are for the most part composed of new and respectable cottages owned by their occupants. Here and there may be seen dilapidated shacks occupied, while alongside stands a new cottage empty and for rent.

Barry Farm is situated on the outskirts of Anacostia; this is another Negro settlement, and is a curious mixture of comfortable cottages, even handsome homes, owned by well-to-do colored people, and tumbledown hovels that bring exorbitant rents.

Garfield and Good Hope are also colored communities on the order of Barry Farm; these villages are situated on the hills to the east of Anascotia. The majority of the houses here are owned by their occupants There are no public service advantages in these outlying regions, with the exception of public water supply in Ivy City; but even here the people do not have water within their houses, nearly always obtaining it from the street hydrant.

The communities just described are the only considerable aggregations of people of the laboring class to be found without the city limits. The character of old dwellings located in them is little better than we would condemn within the city. Nothing is being done to improve the quality of dwellings, and the new dwellings are of the cheapest kind. Moreover, the people who live in these suburban places are not the pick and shovel men, the cart drivers, the hod carriers, the stable men, of the city. They are for the most part more independent folk, such as messengers and skilled laborers in the departments; colored men who work from place to place as porters, waiters, or house-servants, and who keep their wives and children in these little homes. They are the kind who will not rest until they own "a little place in the country," it matters little what sort of dwelling may be upon the "place." The worst hovels are occupied by driftwood: widows who subsist by doing laundry work for the neighbors in better circumstances; old people, supported by sons and daughters in the city, and the children of the sons and daughters. . . .

The company organized under the above charter from Congress [The Washington Sanitary Housing Company] succeeded in securing stock subscriptions sufficient to justify it in commencing building operations and in October, 1904, twenty houses had been completed and were occupied by colored tenants. Seventeen of these houses were on Van Street S. W. The flats of three rooms and a bath were rented for seven dollars per month for lower and seven and one-half dollars per month for upper flats. The four-room flats were rented for eight and eight and one-half dollars per month. This is an average of $2.26 per room. It should be remembered that each of these flats has a good-sized bathroom, with a bathtub and a modern water-closet. There is a good range with water-back in the kitchen, and a small coal stove in the front room. The hot-water boiler connected with the kitchen range is placed in the bathroom and furnishes sufficient heat to make it comfortable. These flats have now been occupied by colored tenants, mostly day laborers, for nearly four years. They are in such demand that there is constantly a waiting list of applicants in case a flat becomes vacant. Many of the present tenants have occupied their flats since the houses were completed. The repairs required have not been excessive, and there has been very little loss from vacancies or failure to collect rents. . . .

In the city of Washington the death rate among the colored population, in 1875, was 42.86 per thousand. In 1906 it had fallen to 28.81 per thousand. Among the whites it was 21.04 in 1875, and in 1906 it had fallen to 15.16. To what extent this decline in death rate is due to improvement in housing conditions it is impossible to say, but no doubt there has been some improvement, and this one of the factors which accounts for one of the gradual reduction of our death rate from the disgracefully high figures of twenty-five or thirty years ago.

Section 12. City Homes of the Better Class. *Atlanta.* Scattered among other homes and gradually segregating themselves in better class districts is a growing class of Negro homes belonging to the rising groups of Negroes. These homes are often unnoticed because they are not distinguishable from corresponding white homes, and so are continually overlooked.

In an address to the Negroes of Boston, Mass., Mr. George W. Cable said: "There is a notion among Southern people, which is not confined to them, . . . but which is upon the tongues of Negro leaders—the notion that it is highly important that the Negro should be kept on the plantation. That is false. I say it because some white man ought to say it. What is civilization? The cityfying of a people or making them what a city makes them. True, the city has many temptations, and many men and women go to shipwreck there. But it only means a more energetic process of selection, and as much as some go down, others go up."

Whatever our views of the influx of Negroes into cities may be, it is clear that there alone can we find a class of Negro homes fully equal to the homes of the whites. This is significant. A determined effort has been made, especially during the reaction of later years, to judge the Negro by his worst and lowest type. Even reputed friends and leaders of the race have been zealous in laying bare the weaknesses of the race and holding its faults up to ridicule and condemnation. Some of this has been justified by a real desire to know the truth, but it has gone so far today as to obscure, almost, in the eyes of the majority of Americans, the existence of a class of intelligent American citizens of Negro blood who represent as good citizenship, as pure homes and as worthy success as any class of their fellows.

They may be found to some extent in the country. But the country was peculiarly the seat of slavery and its blight still rests so heavily on the land that the class of Negro farmers who can compare with the best white farmers of the North and West is very small. In the cities, however, the Negro has had his chance to learn. He has been quickened and taught. He has schools and contact with culture, and in those cases where he has been able to stand normal competition and abnormal prejudice he can, in a large number of cases point to homes which equal the best American homes—not, to be sure, in wealth or size, but in cleanliness, purity and beauty. This class is small and grades quickly down to homes which may be criticized; and still, as representing the best, there is good argument for calling these at least as characteristic of the race, as the alley hovels. A race has a right to be judged by its best.

To illustrate this point let us take the best Negro homes of Atlanta, Georgia. They are largely homes of the graduates of Atlanta University, and their owners are teachers, mail-carriers, merchants and professional men. These homes were thus described in the reports of the class in sociology of this institution in 1900: "They are good-sized one and two-story homes, having bathrooms and water in the house, and in many cases gas and electric-bells. There are seven or eight rooms, each with two or more windows, and both the house and furnishings are in good condition. There are from four to six occupants. The parlors and some of the other rooms have tiled hearths, and there is usually a piano or organ in the home. The walls are painted or papered, the windows have white curtains and shades. In all cases these houses are owned by the occupants." A few houses are more elaborate than this, but this is a fair description of those that are referred to in this section.

A detailed description of two or three of these homes will make the picture more vivid. Number 32 North —— Street is built on brick pillars with lattice-work between. The house is painted without and within, plastered, and the woodwork varnished. The kitchen is ceiled in yellow pine. The house is of two stories on a lot 50 by 100 feet, and has gas and water. On the first floor there is a hall 13 x 12½ x 11 feet, with two windows; a parlor 17½ x 14½, a nursery, pantry, dining-room and kitchen. The parlor has a piano, and there are open fireplaces with tiled mantles, but, as is usual in the South, no other heating apparatus. The second story is like the first, save that there is no room over the kitchen. There are four bedrooms and a bath. There are eight in this family and they own the house.

Another home, 160 —— Street, is a frame house two stories high, with eight rooms. It is a long, narrow house, with a hall running the whole length on one side. Two rooms are papered, the rest white-finished. There is a double parlor with piano, a dining-room and kitchen on the first floor, four bedrooms and a bath on the second. The furniture is good, and all the rooms are carpeted save the kitchen. There are seven inmates, and they own the house.

The favorite type of house here for small families is one-story. The house at 260 —— Street is one-story, weatherboarded, plastered and painted, built on a brick foundation and nicely furnished. It has five rooms: one parlor 16 x 14 with a parlor set, carpet, table, sofa, four chairs and a piano; two bedrooms with sets of furniture; a dining-room, with a nice dining-table, three chairs, a refrigerator and side-board. The kitchen has a stove, table and cupboard. There are two inmates who have owned this property for seven years. Outside is a garden, with henhouse and woodhouse.

Such homes as these are typical of the class with which we are dealing. These are, of course, exceptional, when one considers the great mass of Negroes of Atlanta; and yet, of over a thousand homes of all types studied by Atlanta University students in 1900, about forty were placed in this select class. If among the Negroes of the South two per cent of the homes of the freedmen have reached this type, it is a most extraordinary accomplishment for a single generation. In the country the percentage of comfortable homes is small, certainly not over one per cent and in many places less. In the towns and cities, on the other hand, the percentage must often rise to five per cent and sometimes more. Any more definite statements than these would be purely conjectural.

There are some criticisms that can be brought against this class of homes, although they apply equally well to the similar class of white homes in the South. First, in the economy of space there is a certain lack of coziness and convenience, which can easily be traced to climatic and social reasons. The log-cabin, so prevalent a generation since, was essentially a square box. Other rooms were made by adding, not by subdividing. So that today throughout the South the houses give one the impression of separate rooms in juxtaposition, rather than of a house subdivided according to convenience and relative use of rooms. Long draughty halls, high sombre ceilings, and stiff square walls are the usual thing. Moreover, the kitchen contains a whole social history. In New England, where the mothers and their ancestors for generations have spent most of their time working in kitchens, this important part of the house has developed into a great, clean, sunny room, with abundant ventilation and ample working and storing space. In the South, where the kitchen was the domain of an alien race and servile caste, it was actually cut off entirely from the house, and sat alone cramped and small, in the back yard. Today it has gradually fastened itself to the house again, but with an unobtrusive, apologetic air. It sticks to an out-of-the-way corner, and is usually altogether too small for its purpose. I have seen kitchens, in the homes of well-to-do people, as small as eight or ten feet square, or about the size of my grandmother's pantry. Then, again, the cupboards, closets and storing-rooms of most Southern houses are too small and are ill-arranged. Cellars, owing to the climate, are very exceptional, and good attics are seldom found. There is room for argument as to whether the one or two-story house is most convenient, but certainly for a given amount of money the two-story house furnishes considerably more room space. In a one-story house the temptation always is, among all classes of Southern people, to turn bedrooms into reception-rooms on occasions. This is always objectionable, especially where children are being trained to respect the sanctity of their private rooms. Then, too, the ventilation of the sleeping-rooms is a matter of some difficulty in a one-story house, where windows and doors near the living-rooms cannot be left open long.

The heating problem in the South is serious. Nearly all well-perfected heating systems have been developed to supply the needs of cold climates. In a large part of the South fires are only needed regularly three months or less. Consequently furnaces and base-burners are too costly. On the other hand the open grate, while delightfully cheery, is wasteful, uncomfortable and dangerous. It is responsible for a large number of fires and accidents, and above all it heats the room so unequally that it is a source of colds, rheumatism and consumption. A Southern home, even of the better class, is a dreadfully cheerless place on a cold day. Some cheap heating apparatus in connection with the open grate is really in great demand.

Outside these criticisms of the physical homes there are special moral dangers due to the environments of the best class of Negroes. The best Negro settlements are never free from the intrusion of the worst class of whites. A favorite situation for both white and colored houses of prostitution is in the Negro quarter of the town, and this often brings them near some of the best homes. I have seen a prosperous country town where a prominent white official was not tolerated in the white residence section, but allowed to build and live in a pretty home in the midst of the best Negroes. In Asheville, N. C., one of the best Negro sections is ruined by an open house of ill-fame with white inmates. Again, the Negro sections of the city are usually poorly policed (save in criminal sections), poorly paved and lighted, and, above all, the system of Southern taxation falls heavily on the middle classes: in Atlanta, books, sewing machines, furniture, bicycles, horses and wagons, and all such small luxuries are taxed.

The custom, too, of classing all Negroes together, in law and treatment, leads to carelessness in protecting the best of the Negroes from their own worst elements. A whole Negro district is put under a ban because of the lawlessness of a few, and the lack of purity in some Negro homes is sufficient excuse with many for treating the best of our women with neither courtesy nor decency.

That with such surroundings, and among the mass of poor homes there is growing up a strong beautiful family life, housed decently, and even luxuriously in some cases, is a cause of congratulation and hope.

Section 13.   A Study of Eight Homes.   The class in sociology of Atlanta University, 1908-09, made a detailed study of 32 Negro homes. Plans and descriptions of eight of these homes follow; the scale is one-fourth of that indicated:

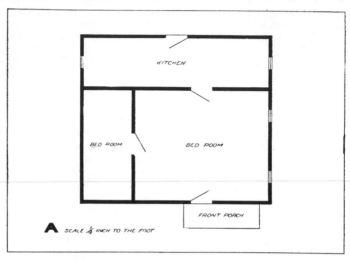

PLAN A.—Family of eleven persons (parents and nine children).

This country house is a wooden structure with the boards running up and down. The roof is shingled with large home-made shingles. None of the walls are plastered, all of the floors are bare, and the windows are without glass panes, curtains or shades. They have wooden shutters.

There are two bedrooms and a kitchen. In the large bedroom are two beds, a dresser, a sewing machine, a cupboard piled with quilts, a table with a bowl and pitcher upon it, a towel-rack and a few chairs. They have newspapers pasted upon the walls and several advertisement pictures—"Fairy Soap," "Baking Powder," "Root Beer"—tacked on. There are no books except the Bibles of the different members of the family and a few old school books. They take "McCaulay's Magazine," "The Yellow Jacket," the "Savannah Tribune," and the "North Georgian." There is a large fireplace.

The second bedroom has no windows and no fireplace. It contains three beds and nothing more. The kitchen has two windows. It contains a stove, two small tables, a cupboard and a few chairs.

The front porch is a mere platform, with no top over it. The house is kept moderately clean. There is a large front yard, bare, clean swept, which merges into woods on one side and into a large kitchen garden on the other; from the front of the yard runs a path leading to another house. The back yard is also large, bare, and clean swept. It leads into woods and cotton fields. There is no other house in sight of this one. They get their water from a spring near by.

PLAN B.—Family of twelve persons (parents and ten children).

This country house is made of pine logs 20 x 15, eight feet high; roofed with split boards. The little room on the side is made of plank 10 x 13, roofed with split boards. The floor is laid with wide plank, 1 x 10. It has one chimney, three windows 2 x 3, with board shutters, three doors 5½ x 3. The porch is just wide enough to make a passage from the

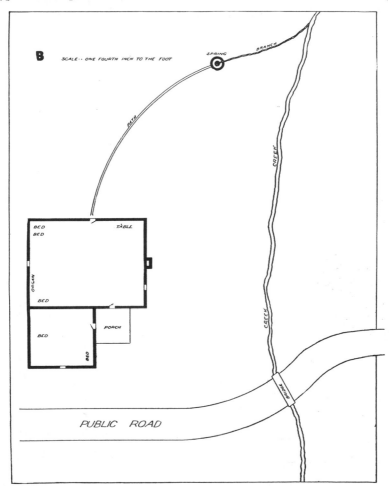

door of the main house to the room, and it is not covered. The yard is very small; cotton rows on one side run almost to the door, and in the rear are weeds and woods.

There are three beds in the main building, with the paint worn off and a large yellow organ near the rear window. There are five home-made chairs and two benches ten feet long, two small trunks, a small table for the lamp and a large one for eating purposes. The dishes are kept in a box, the surplus food is also kept in a box. The cooking utensils are kept on a shelf outside of the window. The cooking is done in this building on the fireplace. The walls are covered with newspapers, with holes showing where mice have been gnawing. The bed is bare, and the bedclothes hang from the joist. No pictures are on the walls and no carpet upon the floor. There is one glass lamp of

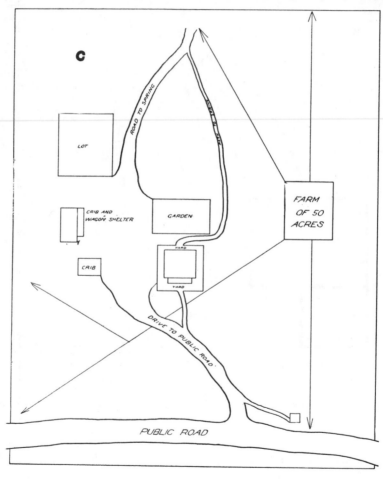

small size and a small tin lamp. A gun is hanging over the door. The water is brought from a spring about 300 yards away.

The little out-room contains two beds and a bench about ten feet long, but no pictures on the wall, no books or carpet. The beds are painted yellow, fairly new. One large box is in the corner to keep clothes packed in. This is called the guest room.

PLAN C.—Family of ten (widow and nine children).

There are four rooms in this country house. In the room that is usually used for the reception of company is a dresser, a washstand, a center-table, straight chairs, one rocker and a bed. The floor has one small rug. There is no plastering on the walls. The inside walls are just the inside of the boards that form the weatherboarding. The window has no glass, but has a lace curtain hanging over it. The other room has two beds in it, a shelf upon which quilts are kept and a big box with things packed in it. In the kitchen is a bed, with a curtain between the bed and the part where the cooking is done, a shelf where the water-bucket stands, and a cupboard where the dishes are kept. In the dining-room is a long table. Chairs are carried from the other rooms to the dining-room as they are needed. In the front room are a few pictures, and on the mantle-shelf, which is a board nailed above the fireplace, is a big clock. There is one trunk in the front room and one in the other bedroom. In the front room the furniture is comparatively new, because the family was recently burned out. Most of the water is taken from a well that is about two hundred yards from the house, and the rest is taken from a spring a little farther away.

This house is heated by fireplaces in which, principally, oak wood is used. A good part of the lighting is done by the fire in these fireplaces in winter and by kerosene lamps in summer. In the yard are flowers and one big oak tree. The house is not painted. On the inside of the house and all around it, everything is kept extremely clean. From the appearance of the fireplace one might think that it is whitewashed three or four times each week.

The periodicals are "The Designer" and the "Delineator." The papers are "The Macon Telegraph," "The Atlanta Independent" and "The Dispatch." In the kitchen is a medium-sized stove.

PLAN D.—Family of six (parents, one child and three brothers).

This country house is a frame structure of four rooms, two on either side of a wide hall. The house is weatherboarded crosswise and painted white, with green bordering. Two windows of eight panes each admit light to each room. The front porch is comparatively wide and the back porch is very wide. The bedrooms are furnished with a wardrobe apiece, made of walnut. Each bedroom contains a bureau of walnut, and a large box upside down, covered neatly with newspaper, with a washpan, soap and towel on the top.

In the front rooms are two beds, and in the back bedroom one bed. All the beds are well kept. The front room on the right has a carpet, somewhat worn, upon the floor. Beside the fireplace is an unpainted tinder-box, containing fat lightwood, chips and wood for making fires. All the rooms have fireplaces. Though some families in that section of the country sleep upon straw-beds, this particular family has feather-beds through the house. The front room on the right has a center-table standing upon three legs with glass feet. The back rooms have lofts stored with hams and dried pumpkins. The other rooms are ceiled overhead, with plastered sides.

The walls of the front room are decked with pictures of "Noah's Ark," "Eternity," "Christ's Blessings," and to sum up the whole array of pictures, those which are not of the immediate family seem to con-tinually impress the fact that death is near. The lights of the house are the common Miller lamps with Rochester burners. The kitchen contains a common cook-stove, a cook-table, milk cans, churn, and general milk apparatus. The bedroom on the back contains also a new food safe, made of oak with doors of flowered wirecloth. Upon the tables of the rooms may be seen copies of the "Truth," an Atlanta Ne-gro publication; copies of cheap novels sold on trains, such as, "A Slow

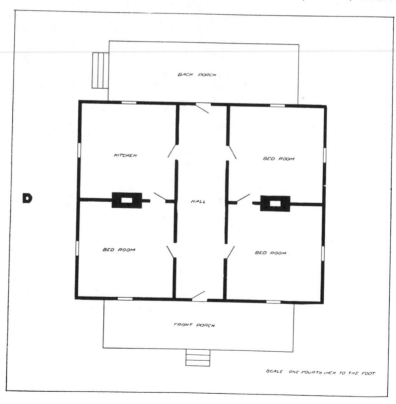

Train through Arkansas," and a book called "Stories from the Ladies' Home Journal." The Atlanta Journal is taken also. The yards are kept as free of obstruction as possible. In the front yard are a few flowers in beds, separated by cleanly-swept walks. The back yard contains a well and a side table, and perhaps half a dozen tubs made from syrup barrels. All water is carried into the house in well-polished cedar buckets.

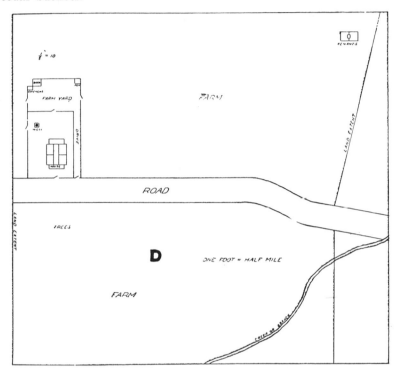

PLAN E.—Family of three (widow and two daughters).

This city house is a frame dwelling of three rooms: two bedrooms and a kitchen. One bedroom, 18 x 14½, has two windows and two doors, one leading to the next room and the other to some steps in front. The windows have no curtains nor shades. The walls are unplastered and, save for a few calendars, are bare. The floor has no covering. Within the room are a bed, a table, a bureau and a wardrobe. There is also a fireplace, with a mantel above upon which are two vases, a calendar and one or two Sunday-school cards. The other bedroom is 18 x 12. The walls are bare and the floors uncovered. There are two windows without shades and curtains. Within the room are a bed, a table and one or two chairs. There is a fireplace, with a mantel above upon which irons are kept. The kitchen, which is detached, is 12 x 7. The

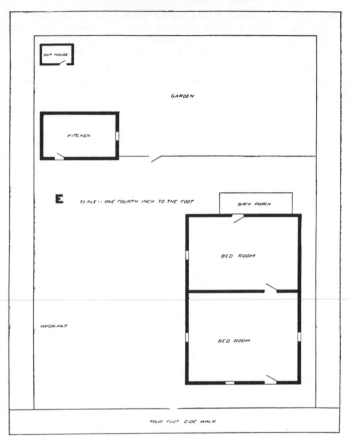

walls are bare and unplastered and the floors uncovered. In it are a
small cooking stove, a table, a food safe, a bench and four chairs.
There is one window without shade or curtain, and one door. This
family does not subscribe for any paper or magazine, and the books
consist of some school books once used by children of the family. The
yard in front is used as a place for washing, and the tubs and
clothes-lines are there. The yard in the back is used for a garden.
There are several trees and an outhouse in it. A hydrant supplies city
water.

PLAN F.—Family of four (parents and two daughters).

This city cottage is built of boards ½ x 12 in., with shingle roof and
wooden supporting pillars. The walls of the room are made out of
regular flooring lumber. The front room has paper on the walls, carpet on the floor, and curtains at the windows. On the walls are two
or three pictures of the members of the family. This room is used as

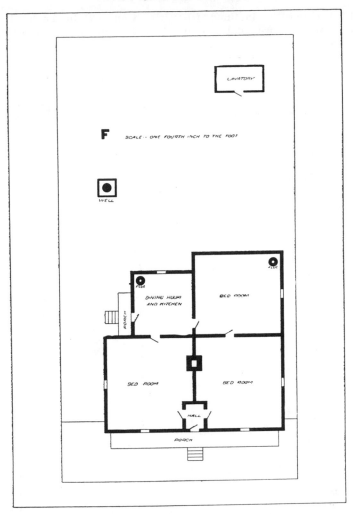

a bedroom as well as a parlor, and contains a bed, bureau, washstand, bowl and pitcher. The walls of the other two rooms and kitchen are destitute of paper, plaster and pictures, and the floors are bare. In one of these rooms is an old-fashioned bed and a bureau. In the other is an iron bed, a piano and a bureau. In the kitchen is a table, a safe and a range. There are eight chairs in the house and one rocking-chair. There are a few books in the main room, such as: the Bible, and "Life of Fred Douglas"; there is also the Atlanta "Constitution." Coal and wood is used for heating purposes. The front room has a grate and the other two have fireplaces. For light, kerosene lamps are used. The yard is inclined from the front to the back. In the back is an outhouse and a well. In the front is a rosebush and a peachtree.

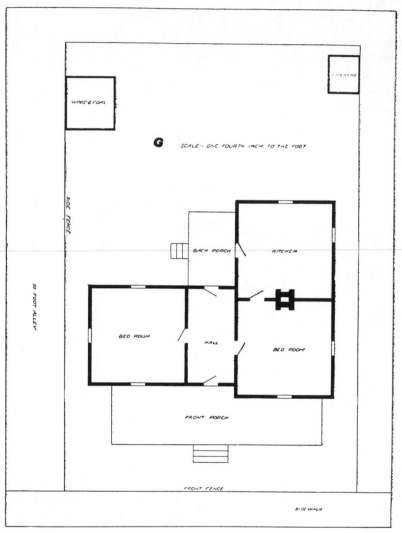

PLAN G.—Family of seven (parents, two children, grandfather, uncle and nephew).

This city house is a frame structure of three rooms, two on one side of a hall and one on the other. The house is weatherboarded crosswise and painted green. The front room on the right has two windows, the front window being a large one-pane sash, with transom. The side window has four lights in two sashes. The rest of the rooms have two and three windows each. The front porch is ten feet wide at the widest part. The back porch is five feet wide. The front room contains an oak suit of furniture, with four straight-back chairs and two rockers. There is a rug upon the oak-stained floor. The casings of the room are cherry colored. The mirrored mantel is cherry with vari-colored tile hearth, and club-house grate. The bed mattress is of cotton felt. On the under shelf of a center-table are the daily issues of the Atlanta "Georgian," an Atlanta daily, together with weekly issues of the Atlanta Independent, a Negro weekly published here. On a small bookcase are various books: novels like "Ishmael," a Webster's abridged dictionary, and the "Home Encyclopædia." The room back of this is the kitchen; it contains a common cook-stove, an iron bed used for "lounging," a cheap safe, an eating-table, a side table, a combination affair for holding flour, meal, coffee, spices, sugar, salt, etc.; the floor is kept well scoured. In the room across the hall are two beds, a washstand, a dresser, and a center-table. In this room is a small heater of ordinary style; nothing is upon the floor. Common cotton mattresses are upon the beds. The pictures are mostly of landscapes and portraits of the immediate family. In the hall is a common sideboard. The lights are Miller lamps with Rochester burners. There are three or four alarm clocks in the house. There is a stand-pipe on the back porch, furnishing water for the house. The walls are all plastered, also overhead with scratchcoat finish. The front yard has grass, but no flowers. The back yard contains a coalhouse, chicken-house, water-closet and storeroom, a washbench and three tubs.

PLAN H.—Family of eleven (parents and nine children).

A City Home:

Parlor.—The walls are kalsomined in pink and blue. There are six painted pictures on the walls, two of the mother, one of the husband and four of rural scenes. The floor is carpeted with Brussels carpet and three rugs. The furniture consists of one parlor suite, mahogany-finished and leather-bottomed, and two bookcases, one in oak and one in oil-finish, with books such as the works of George Eliot, Dickens, Shakespeare, Irving, Poe; Latin, Greek, German and French textbooks, and others. The room is heated by an open grate and lighted by gas.

Reception Hall.—The walls are sand-finished, and kalsomined in blue and pink. There are six framed pictures, two of grandparents, one of sister, one of Fred Douglass, one of Booker Washington, and one rural scene. The floor is carpeted with Brussels carpet and three rugs. The furniture consists of four straw-bottomed chairs, cherry-colored, one table, and one piano ebony-finished. The books consist of collections of music. The room is heated by an open grate and lighted by gas. The woodwork of both these rooms is oil-finished.

Dining-Room.—The walls are sand-finished, and kalsomined in pink.

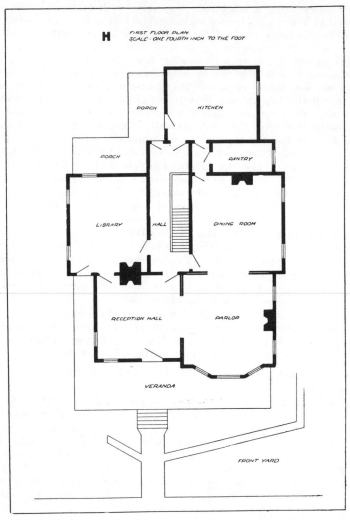

The pictures consist of four framed pictures, chiefly of fruits. The floor is painted red and has a rug. The furniture consists of twelve chairs, one table, one sideboard, oak-finished, and china closet oil-finished. The room is heated by open grate and lighted by gas.

Study.—The walls are kalsomined in blue and cream. There are four framed pictures and one framed mirror on the wall. The floor is covered with linoleum. The furniture consists of six chairs, one table, one desk and one piano. The books consist for the most part of school books—of grammar school and preparatory course—with magazines,

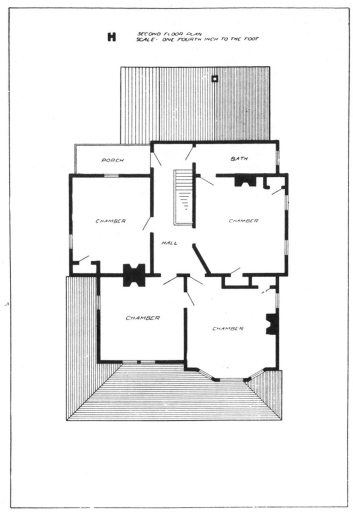

such as "The Ladies' Home Journal," "Woman's Home Companion," "Harper's," and others. The room is heated by a small heater and lighted by gas.

Kitchen.—The walls are of painted wood. The floor is bare, painted. The furniture consists of one table, range, sink, drawboard. It is lighted by gas.

Halls.—The walls are kalsomined in blue and yellow. The floors are covered with linoleum; the steps are carpeted. The halls are lighted with gas.

Bedrooms.—The bedroom over the parlor has walls kalsomined in blue and yellow. The floor is carpeted. The pictures consist of four framed pictures. The furniture consists of one bed, one washstand, table, one dresser and four chairs, oak-finished. The room is heated by an open grate and lighted by gas. The bedroom over the reception hall has similar walls, the floor is covered with matting; the pictures consist of three framed pictures, two of parents and one of country scene. The furniture consists of one iron bed, dressing-table, chiffonier and three chairs. It is heated by an open grate and lighted by gas. The bedroom over the study has similar walls, is covered with matting and has four pictures of relatives and scenes. The furniture consists of a double bed, dresser, washstand, table and three chairs. It is heated and lighted as the others. The bedroom over the dining-room has similar walls, is covered with matting, and has one framed picture of a group of boys. The furniture consists of one ordinary bed, one folding-bed and dresser. It is heated by one small fireplace and lighted by gas. Next to this bedroom is the bathroom, 5 x 10 feet.

Building Material.—The house is built of wood, with all the inside walls plastered with the exception of the kitchen. There is water through the house and in the yard. The house is lighted by gas; there is only one outhouse, the coalhouse. The house has had a recent coat of paint upon it.

Section 14. Evolution of the Negro Home. The pictures on the following pages present a series which illustrates partially the evolution of the Negro home:

No. 1—Group of African huts (loaned by the *Southern Workman*).

No. 2—Storehouse for corn—Bongo (Schweinfurth).

No. 3—Two dwelling-huts, 5–7 metres high—Bongo (Schweinfurth).

No. 4—Corn warehouses—Niam-Niam (Schweinfurth).

No. 5—Sleeping-hut for boys, kitchen-hut and dwelling-hut—Niam-Niam (Schweinfurth).

No. 6—Dwelling-hut (6 x 10 metres) and palace of the king (25 x 50 metres, 17 metres high)—Monbuttos (Schweinfurth).

Nos. 7–10—Slave-cabins, Southern United States (loaned by *Southern Workman*).

Nos. 11–13—Negro city tenements, Atlanta (photo. by A. J. Williams, '09.)

Nos. 14–19—Negro city tenements, Atlanta, poorer class (photo. by A. J. Williams, '09).

Nos. 20–27—Negro city tenements, Atlanta, better class (photo. by A. J. Williams, '09).

Nos. 28–35—Homes owned by Atlanta Negroes (photo. by A. J. Williams, '09).

No. 36—Residence of a Negro minister, Decatur (photo. by Askew).

No. 37—Residence of a Negro lawyer, Atlanta (photo. by Askew).

No. 38—Residence of a Negro tailor, Atlanta (photo. by Askew).

No. 39—Residence of a Negro working-woman, Atlanta.

No. 40—Residence of a Negro railway postal-clerk, South Atlanta.

No. 41—Residence of a Negro contractor and builder, Atlanta.

No. 42—Residence of a Negro grocer.

No. 43—Residence of a Negro business man, insurance manager and proprietor of barber shops; now building and said to be the finest Negro residence in the South. It will have electric bells and lights, fireplaces, steam-heat, roof-garden, and 15 rooms. (Photographs 39-43 by Askew).

Reproduced, by permission, from Stanley's "Through the Dark Continent."—Copyright, 1878, by Harper & Brothers.

1

Reproduced, by permission, from Stanley's "Through the Dark Continent."—Copyright, 1878, by Harper & Brothers

2

5

6

7

8

9

10

11

12

13

14 15

16

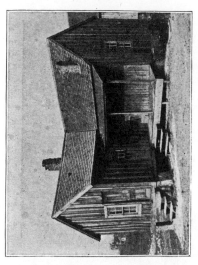

17

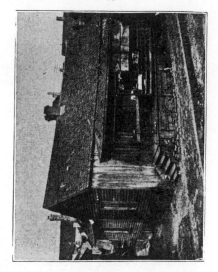

18

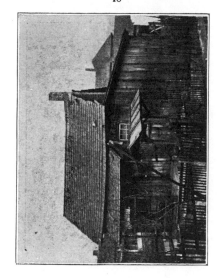

19

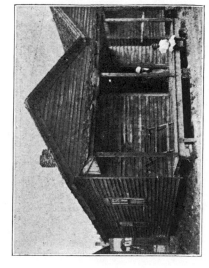

20

21

22

23

24

25

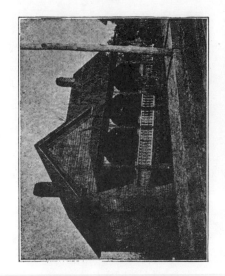

26

27

28

29

30

31

32

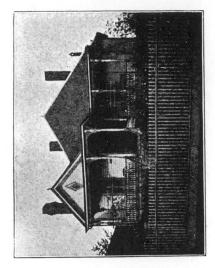

33

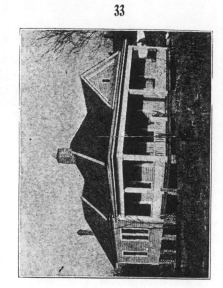

34

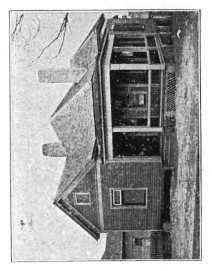

35

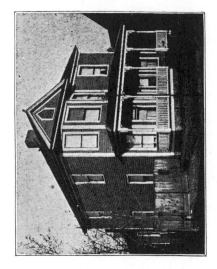

36

37

38

39

40

41

42

43

Part 3.   The Economics of the Family

Section 15.   Africa. The family economy of Africa is simple and primitive, and may be described briefly in the words of Bücher: [1]

The economy of many Negro tribes shows . . . a sharp division of the production and of many parts of the consumption according to sex; indeed even the extension of this distinction to the sphere of barter. As P. Pogge, one of our most reliable observers, says concisely of the Congo Negroes: "The woman has her own circle of duties independent of that of her husband." And in the description of the Bashilangas he observes: "No member of the family troubles himself about another at meal-times; while some eat the others come and go just as it suits them; but the women and the smaller children generally eat together." And finally he reports further regarding the Lundas: "Under ordinary conditions, when a caravan has pitched its camp in a village, the women of the place are accustomed to bring vegetables and fowl into the camp for sale, while goats, pigs and sheep are usually sold only by the men. It is similarly related by L. Wolf that in the market of Ibaushi all the agricultural products and materials, mats and pottery are sold by the women and only goats and wine by the men. Each sex is thus possessor of its special product of labor, and disposes of it independently.

The division of the labor production between the two sexes in Africa varies in detail from tribe to tribe; as a rule, however, agriculture and the preparation of all the vegetable foods are also assigned here to the woman, and hunting, cattle-raising, tanning, weaving to the man. This arrangement is often supported by superstitious usages. In Uganda the milking of the cows falls exclusively to men; a woman is never permitted to touch the udder of a cow. In the Lunda territory, again, no man is allowed to take part in the extraction of oil from the ground-nut, as his presence is thought to frustrate the success of the operation. As a rule the carriers whom Europeans engage refuse to do women's work; Livingstone even reports a case of famine among the men in a certain district because no women were there to grind the corn they had on hand. The separation of the two sexes in the preparation and consumption of food is often made still more rigid by regulations of a semi-religious character, forbidding the women the use of certain kinds of meat, which are thus reserved for men alone.

Everywhere among primitive peoples the children become independent very early in youth and desert the society of their parents. They often live then for some years in special common houses, of which there are others for married men. These common-houses for men-folk grouped according to age, and frequently also for the unmarried women grouped in the same way, are found very widely distributed in Africa and America, and especially in Oceania. They serve as common places of meeting, work, and amusement and as sleeping-places for the younger people, and are used also for lodging strangers. They naturally form a further obstacle to the development of a common household economy based upon the family, for each family is generally subdivided into different parts with separate dwellings.

It may be asserted as a general rule for primitive peoples practising polygamy that each wife has her own hut. Among the Zulus they go so far as to build a separate hut for almost every adult member of the household—one for the husband, one for his mother, one for each of his wives and other adult members of his family. These huts all stand in a semi-circle about the en-

---

[1] Carl Bucher: Industrial Evolution (translated by Wickett), chap. 1, pp. 35-38.

closed cattle-kraal in such a way that the man's dwelling is in the center. Of course it is to be remembered that a hut of this kind can be constructed in a few hours. [1]

Miss Kingsley says: [2]

The House is a collection of individuals; I should hesitate to call it a developed family. I cannot say it is a collection of human beings, because the very dogs and canoes and so on that belong to it are a part of it in the eye of the law, and capable therefore alike of embroiling it and advancing its interests. These Houses are bound together into groups by the Long ju-ju proper to the so-called secret society, common to the groups of houses. The House is presided over by what is called in white parlance, a king, and beneath him there are four classes of human beings in regular rank, that is to say influence in council: firstly, the free relations of the king, if he be a free man himself, which is frequently not the case; if he be a slave, the free people of the family he is trustee for; secondly, the free small people who have placed themselves under the protection of the House, rendering it in return for the assistance and protection it affords them service on demand; the third and fourth classes are true slave classes, the higher one in rank being that called the Winnaboes or Trade boys, the lower the pull-away boys and plantation hands. The best point in it, as a system, is that it gives to the poorest boy who paddles an oil-canoe a chance of becoming a king.

Property itself in West Africa, and as I have reason to believe from reports in other parts of tropical Africa that I am acquainted with, is firmly governed and is divisable into three kinds. Firstly, ancestral property connected with the office of headmanship, the Stool, as this office is called in the true Negro state, the Cap as it is called down in Bas Congo; secondly, family property, in which every member of the family has a certain share, and on which he, she or it has a claim; thirdly, private property, that which is acquired or made by a man or woman by their personal exertions, over and above that which is earned by them in co-operation with other members of their family which becomes a family property, and that which is gained by gifts or made in trade by the exercise of a superior trading ability.

Every one of these forms of property is equally sacred in the eye of the African law. The property of the Stool must be worked for the Stool; working it well, increasing it, adds to the importance of the Stool, and makes the king who does so popular; but he is trustee not owner of the Stool property, and his family does not come in for that property on his death, for every profit made by the working of Stool property is like this itself the property of the Stool, and during the king's life he cannot legally alienate it for his own personal advantage, but can only administer it for the benefit of the Stool.

The king's power over the property of the family and the private property of the people under this rule, consists in the right of Ban, but not arriere Ban. Family property is much the same as regards the laws concerning it as Stool property. The head of the family is trustee of it. If he is a spendthrift, or unlucky in its management, he is removed from his position. Any profit he may make with the assistance of a member of his own family becomes family property; but of course any property he may make with the assistance of his free wives or wife, a person who does not belong to his family, or with the assistance of an outsider, may become his own. Private property acquired in the ways I have mentioned is equally sacred in the eyes

---

[1] Carl Bucher: Industrial Evolution (translated by Wickett), chap. 1, p. 38.
[2] West African Studies, 2d ed., pp. 365-366.

of the law. I do not suppose you could find a single human being, slave or free, who had not some private property of his or her very own.

Section 16. Slavery. The economic revolution of slavery, so far as the family was concerned, was far-reaching. Newly imported Africans were in the West Indies often portioned off among the older slave families. These families were supposed to support themselves by food which they raised on plots of ground given them, the masters only helping out in case of drought. This, however, did not always work well, as the harder the slaves were driven the less time and inclination they had to raise food of the proper amount and kind. Gradually, therefore, on the continent, the system of "rations" came into use: every week or fortnight each slave family presented themselves at the master's storehouse and received an allowance of pork and corn-meal, and perhaps other food. Once a year, usually at Christmas-time, clothing was distributed. The following extracts will illustrate conditions:

Rev. George Whitefield, in his letter to the slaveholders of Maryland, Virginia, North Carolina, South Carolina and Georgia, published in 1739, said:

My blood has frequently run cold within me, to think how many of your slaves have not sufficient food to eat; they are scarcely permitted to pick up the crumbs that fall from their master's table.

The Maryland *Journal*, and Baltimore *Advertiser*, May 30, 1788, says:

A single peck of corn a week, or the like measure of rice, is the ordinary quantity of provision for a hard-working slave; to which a small quantity of meat is occasionally, though rarely, added.

Hon. Alexander Smyth, a slaveholder, and for ten years a Member of Congress from Virginia, in his speech on the Missouri question, said January 28, 1820:

By confining the slaves to Southern States, where crops are raised for exportation and bread and meat are purchased, you doom them to scarcity and hunger. It is proposed to hem in the blacks where they are ill-fed.

The report of the Gradual Emancipation Society, of North Carolina, 1826, speaking of the condition of slaves in the eastern part of that State, says:

The master puts the unfortunate wretches upon short allowances, scarcely sufficient for their sustenance, so that a great part of them go half-starved much of the time.

Hon. Robert Turnbull, a slaveholder of Charleston, S. C., says:

The subsistence of the slaves consists, from March until August, of corn ground into grits, or meal, made into what is called hominy, or baked into cornbread. The other six months they are fed upon the sweet potato. Meat when given is only by the way of indulgence or favor.

Others testify: [1]

The food of the slaves was generally cornbread, and sometimes meat or molasses.

---

[1] American Slavery as it Is, p. 28.

The slaves had no food allowed them besides corn, excepting at Christmas, when they had beef.

On my uncle's plantation the food of the slaves was cornpone and a small allowance of meat.

Angelina Grimke Weld says: [1]

Only two meals a day are allowed the house-slaves—the first at twelve o'clock. If they eat before this time, it is by stealth, and I am sure there must be a good deal of suffering among them from hunger, and particularly by children. Besides this they are often kept from their meals by way of punishment. No table is provided for them to eat from. They know nothing of the comfort and pleasure of gathering round the social board—each takes his plate or tin pan and iron spoon, and holds it in the hand or on the lap. I never saw slaves seated around a table to partake of any meal.

Mr. Eleazar Powell, Chippewa, Beaver county, Penn., who resided in Mississippi in 1836 and 1837, said:

The slaves received two meals during the day. Those who have their food cooked for them get their breakfast about eleven o'clock, and their other meal about midnight.

Philemon Bliss, Esq., a lawyer in Elyria, Ohio, and a member of the Presbyterian church, who lived in Florida in 1834 and 1835, said:

The slaves go to the field in the morning; they carry with them cornmeal wet with water, and at noon build a fire on the ground and bake it in the ashes. After the labors of the day are over, they take their second meal of ash-cake.

"The legal allowance for food in North Carolina is, in the words of the law, 'a quart of corn per day.' See Haywood's Manual, page 525. The legal allowance in Louisiana is more, a barrel [flour barrel] of corn (in the ear), or its equivalent in other grain, and a pint of salt a salt a month. In the other slave States the amount of food for the slaves is left to the option of the master." (1839.)

Thos. Clay, Esq., of Georgia, a slaveholder, in his address before the Presbytery, 1833, said:

The quantity allowed by custom is a peck of corn a week.

An observer who lived twelve years in the South says:

In lower Tennessee, Mississippi and Louisiana, the clothing of the slaves is wretchedly poor; and grows worse as you go south, in the order of the States I have named. The only material is cotton bagging, i. e., bagging in which cotton is baled, not bagging made of cotton. In Louisiana, especially in the lower country, I have frequently seen them with nothing but a tattered coat, not sufficient to hide their nakedness. In winter their clothing seldom serves the purpose of comfort, and frequently not even of decent covering. In Louisiana the planters never think of serving out shoes to slaves. In Mississippi they give one pair a year generally. I never saw or heard of an instance of masters allowing them stockings. A small poor blanket is generally the only bed clothing, and this they frequently wear in the field when they have not sufficient clothing to hide their nakedness or to keep them warm. Their manner of sleeping varies with the season. In hot weather

---

[1] American Slavery, etc., pp. 55-56.

they stretch themselves anywhere and sleep. As it becomes cool they roll themselves in their blankets, and lay scattered about the cabin. In cold weather they nestle together with their feet towards the fire, promiscuously. [1]

The masters [in Georgia] make a practice of getting two suits of clothes for each slave per year, a thick suit for winter and a thin one for summer. They provide also one pair of Northern-made sale shoes for each slave in winter. [2]

The males and females have their suits from the same cloth for their winter dresses. These winter garments appear to be made of a mixture of cotton and wool, very coarse and sleazy. The whole suit for the men consists of a pair of pantaloons and a short sailor jacket, without shirt, vest, hat, stockings, or any kind of loose garments! These, if worn steadily when at work, would not probably last more than one or two months; therefore, for the sake of saving them, many of them work, especially in the summer, with no clothing on them except a cloth tied around their waist, and almost all with nothing more on them than a pantaloons, and these frequently so torn that they do not serve the purposes of common decency. The women have for clothing a short petticoat, and a short loose gown, something like the male's sailor-jacket, without any under garment, stockings, bonnets, hoods, caps, or any kind of over-clothes. When at work in warm weather they usually strip off the loose gown, and have nothing on but a short petticoat with some kind of covering over their breasts. Many children may be seen in summer months as naked as they came into the world. [3]

The allowance of clothing on this plantation to each slave, was given out at Christmas for the year, and consisted of one pair of coarse shoes and enough coarse cloth to make a jacket and trousers. If the man has a wife she makes it up; if not, it is made up in the house. The slaves on this plantation, being near Wilmington, procured themselves extra clothing by working Sundays and moonlight nights, cutting cordwood in the swamps, which they had to back about a quarter of a mile to the river; they would then get a permit from their master and, taking the wood in their canoes, carry it to Wilmington and sell it to the vessels, or dispose of it as best they could, and with the money buy an old jacket of the sailors, some coarse cloth for a shirt, etc. They sometimes gather the moss from the trees, which they cleanse and take to market. The women receive their allowance of the same kind of cloth that the men have. This they make into a frock; if they have any under garment they must procure them for themselves. . . .

Every Saturday night the slaves receive their allowances of provisions, which must last them till the next Saturday night. "Potato time," as it is called, begins about the middle of July. The slave may measure for himself, the overseers being present, half a bushel of sweet potatoes, and heap the measure as long as they will lie on; I have, however, seen the overseer, if he thinks the Negro is getting too many, kick the measure; and if they fall off tell him he has got his measure. No salt is furnished them to eat with their potatoes. When rice or corn is given they give them a little salt; sometimes half pint of molasses is given, but not often. The quantity of rice, which is of the small broken, unsaleable kind, is one peck. When corn is given them their allowance is the same, and if they get it ground (Mr. Swan had a mill on his plantation), they must give one quart for grinding, thus reducing their weekly allowance to seven quarts. When fish (mullet) were plentiful they were allowed in addition one fish. As to meat they seldom had any. I do not

---

[1] American Slavery as it Is, p. 42.   [2] Ibid., p. 19.   [3] Ibid., p. 19.

think they had any allowance for meat oftener than once in two or three months, then the quantity was very small. When they went into the field to work they took some of the meat or rice and a pot with them; the pots were given to an old woman who placed two, poles parallel, set the pots on them and kindled a fire underneath for cooking; she took salt with her and seasoned the messes as she thought proper. When their breakfast was ready, which was generally about ten or eleven o'clock, they were called from labor, ate, and returned to work; in the afternoon dinner was prepared in the same way. They had but two meals a day while in the field; if they wanted more, they cooked for themselves after they returned to their quarters at night. At the time of killing hogs on the plantation, the pluck, entrails and blood were given to the slaves. [1]

Mr. George W. Westgate, who had been engaged in the low-country trade for twelve years, more than half of each year, principally on the Mississippi, and its tributary streams in the southwestern slave States, said:

Feeding is not sufficient—let facts speak. On the coast, i. e., Natchez and the Gulf of Mexico, the allowance was one barrel of ears of corn and a pint of salt per month. They may cook this in what manner they please, but it must be done after dark; they have no daylight to prepare it by. Some few planters, but only a few, let them prepare their corn on Saturday afternoons. Planters, overseers and Negroes have told me that in pinching times, i. e., when corn is high, they did not get near that quantity. In Mississippi I know some planters who allowed their hands three and a half pounds of meat per week when it was cheap. Many prepare their corn on the Sabbath, when they are not worked on that day, which however is frequently the case on sugar plantations. There are very many masters on "the coast" who will not suffer their slaves to come to the boats, because they steal molasses to barter for meat; indeed, they generally trade more or less with stolen property. But it is impossible to find out what and when, as their articles of barter are of such trifling importance. They would often come on board to beg a bone, and would tell how badly they were fed, that they were almost starved; many a time I have sat up all night to prevent them from stealing something to eat. [2]

Slaves belonging to merchants and others in the city often hire their own time, for which they pay various prices, per week or month, according to the capacity of the slave. The females who thus hire their time pursue various modes to procure the money; their masters making no inquiry how they get it, provided the money comes. If it is not regularly paid they are flogged. Some take in washing, some cook on board vessels, pick oakum, sell peanuts, etc., while others, younger and more comely, often resort to the vilest pursuits. [3]

This is all that good or bad masters allow their slaves round about Savannah on the plantations: One peck of gourd seed-corn is to be measured out to each slave once every week. One man with whom I labored, however, being desirous to get all the work out of his hands he could before I left (about fifty in number), bought for them every week, or twice a week, a beef's head from market. With this they made a soup in a large iron kettle, around which the hands came at meal time, and dipping out the soup would mix it with their

---

[1] Narrative of Mr. Caulkins on estate of John Swan, near Wilmington, N. C., 1838. American Slavery as it Is, p. 13.

[2] American Slavery as it Is, p. 30.   [3] Ibid., p. 16.

hommony, and eat it as though it were a feast. This man permitted his slaves to eat twice a day while I was doing a job for him. [1]

The custom was to blow the horn early in the morning, as a signal for the hands to rise and go to work, when commenced; they continued work until about eleven o'clock, a. m., when at the signal all-hands left off and went into their huts, made their fires, made their corn-meal into hommony or cake, ate it, and went to work again at the signal of the horn, and worked until night or until their tasks were done. Some cooked their breakfast in the field while at work. Each slave must grind his own corn in a hand-mill after he has done his work at night. There is generally one hand-mill on every plantation for the use of the slaves.

Some of the planters have no corn, others often get out. The substitute for it is the equivalent of one peck of corn either in rice or sweet potatoes; neither of which is as good for the slave as corn. They complain more of being faint who feed on rice and potatoes than when fed on corn. I was with one man a few weeks who gave me his hands to do a job of work, and to save the time one cooked for all the rest. The following course was taken: Two crotched sticks were driven down at one end of the yard, and a small pole being laid on the crotches, they swung a large iron kettle on the middle of the pole; then made up a fire under the kettle and boiled the hommony; when ready the hands were called around this kettle with their wooden plates and spoons. They dipped out and ate standing around the kettle, or sitting upon the ground, as best suited their convenience. When they had potatoes they took them out with their hands, and ate them. As soon as it was thought they had had sufficient time to swallow their food they were called to their work again. This was the only meal they ate through the day. [2]

The general allowance of food was thought to be a peck and a half of meal and three pounds of bacon a week. This it was observed is as much meal as they can eat, but they would be glad to have more bacon; sometimes they receive four pounds, but it is oftener that they receive less than three. It is distributed to them on Saturday nights, or on the better-managed plantations sometimes Wednesday, to prevent their using it extravagantly, or selling it for whiskey on Sunday.

Olmsted says that the slaves take their breakfast at sunrise or a little before, then go to the field and work until noon; their dinner is brought to them, and when the work is not too pressing they have two hours to rest. Promptly at sundown they stop work and return to their cabins. Then they go to the woods, bring wood and cook their supper, which will be a bit of bacon fried often with eggs, corn-bread baked in the spider, after the bacon to absorb the fat, and perhaps some sweet potatoes roasted in the ashes. [3]

The ploughmen got their dinner at twelve o'clock: those not using horses do not usually dine till they have finished their tasks; but this, I believe, is optional with them. They commence work at sunrise and at about eight o'clock have their breakfast brought to them in the field, each hand having left a bucket with the cook for that purpose. All who are working in connection leave their work together and gather in a social company about a fire, where they spend about half an hour, at breakfast time. The provisions furnished them consist mainly of meal, rice, and vegetables, with salt and molasses, and occasionally bacon, fish and coffee. The allowance is a peck of meal or an equivalent quantity of rice per week, to each working hand old or young, besides small stores. [4]

---

[1] American Slavery as it Is. p. 18.   [2] Ibid., pp. 18-19.
[3] Olmsted: Seaboord Slave States, I, pp. 120-122.   [4] Ibid, I, p. 60

The slaves were furnished with a coat and trousers of coarse woollen, or woollen and cotton stuff for winter, and trousers of cotton osnaburg for summer. They had two pairs of shoes, or a pair of shoes and a pair of boots each year. The women have two dresses of striped cotton, three shifts, two pairs of shoes, etc. [1]

Section 17. General Economic Condition. The chief occupations of Negroes in 1890 and 1900 were as follows:

Negro Population, at least Ten Years of Age, Engaged in Specified Occupations: 1890 and 1900

OCCUPATION	1890	1900	Per cent of Increase
Continental United States:			
All occupations....................	3,073,164	3,992,337	29.9
Occupations giving employment to			
at least 10,000 Negroes in 1900.......	*2,917,169	3,807,008	*29.8
Agricultural laborers.................	1,106,728	1,344,125	21.5
Farmers, planters and overseers.....	590,666	757,822	28.3
Laborers (not specified)........	349,002	545,935	56.4
Servants and waiters	401,215	465,734	16.1
Launderers and Laundresses	153,684	220,104	43.2
Draymen, hackmen, teamsters, etc...	43,963	67,585	53.7
Steam railroad employees...	47,548	55,327	16.4
Miners and quarrymen	19,007	36,561	92.4
Saw and planing-mill employees.....	17,276	33,266	92.6
Porters and helpers (in stores, etc.)..	11,694	28,977	147.8
Teachers, professors in colleges, etc..	15,100	21,267	40.8
Carpenters and joiners	22,581	21,113	†6.5
Turpentine farmers and laborers.....	‡	20,744	....
Barbers and hairdressers............	17,480	19,942	14.1
Nurses and midwives	5,213	19,431	272.7
Clergymen	12,159	15,528	27.7
Tobacco and cigar factory operatives	15,004	15,349	2.3
Hostlers..............................	10,500	14,496	38.1
Masons (brick and stone).............	9,760	14,386	47.4
Dressmakers	7,586	12,569	65.7
Iron and steel workers...............	6,579	12,327	87.4
Seamstresses	11,846	11,537	†2.6
Janitors and sextons.................	5,945	11,536	94.0
Housekeepers and stewards..........	9,248	10,596	14.6
Fishermen and oystermen	10,071	10,427	3.5
Engineers, firemen, (not locomotive)	6,326	10,224	61.6
Blacksmiths..........................	10,988	10,100	†8.1
Other occupations	§155,995	185,329	§32.1

* Excludes turpentine farmers and laborers.   † Decrease.
  ‡Turpentine farmers and laborers were included in "other agricultural pursuits" in 1890.   § Includes turpentine farmers and laborers. [2]

Turning our attention specifically to the Negro farmer we may say: There was some ownership of land by Negroes before the war, but not much. During and after the war lands in Georgia and South Carolina were sold to Negroes on easy terms and Negroes bought land elsewhere. In 1875, there is reason to believe, Negroes held between two and four million acres of land; by 1880 this had increased to about six millions; to about eight millions in 1890, and to about twelve millions in 1900.

---

[1] Olmsted, I, p. 129.
[2] Bulletin No 8, p. 58.

In 1900 there were 187,799 farms in the United States owned by Negroes, comprising about 12,000,000 acres. The owned farms constitute 25.2% of all Negro farms; the private farm-owning families 25.3% of all Negro-farms families. Taking all homes, both farm homes and others, we · find that 20.3% of them are owned. There were 190,111 private farm-owning Negro families in 1900, and a somewhat larger number of farm-owning families of all sorts. Since 1890 the number of Negro farmers probably increased by about 36 or 38 per cent, the number of Negro owners increased over 57 per cent, and the percentage of ownership increased by 3.5. These percentages, although based on figures which are not entirely comparable, are sufficiently exact to measure approximately the advance toward farm ownership made by the Negroes during the decade 1890 to 1900. These owners—including Indians and Mongolians, who constitute but 3% of all—have 15 million acres worth $179,796,639, and raised in 1899 products worth $57,422,983. They expended $2,624,595 for hired labor, and $1,197,180 for fertilizers. The black tenant farmer of the South is half way between slavery and free-ownership of the soil. The crop-lien system binds him in a black-belt of farming which is growing blacker. Under favorable conditions share tenants become cash renters and eventually owners, but this evolution is difficult. There are 283,614 Negro share tenant farmers in the United States and 273,560 cash tenants, and although the separate farms they cultivate are small, there is great concentration in owner-ship of land by the landlords. The colored tenants control 25 million acres of land and 360 million dollars of farm property; they raise 200 million dollars worth of products annually, including 3 million bales of cotton, 73 million bushels of corn, 6 million bushels of sweet potatoes, 200,000 tons of hay and forage, $1\frac{1}{2}$ million bushels of wheat, 2 million bushels of oats, 31 million pounds of rice and $62\frac{1}{2}$ million pounds of tobacco. The average share-tenant's farm is worth $628. It has land worth $435, $84 in buildings, $19 in tools, and $90 in live stock. It raises on an average $311 worth of products, or $7.33 worth per acre.

Considering all·Negro farmers, owners and tenants, we have in the United States 746,717 farms conducted by them, with an acreage about the size of New England. Of this acreage less than a million acres are in the North and 37 millions in the South. Of these farms 716,514 were improved by buildings, and they contained 38,233,933 acres, or 59,741 square miles, an area about equal to that of the State of Georgia or that of New England; 23,362,798 acres, or 61 per cent of the total area, was improved for farming purposes. The total value of property on these farms was $499,943,734, of which $324,244,397 represented the value of land and improvements, $71,903,315 that of buildings, $18,859,757 that of implements and machinery, and $84,936,265 that of live stock. The gross value of all products on farms of Negroes in 1899 was $255,751,145. Of this sum, however, $25,843,443 represents products fed to live stock, the value of which reappears and is to that extent duplicated in the reported value of animal products, such as meat, milk, butter, eggs and poultry; subtracting this amount we have a net value of $229,907,702, or 46 per cent of the total value of farm property in farms cultivated by Negroes. This sum represents the gross farm income. The total expenditure for labor on farms of Negroes in 1899 was $8,789,792, and the expenditure for fertilizers was $5,614,844.

A third of the Negro farms yielded $100 to $250 income; another third $250 to $500 income; something over a seventh yielded over $500. The rest, 18 per cent, yielded less than $100. Estimating the net income after the rent has been subtracted, it is probable that 560,000 Negro-farm families have incomes between $150 and $170 a year, while about 200,000 families average $250 to $275 a year.

The colored farmer conducts a little less than $\frac{1}{7}$ of all the farms in the United States; controls $\frac{1}{20}$ of the total farm acreage and $\frac{1}{37}$ of all farm property in value, and raises $\frac{1}{15}$ of the products in value. In the South the Negro holds a third of the farms, a tenth of the acreage and a ninth of the property, and raises $\frac{1}{5}$ of the products. He conducts half the farms on which cotton is the chief crop, over a third of the rice farms, nearly a fifth of the tobacco farms, a seventh of the sugar farms and a tenth of the vegetable farms. Colored farmers raised, in 1899, 39.4% of the cotton on their own farms, besides what they raised as laborers on white farms; 9% of the rice, 21% of the sweet potatoes, 10% of the tobacco, and 4% of the corn. They owned 3% in value of the stock. The average Negro farm is worth 16% as much as the average white farm. The Negro is thus seen to be relatively a small economic factor according to his numbers, but nevertheless a factor that cannot be ignored and which is absolutely of great importance.

To estimate the total property held by Negroes we may quote a report of a committee of the American Economic Association based on the census of 1900:

It is the opinion of your committee that the census farm returns furnish a better basis for estimating the total accumulated wealth possessed by the Negroes in 1900 than is found in the only other source that has been used, namely, the assessors' returns for a few Southern States. The Census Bureau estimate is $200,000,000 fqr the value of (1) the farms, live-stock and implements on the farms owned and operated by Negroes and of (2) the live-stock on the farms rented by Negroes. This should be increased by (3) the farm property owned by Negroes and rented by them either to Negroes or to whites, and also by (4) the farm property other than live-stock owned by Negro farm tenants. It should be decreased by (1) the various unknown liabilities against this property in the hands of whites and by (2) the value of the live-stock of Negro tenants which is owned by white landlords. It is the belief of your committee that the subtractions would at least equal the additions, and that $200,000,000 may be deemed an outside estimate of the net value of the accumulated property owned by Negro farmers. Indeed it seems to us probable that this estimate would be large enough to include also the wealth owned by the 550,000 families of agricultural laborers. In other words, we believe that the total property held by these families is not greater than the legal claims held by whites against Negro farm property plus the proportion of the $50,000,000 worth of live-stock on the farms of Negro tenants which is owned by whites, of neither of which is any account taken in the Census Bureau estimate.

If this be granted, then the further assumption may be ventured that the other 500,000 Negro families in the United States are no better off on the average in the matter of accumulated wealth than are the 1¼ million families occupied in agricultural pursuits. On that assumption the total accumulated wealth of Negro families in 1900 was in the neighborhood of $275,000,000.

An inquiry into the value of the property held by Negro churches in 1890 gave as a result $26,600,000. As the Negro population of the United States increased between 1890 and 1900 by 18.0 percent and the number of Negro churches only about two-thirds as fast, the value of property held by Negro churches can hardly be supposed to have increased during the decade by more than 20 per cent. In that case the value of such property in 1900 was approximately $32,000,000. The legal claims against it owned by whites cannot be estimated. Nor does your committee see any way in which the amount of property held by Negroes other than family or church property can be approximated.

The evidence in hand leads your committee to the conclusion that the accumulated wealth of the Negro race in the United States in 1900 was approximately $300,000,000, and probably neither less than $250,000,000 nor more than $350,000,000.

Section 18. Georgia. A more detailed picture of property owned by Negroes is furnished by the reports of the Comptroller-General of Georgia:

Number of Acres and Assessed Value of Land Owned by Negroes of Georgia, 1874 to 1907

YEAR	Acres owned	Assessed value	YEAR	Acres owned	Assessed value
1874	338,769	(a)	1891	1,004,305	$3,914,143
1875	396,658	$1,263,902	1892	1,063,649	4,477,183
1876	457,635	1,234,104	1893	1,043,860	4,450,121
1877	458,999	1,262,723	1894	1,064,431	4,386,366
1878	501,890	1,294,383	1895	1,038,824	4,158,960
1879	541,199	1,348,758	1896	1,043,847	4,234,848
1880	586,664	1,522,173	1897	1,057,567	4,353,798
1881	600,358	1,754,800	1898	1,097,087	4,340,100
1882	692,335	1,877,861	1899	1,062,223	4,220,120
1883	666,583	2,065,938	1900	1,075,073	4,274,549
1884	756,703	2,262,185	1901	1,141,135	4,656,042
1885	788,376	2,362,889	1902	1,175,291	4,779,263
1886	802,939	2,508,198	1903	1,251,714	5,181,471
1887	813,725	2,598,650	1904	1,284,336	5,455,328
1888	868,501	2,822,943	1905	1,336,821	6,282,436
1889	877,112	3,047,695	1906	1,420,888	7,149,925
1890	967,234	3,425,176	1907	1,449,624	7,972,787

(a) Not reported.

An examination of the records of typical counties show that this land was distributed about as follows:

Farm Land, 1899, Approximate Distribution by Assessed Value

	Per cent of Owners	Per cent of Value
Under $100	46.9	9.4
$100 or under $300	31.1	23 8
$300 or under $500	11.3	19.2
$500 or under $1000	7.7	23.4
$1000 or under $2000	2.2	12.9
$2000 and over.	.8	11.8
	100.0	100.0

Farm Land, 1906

	Per cent of Owners	Per cent of Value
Under $100	36.5	5.5
$100 or under $300	32.7	18.5
$300 or under $500	14.3	17.8
$500 or under $1000	11.2	25.1
$1000 or under $2000	4.1	17.8
$2000 and over.................	1.2	15.3
	100.0	100.0

Farm Land, 1899: Approximate Distribution by Acres

	Per cent of Owners	Per cent of Acreage
Under 10 acres.................	30.5	1.6
10 acres or under 50	32.4	12.1
50 acres or under 100..........	16.5	16.9
100 acres or under 300	17 4	42.2
300 acres or under 500	2.3	13 9
500 acres and over.............	9	13.3
	100.0	100.0

Farm Land, 1906

	Per cent of Owners	Per cent of Acreage
Under 10 acres.....	30.3	1.5
10 acres or under 50	31.7	12.1
50 acres or under 100	16.4	17.1
100 acres or under 300	18.5	44 9
300 acres or under 500	2.2	12.7
500 acres and over.............	.9	11.7
	100.0	100.0

Assessed Value of Town and City Real Estate and Per Cent of Town and City Real Estate of Total Property Owned by Negroes of Georgia, 1875 to 1907

YEAR	Assessed value	Per cent of total property	YEAR	Assessed value	Per cent of total property
1875.	$1,203,202	22.31	1892.	$4,668,733	31.40
1876	1,192,609	21.73	1893.	4,851,144	32.43
1877.	1,154,422	21.26	1894.	4,635,055	32.22
1878.	1,110,147	21.66	1895.	3,436,778	34.28
1879.	1,094,435	21.12	1896.	4,437,329	33.38
1880.	1,201,992	20.85	1897.	4,321,620	31.73
1881.	1,323,045	20.42	1898.	4,374,565	31.89
1882.	1,478,623	22.44	1899.	4,346,396	32.32
1883.	1,657,101	21.85	1900.	4,361,390	30.89
1884.	1,921,801	23.96	1901.	4,351,935	27.84
1885.	2,098,787	25.74	1902.	4,389,422	28.89
1886.	2,328,962	26.91	1903.	4,668,620	27.93
1887.	2,499,389	27.97	1904.	5,165,000	28.55
1888.	2,752,024	28.57	1905.	5,512,217	26.73
1889.	3,103,486	29.80	1906.	5,950,036	25.05
1890.	3,642,586	29.56	1907.	6,710,189	25.90
1891.	4,131,216	29.10			

**Georgia Town and City Property, 1899,
Approximate Distribution by Value**

	Per cent of Owners	Per cent of Value
Under $100	26.7	4.1
$100 or under $300	38.0	19.0
$300 or under $500	16.0	17.4
$500 or under $1000	13.9	27.2
$1000 or under $2000	3.0	10.4
$2000 and over	2.4	21.9
	100.0	100.0

Town and City Property, 1906

	Per cent of Owners	Per cent of Value
Under $100	17.9	2.5
$100 or under $300	39.2	18.3
$300 or under $500	21.7	21.8
$500 or under $1000	15.4	27.2
$1000 or under $2000	4.3	15.2
$2000 and over	1.5	15.0
	100.0	100.0

Assessed Value of Horses, Mules, Cattle, and Other Stock, and of Plantation and Mechanical Tools, Owned by Negroes of Georgia, 1875 to 1907

YEAR	Assessed Value		YEAR	Assessed Value	
	Horses, mules, cattle, and other stock	Plantation and mechanical tools		Horses, mules, cattle, and other stock	Plantation and mechanical tools
1875	(a)	$20,017	1892	$3,180,322	$590,902
1876	$241,106	125,120	1893	3,130,818	547,739
1877	1,926,942	162,647	1894	2,997,587	511,316
1878	1,641,367	166,780	1895	2,288,850	402,040
1879	1,704,230	143,258	1896	2,494,390	416,091
1880	2,054,787	163,086	1897	2,676,186	491,956
1881	2,213,021	225,973	1898	2,579,770	479,520
1882	2,031,361	193,898	1899	2,213,905	433,125
1883	2,361,662	238,308	1900	2,424,674	469,637
1884	2,387,282	242,222	1901	3,078,444	645,451
1885	2,245,801	228,894	1902	2,985,831	652,583
1886	2,166,569	260,549	1903	3,531,471	810,553
1887	2,178,518	304,815	1904	3,889,441	880,599
1888	2,314,356	331,876	1905	4,633,124	1,108,534
1889	2,315,480	384,827	1906	5,880,761	1,402,033
1890	2,915,635	474,386	1907	6,080,657	1,407,865
1891	3,429,223	645,261			

(a) Not reported.

Assessed Value of Household and Kitchen Furniture Owned by Negroes of Georgia, 1875 to 1907

YEAR	Assessed value	YEAR	Assessed value	YEAR	Assessed value
1875	$21,186	1886	$858,329	1897	$1,429,247
1876	489,522	1887	901,765	1898	1,453,619
1877	535,291	1888	951,177	1899	1,434,975
1878	502,699	1889	1,017,439	1900	1,655,092
1879	448,713	1890	1,173,624	1901	1,811,113
1880	498,532	1891	1,365,468	1902	1,688,541
1881	600,892	1892	1,474,220	1903	1,822,551
1882	579,736	1893	1,486,821	1904	1,935,409
1883	676,346	1894	1,446,926	1905	2,080,444
1884	699,182	1895	1,322,694	1906	2,393,402
1885	736,170	1896	1,363,842	1907	2,581,645

Assessed Value of Total Property Owned by Negroes of Georgia, 1874 to 1907

YEAR	Assessed value	YEAR	Assessed value	YEAR	Assessed value
1874	$6,157,798	1886	$8,655,298	1898	$13,719,200
1875	5,393,885	1887	8,936,479	1899	13,447,423
1876	5,488,867	1888	9,631,271	1900	14,118,720
1877	5,430,844	1889	10,415,380	1901	15,629,811
1878	5,124,875	1890	12,322,003	1902	15,188,069
1879	5,182,398	1891	14,196,735	1903	16,714,334
1880	5,764,293	1892	14,869,575	1904	18,087,934
1881	6,478,951	1893	14,960,675	1905	20,616,468
1882	6,589,876	1894	14,387,780	1906	23,750,109
1883	7,582,395	1895	12,941,230	1907	25,904,822
1884	8,021,525	1896	13,292,816		
1885	8,153,390	1897	13,619,690		

Since 1900 Negro property in Georgia has increased 83.4%. If Negro property throughout the Nation has increased in like proportion (and this is wholly conjectural), then, to use the phraseology of the American Economic Association Committee: "The accumulated wealth of the Negro race in the United States in 1907 may be approximately $550,000,000 and possibly neither less than $550,000,000 nor more than $600,000,000."

The economic situation of Negro Americans is thus summed up:

To sum then the conclusions of this paper: half the Negro breadwinners of the nation are partially submerged by a bad economic system, an unjust admiration of the laws and enforced ignorance. Their future depends on common schools, justice, and the right to vote. A million and three-quarters of men just above these are fighting a fierce battle for admission to the industrial ranks of the nation—for the right to work. They are handicapped by their own industrial history which has made them often shiftless and untrustworthy, but they can, by means of wise economic leadership, be made a strong body of artisans and landowners. A quarter of a million men stand economically at the head of the Negroes, and by a peculiar self-protecting group economy are making themselves independent of prejudice and competition. This group economy is extending to the lower economic strata." [1]

Section 19. Income. Some ideas of the income of Negro families may be gathered from the following figures:

Number of Families by Size of Family and Annual Income. Farmville, Va., 1897

ANNUAL INCOME	FAMILIES OF									Total Families
	One Member	Two Members	Three Members	Four Members	Five Members	Six Members	Seven Members	Eight Members	Nine to Eleven Members	
$50 or less	3	..	1	..	1	..	..	..	..	5
$50 to $75	5	4	1	1	..	..	..	..	..	11
$75 to $100	1	6	..	3	..	1	..	..	..	11
$100 to $150	1	7	6	..	2	2	1	..	..	19
$150 to $200	..	8	4	5	4	3	3	2	..	29
$200 to $250	1	14	5	9	3	4	2	..	2	40
$250 to $350	..	10	7	12	5	7	6	1	5	53
$350 to $500	..	1	7	13	7	1	4	5	6	44
$500 to $750	..	2	1	3	6	7	3	8	5	35
$750 or over	..	..	..	..	1	..	..	..	5	6
Not reported	2	..	2	2	2	1	..	..	..	9
Total Families	13	52	34	48	31	26	19	16	23	262

[1] From Papers and Proceedings of the Eighteenth Annual Meeting American Economic Association, December, 1906.

Number of Families by Size of Family and Annual Income
Negroes of Xenia, Ohio, 1903

ANNUAL INCOME	FAMILIES OF										
	One Member	Two Members	Three Members	Four Members	Five Members	Six Members	Seven Members	Eight Members	Nine Members	Ten Members or over	Total Families
Under $50	2	2	1	....	....	....	....	....	....	....	5
$50 to $75	4	3	4	....	....	....	....	....	....	....	11
$75 to $100	8	4	2	....	1	....	....	....	....	....	15
$100 to $150	7	12	8	2	2	....	....	....	....	....	31
$150 to $200	7	17	1	3	3	....	2	....	....	....	33
$200 to $250	7	8	14	12	4	1	1	3	....	....	50
$250 to $350	2	29	22	11	9	5	3	2	3	....	86
$350 to $500	3	21	35	23	18	15	3	2	2	1	123
$500 to $750	....	7	10	8	15	6	2	3	2	4	57
$750 to $1000	....	4	6	4	8	3	1	1	....	1	28
$1000 or over	....	....	3	5	3	....	2	1	....	4	18
Not reported	11	5	19	4	1	2	1	1	....	....	14
Total	51	112	125	72	64	32	15	13	7	10	501

Estimated Annual Income and Expenditure of a Family of Five
Negroes of Xenia, Ohio, 1903

INCOME		EXPENDITURE	
Items	Amt.	Items	Amt.
11 weeks @ $6.50 per week	$71 50	Rent @ $3.00 per month	$36 00
26 weeks @ 7.50 per week	195 00	Clothing (two suits)	20 00
		Underclothes	3 00
		Shoes and stockings	9 50
		Groceries and meat @ 80c. per week	93 60
		Doctor's bill and medicine	15 00
		Life Insurance for 4 @ 5c pr. wk. ea.	10 40
		Incidentals and miscellaneous	12 10
		Moving to Xenia	37 00
		Fuel and lighting	30 00
Total	$266 50	Total	$266 50

Incomes According to Size of Family in Seventh Ward. 1896. Philadelphia

Amount of Income Per Year	Size of Family											Total Number of Families
	1	2	3	4	5	6	7	8	9	10	11 to 15	
$50	7	5	1	....	....	....	1	....	....	....	....	14
100	22	18	2	2	1	....	....	....	....	....	....	45
150	31	69	19	4	6	4	....	....	....	....	....	133
200	23	105	35	12	8	4	....	....	....	....	....	187
250	32	95	46	26	7	1	5	2	....	....	....	214
300	10	108	49	33	9	3	1	....	....	....	....	213
350	9	121	46	30	11	10	2	1	....	....	....	230
400	4	95	39	34	22	9	6	....	....	....	....	209
450	1	79	40	26	14	7	3	1	1	....	....	172
500	7	115	47	37	26	17	1	3	2	....	1	256
550	....	23	12	8	4	4	1	0	3	....	....	55
600	1	17	14	8	7	3	3	....	1	....	....	54
650	1	45	26	27	11	7	4	2	1	...	1	125
700	....	10	16	12	9	5	6	3	2	....	....	63
750	3	23	19	16	13	7	9	3	1	....	....	94
800	....	7	7	7	3	2	2	1	....	1	1	31
850	....	3	2	1	3	1	4	2	2	....	....	18
900	....	5	4	8	3	3	5	9	1	1	1	40
1000 to 1200	....	1	1	1	4	....	....	....	1	3	1	12
1200 to 1500	1	3	10	3	5	7	6	2	5	3	1	46
1500 and over	2	6	10	12	6	5	10	3	2	4	5	65
Unknown	15	67	17	6	2	2	1	....	....	....	....	110
Unknown size	....	....	....	....	....	....	....	....	....	....	....	55

The income according to size of family is indicated in the next table. From this, making the family a standard of five, and making some allowance for large and small families, we can conclude that 19 per cent of the Negro families in the Seventh Ward earn five dollars and less per week on the average; 48 per cent earn between $5 and $10; 26 per cent, $10–$15, and 8 per cent over $15 per week.

Philadelphia, 1896

Average Earnings Per Week	No. of Families	Per Cent	Remarks
$5 and less	420 { 192... / 228...	8.8 / 9.6	Very poor. / Poor.
$5 to 10	1088	47.8	Fair.
$10 to 15	581	25.5	Comfortable.
$15 to 20	91	4.0	Good circumstances.
$20 and over	96	4.2	Well-to-do.
Total	2276	100.0	

The following tables of Atlanta Negro budgets were made up in 1900:

Annual Income of 124 Representative Families of Atlanta, and Amount and Per Cent of Expenditure for Various Items

CLASSIFIED INCOME	Number of Families (N)	ANNUAL INCOME		ANNUAL EXPENDITURE									
		Total	Average	Rent		Food		Clothing		Taxes		Other Expenses and Savings	
				Amt.	Per Cent of Total	Amt.	Per Cent of Total	Amt.	Per Cent of Total	Amt.	Per Cent of Total	Amt.	Per Cent of Total
$ 100 or under $ 200	18	$ 2,504	$ 139	$ 288	11.50	$ 928	37.06	$ 570	20.37	$ 3	0.12	$ 775	30.95
200 " 300	34	8,480	249	1,088	12.24	4,198	49.50	1,800	21.23	184	2.17	1,200	14.88
300 " 400	30	10,004	333	864	8.63	4,248	42.46	2,060	20.59	264	2.64	2,568	25.68
400 " 500	19	8,234	433	770	9.35	2,940	35.71	1,285	15.61	243	2.95	2,996	36.38
500 " 750	20	11,288	564	804	7.12	3,448	30.54	1,755	15.55	328	2.91	4,953	43.88
750 " 1,000	2	1,760	880	....	....	660	37.50	350	19.89	150	8.52	600	34.09
1000 or over	1	1,125	1,125	....	....	360	32.00	200	17.78	50	4.44	515	45.78

Section 20. Budgets. There follow budgets showing the expenditures of seventeen Negro families. All of these except the first three were collected in 1909 by Senior and Junior students of Atlanta University:

No. 1. Merchant's Account with a Farm Tenant. Alabama

Dr.	A. B. 1898.	Cr.
To Balance .... $ 59 13		By Credit 47 91 $117 27
Rent 20 00		Cash 69 36
Taxes 8 71		3 bales Cotton
Interest 17 34		
Cash 6 75		
Tools—		
3 prs. plow lines .. 45		
1 plow 40		
85		
Shop work............. 25		
Food—		
147¾ lbs. meat..$13 20		
12 bu. meal..... 5 85		
4 lbs. sugar.... 28		
42 lbs. flour... 1 40		
20 73		
Carried forward....$133 76		Carried forward....$117 27

Dr.	A. B. 1898.	Cr.
Brought forward..$133 76		Brought forward.....$117 27
Feed—Corn...... 13 85		
4 bu. Oats ... 2 00		
15 85		
Clothing—		
1 pr. Suspenders 10		
1 hat 75		
2 pr. pants..... 1 85		
6 pr. shoes..... 6 70		
22 yds. cloth... 1 45		
10 85		
Seeds—		
11¼ bu. cotton seed ... 1 70		
$162 16		$117 27

No. 2. Farm-Hand,[1] Five Persons

INCOME		EXPENDITURE	
Items	Amount	Items	Amount
Man: 12 months' labor @ $12...	$144 00	Food per week @ $1.70 for 52 weeks.......................	$88 40
Woman: 52 weeks' labor @ $1...	52 00		
Boy: 6 months' labor @ $3......	18 00	Fuel and lighting:	
		7 cords of wood @ $3.00, $21.00; oil @ 10c. a week for 52 weeks, $5.20..........	26 20
		Clothing	50 00
		Miscellaneous.................	10 00
		Rent........................	18 00
		Doctor and medicine..........	10 00
		Surplus	11 40
Total	$214 00	Total	$214 00

No. 3. Laborer,[2] Five Persons

INCOME		EXPENDITURE	
Items	Amount	Items	Amount
Man: 39 wks. work @ $9........	$351 00	Rent 12 mos. @ $3 per mo	$ 36 00
Wife: 12 wks. cooking @ $2.50 per wk.; 18 wks. washing @ $1 per wk......	48 00	Groceries and meat @ $4.00 per wk.....................	208 00
		Dresses for wife and daughter	7 00
		2 suits for boys	4 50
		1 suit for husband............	5 50
		Shoes and stockings for all...	8 75
		Underclothes for all..........	2 00
		Doctor's bill and medicine...	21 00
		Funeral expenses..............	20 00
		Life expenses @ 25c per wk....	13 00
		Fuel	33 00
		Tobacco @ 20c per wk..........	10 40
		Miscellaneous.................	14 45
		On hand.......................	15 40
Total	$399 00	Total	$399 00

No. 4. Farmer and Laborer, Four Persons

INCOME		EXPENDITURE	
Items	Amount	Items	Amount
Cotton..........................	$300 00	Clothes..........................	$50 00
Other work	100 00	Food	100 00
		Tax	10 00
		Amusements	20 00
		Other purposes.	25 00
			$205 00
		[3]Unaccounted for.......	195 00
Total	$400 00	Total	$400 00

[1] Estimated, see U. S. Bulletin of the Bureau of Labor No. 32.

[2] Estimated, Xenia, Ohio, Bureau of the U. S. Bureau of Labor No. 48.

[3] This portion includes a part which is spent upon drink.

No. 5. Farmer and Teacher, Nine Persons

INCOME		EXPENDITURE		
Items	Amount	Items	Amt.	Pr. ct.
8 bales of cotton weighing 500 lbs. @ 9c	$360 00	Food	$230 10	41.2
2 cows @ $20	40 00	Fuel and light	2 50	.4
For teaching 8 months	160 00	Clothes	82 00	14.6
		Sickness	25 00	} 7.1
		Other purposes	15 00	
		Balance on hand	205 40	36.7
Total	$560 00	Total	$560 00	100%

No. 6. Laborer, Six Persons

INCOME		EXPENDITURE		
Items	Amount	Items	Amt.	Pr. ct.
Labor and income	$650 00	Food	$250 00	38.5
		Clothes	100 00	15.25
		Taxes	13 00	2.00
		Light	3 00	.5
		Other things	284 00	43.75
Total	$650 00	Total	$650 00	100%

No. 7. Laborer, Five Persons

INCOME		EXPENDITURE		
Items	Amount	Items	Amt.	Pr. ct.
Labor	$625 00	Food	$250 00	40.0
		Clothes	125 00	16 0
		Rent and taxes	121 00	15.75
		Fuel and light	30 00	4.8
		Family savings	27 00	4.2
		Other things	72 00	19.25
Total	$625 00	Total	$625 00	100%

No. 8. Farmer, Eleven Persons

INCOME		EXPENDITURE		
Items	Amount	Items	Amt.	Pr. ct.
Cotton	$500 00	Paid out on land and stock	$200 00	} 55.6
Beans and potatoes	12 50	Balance saved up	147 50	
Chickens	12 50	Food	150 00	24.0
Tobacco	20 00	Clothing	100 00	16.0
Peas	5 00	Church and secret orders	25 00	4.0
Odd work on other farms	75 00	Taxes	2 50	.4
Total	$625 00	Total	$625 00	100%

No. 9. Brickmason and Driver, Seven Persons

INCOME		EXPENDITURE		
Items	Amount	Items	Amt.	Pr. ct.
Average yearly returns as brickmason and driver....	$800 00	Food	$400 00	50.00
		Fuel	50 00	6.25
		Clothes......................	75 00	9.375
		Payments on home and taxes	175 00	.875
		For amusements...........	25 00	
		Running house and payments of water bills....	25 00	
		For church purposes	6 00	} 12.50
		Sickness and tooth bill...	30 00	
		Societies	6 00	
		Books, paper, periodicals.	8 00	
		Savings		21.00
Total	$800 00	Total	$800 00	100%.

No. 10. Farm-hand (Georgia), 12 Persons

INCOME		EXPENDITURE		
Items	Amount	Items	Amt.	Pr. ct.
½ of 30 bales cotton $47........	$705 00	Food	$329 75	40.3
5 tons cotton seeds @ 16.50......	82 50	20 bbls. flour @ $6....$120 00		
Balance due landlord	21 85	70 bu. meal @ $1.10.. 77 00		
		75 gal. molasses @ 45 33 75		
		825 lbs. meat @ 12 ... 99 00		
		$329 75		
		Clothes....	135 00	16.4
		7 suits @ 16.25.. .....$113 75		
		Sunday dresses...... 21 25		
		$135 00		
		Borrowed $25 note for	30 00	
		Mending shoes..............	5 20	
		2 boxes tobacco.............	6 00	
		Gun (second-hand).........	12 80	} 42.2
		Buggy (second-hand)	80 00	
		Organ	75 00	
		6 tons guano @ 22.50........	135 00	
		2 boxes shells @ 55	1 10	
		Taxes........................	9 50	1.1
Total	$819 35	Total	$819 35	100%

No. 11. Janitor, Three Persons

INCOME		EXPENDITURE		
Items	Amount	Items	Amt.	Pr. ct.
Man's salary	$520 00	Food	$369 00	41.7
Woman's sewing..........	216 00	Clothes......................	115 00	13.0
House rent	151 00	Insurance and church	79 00	
		Amusements...............	3 00	} 21.2
		Medicine and toilet articles	5 00	
		Other things................	100 00	
		Taxes.......................	44 00	5.0
		Balance saved up..........	172 00	19.1
Total	$887 00	Total	$887 00	100%

No. 12.   Brickmason, Nine Persons

INCOME		EXPENDITURE		
Items	Amount	Items	Amt.	Pr. ct.
For laying bricks..............	$907 20	Food	$278 30	29.00
For washing and ironing......	52 00	Fuel and light..............	48 90	5.08
		Clothes.....................	85 00	8.85
		Amusements	1 20	⎫
		Sickness	12 00	⎬ 7.16
		Society dues...............	55 60	⎭
		Taxes......................	20 25	2.10
		Savings and unaccounted	467 95	48.81
Total..........................	$959 20	Total	$959 20	100%

No. 13.   Teacher, Ten Persons

INCOME		EXPENDITURE		
Items	Amount	Items	Amt.	Pr. ct.
Rent.... ⎱ A	$240 00	Clothes....................	$175 00	11.4
Nursing ⎰	80 00	Food	432 00	27.9
Teaching ⎱ B	384 00	Taxes......................	112 00	7.2
Secretary ⎰	60 00	Fuel	52 00	3.3
Wages ⎱ C	600 00	Repair	8 00	⎫
Rent.. ⎰	180 00	Insurance	54 00	⎬
		Amusement	45 00	31.9
		Sickness	70 00	⎭
		Other purposes............	314 00	
		Savings	282 00	18.3
Total	$1544 00	Total	$1544 00	100%

No. 14.   Mail Carrier, Nine Persons

INCOME		EXPENDITURE		
Items	Amount	Items	Amt.	Pr. ct.
Man's salary @ $95 per month for 1 year....................	$1140 00	Food supplies @ $35 per month..................	$420 00	26.9
Daughter's salary @ $20 per month for 1 year...........	240 00	Water and gas..	60 00	⎱ 6.0
Rent for 1 house @ $15 per mo..	180 00	Coal and fuel..............	35 00	⎰
		Taxes......................	100 00	6.4
		Clothes	300 00	19.2
		Incidentals and repairs...	369 00	23.7
		Other things...............	169 00	10.9
		Savings	107 00	6.9
Total	$1560 00	Total	$1560 00	100%

No. 15.· Farmer, Eleven Persons

INCOME		EXPENDITURE	
Items	**Amount**	**Items**	**Amount**
Food.............................	$310 20	Food.............................	$209 12
22 bu. peas @ $2.......... $44 00		15 bbls. flour........... $82 50	
8 gal. vinegar @ 40c....... 3 20		40 bu. corn.......... 41 62	
4 turkeys @ $1.25 .... 5 00		20 gal. syrup @ 35c..... 7 00	
400 lbs. butter @ 15c.... 60 00		330 lbs. bacon @ 11c ... 33 00	
150 gal. buttermilk @ 10c 15 00		Sugar.............. .... 16 00	
105 doz. eggs @ 20c 21 00		Pepper................. 25	
225 chickens @ 20c 45 00		20 lbs. soda @ 5c....... 1 00	
Fruit 15 00		Spice.................. 20	
Watermelons........... 17 00		2 sacks of salt @ 80c... 1 60	
175 gal. molasses........ 85 00		Lemon extract 30	
		2 gal. vinegar @ 40c.... 80	
Total $310 20		50 lbs. beef @ 10c. 5 00	
Live stock	72 25	Lard.... .... 6 25	
22 pigs @ $2.............. $44 00		Ginger................. 35	
1 cow.................... 28 25		Coffee................. 5 75	
		Grits.................. 3 75	
Total $72 25		Irish potatoes 3 73	
18 cords of wood @ $2.50......	45 00		
3 tons of cotton seed @ $21....	63 00	Total $209 12	$203 90
38 bales of cotton @ $52	1976 00	Clothes.........................	
		5 suits @ $15 .... $75 00	
		8 prs. shoes (Sunday)	
		@ $2.50................ 20 00	
		10 prs. shoes (everyday)	
		@ $2 .... 20 00	
		Dress goods (Sunday) 60 00	
		do (everyday) 25 50	
		Pins 15	
		Socks and stockings.. 3 25	
		Total $203 90	103 50
		Rents and taxes...............	
		Road tax.. .... $6 00	
		State tax 12 50	
		Interest 85 00	
		Total $103 50	22 70
		Horse Food	
		20 bu. oats @ 65c $13 00	
		2 bu. rye @ $1.25... ..... 2 50	
		6 sacks bran @ $1.20.... 7 20	
		Total................. $22 70	66 90
		Medicine	
		Doctor's bill (sickness) $35 75	
		Turpentine 75	
		Saltpetre 1 00	
		Alum 15	
		2 gal. whiskey @ $2.75.. 5 50	
		Patent medicine...... 5 50	
		To dentist..., ... 17 50	
		3 pkgs. home powder.. 75	
		Repairs	31 40
		1 watch $1 00	
		7 prs. shoes @ 45c 3 15	
		Shoeing horses 6 00	
		Mows 5 25	
		General shop work.... 10 75	
		On house dwelling 5 26	
		Total $31 40	
Total	$2466 45	Total	$637 52

No. 15 (Continued)

INCOME		EXPENDITURE	
Items	Amount	Items	Amount
Brought forward..............	$2466 45	Brought forward..............	$637 52
		Personal service..............	56 60
		Field labor $50 50	
		27 hair cuts @ 20c...... 5 40	
		7 shaves @ 10c..... 70	
		Total $56 60	
		Luxuries	20 20
		60 sacks smoking to-	
		bacco $3 00	
		1 doz. photos........... 2 25	
		½ box cigars.......... 1 00	
		Candy 1 50	
		4 doz. oranges @ 30c... 1 20	
		Jewelry 11 25	
		Total................. $20 20	
		Farming implements........	198 10
		Gear, harness, hoes.... $7 85	
		16 baskets @ 75c........ 12 00	
		1 disc harrow.......... 24 00	
		1 mower 75 00	
		1 two-horse wagon 65 00	
		2 axes @ 75c............ 1 50	
		3 buggy whips......... 1 50	
		Plows 11 25	
		Total........... ....$198 10	
		Household purposes..........	31 50
		Furniture............... $16 85	
		3 lamps 4 25	
		Soap.... .... 3 25	
		Matches.. 40	
		Lamp oil 6 75	
		Total.................. $31 50	
		Live animals.................	450 00
		2 mules @ $225..........$450 00	
		Seed trees.....	19 85
		20 fruit trees........... $18 25	
		Garden seeds 45	
		Watermelon seed..... 50	
		Flower seed........... 65	
		Total.................. $19 85	
		Guano, 10 tons @ $20	200 00
		Improvements.................	141 10
		Lightning rods.......$110 00	
		28 gal. paint @ $1.10.... 30 80	
		3 qts. machine oil @ 10c 30	
		Total $141 10	
		Incidentals....................	109 55
		Church assessment... $15 00	
		School funds.......... 5 75	
		Railroad fare......... 5 55	
		Charity................ 1 50	
		Stamps and stationery 2 60	
		Books............. ... 12 75	
		Newspaper............ 6 50	
		Daughter's education. 60 00	
		Total $109 55	
		Paid on old debt	602 43
Total	$2466 45	Total	$2466 85

No. 15 (Continued)

INCOME		EXPENDITURE	
Items	Amount	Items	Amount
Brought forward.............. Balance	$2466 45 40	Brought forward..............	$2466 85
Total	$2466 85		

RECAPITULATION

Items	Amt.	Pr. ct.
Food	$209 12	8.5
Clothes.	203 90	8.2
Rents and taxes............	103 50	4.1
Savings (includ'g amount paid on old debt........	602 43	24.5
Other purposes (including horse food, medicine, repairs, personal service, luxuries, farming implements, household purposes, live animals, guano, seed trees, and incidentals)	1347 90	54.7
Total	$2466 85	100%
Income (yearly)	2466 45	
Balance	40	

Total (Expenditure) $2446 85

No. 16. Farmer, Ten Persons

INCOME		EXPENDITURE		
Items	Amount	Items	Amt.	Pr. ct.
Father for one year....	$1000 00	Food @ $30 per month.....	$360 00	15.0
Two sons for one year..........	500 00	Clothes.....................	300 00	12.5
Income for rent of 600 acres @ $1.50 per acre................	900 00	Farm labor @ $50 per mo..	600 00	
		Periodicals and papers....	5 00	
		Amusements	50 00	
		Railroad travels	100 00	
		House insurance...........	75 00	45.0
		Incidentals (house repairing, new furniture, etc.)...............	150 00	
		Money spent on wagons..	100 00	
		Taxes (State and county).	200 00	8.3
		Life insurance	150 00	19.2
		Family savings...........	310 00	
Total	$2400 00	Total	$2400 00	100%

No. 17. Farmer, Six Persons

INCOME		EXPENDITURE		
Items	Amount	Items	Amt.	Pr. ct.
Cotton raised on farm, and fertilizer......................	$1837 50	For food	$200 00	} 30.37
Restaurant in town....	1825 00	Restaurant food	912 50	
		Fuel and lights	50 00	1.36
		Clothes......................	350 00	9.55
		Rent and taxes..............	200 00	5.46
		Unaccounted for............	1118 75	
		Amusements...............	50 00	
		Sickness	50 00	
		Helper in restaurant......	117 00	
		For running house and keeping up rolling stock	175 00	} 42.88
		Societies, church, lodges, and charity, papers, etc.	60 00	
		Savings	379 25	10.38
Total	$3662 50	Total	$3662 50	100%

One indication of the strengthening of family life and sounder economic conditions is found in the proportion of students in a school like
Atlanta University who are supported by their families. A search of
the University records reveals the following approximate results:

ATLANTA UNIVERSITY	PROPORTION OF STUDENTS	
Date	Supported by family	Self-supported
1887–1888	42.3%	57.7%
1897–1898	51.4%	48.6%
1907–1908	68.8%	31.2%

Section 21. Rents. Two heavy items of expense for the poor are
rent and food. The following tables show certain typical rents. In
the country it is not possible to distinguish the rent from the wages in
most cases:

Farmville, Va.

Families Owning and Renting Homes, by Number of Rooms to a Dwelling

TENURE	FAMILIES OCCUPYING DWELLINGS OF								
	One Room	Two Rooms	Three Rooms	Four Rooms	Five Rooms	Six Rooms	Seven Rooms	Eight or Nine Rooms	Total Families
Owners.............................	3	25	31	22	18	8	3	4	114
Renters	14	109	14	9	1	....	....	1	148
Total families................	17	134	45	31	19	8	3	5	262

Of these 148 tenants, 15 rent from Negroes and 133 from whites. Several of the tenants own land. The rents paid by 83 typical tenants are reported in the following table, and from these the total annual rent charge of this community is estimated at about $5000.

Rents paid by Typical Families, by Number of Rooms to a Dwelling

MONTHLY RENT	FAMILIES OCCUPYING DWELLINGS OF					Total Families	Annual Rent Paid
	One Room	Two Rooms	Three Rooms	Four Rooms	Five or more Rooms		
Free	....	1	....	....	....	1	....
$1.00	2	....	....	....	....	2	$24
$1.25	1	....	....	....	....	1	15
$1.50	3	....	1	....	....	4	72
$2.00	1	9	1	....	....	11	264
$2.50	....	15	1	....	....	16	480
$2.75	....	1	....	....	....	1	33
$3.00	....	38	5	....	....	43	1548
$3.50	....	....	1	3	....	4	168
Total	7	64	9	3	....	83	2604
Not reported	7	45	5	6	2	65	*2268

* Estimated.

Philadelphia. The inquiry of 1848 returned quite full statistics of rents paid by the Negroes. In the whole city at that date 4019 Negro families paid $199,665.46 in rent, or an average of $49.68 per family each year. Ten years earlier the average was $44.00 per family. Nothing better indicates the growth of the Negro population in numbers and power when we compare with this the figures of 1896 for one ward; in that year the Negroes of the Seventh Ward paid $25,699.50 each month in rent, or $308,034.00 a year, an average of $126.19 per annum for each family. This ward may have a somewhat higher proportion of renters than most other wards. At the lowest estimate, however, the Negroes of Philadelphia pay at least $1,250,000 in rent each year.[1]

A table of rents is as follows:[2]

Under $5 per month............490 families, or 21.9 per cent
$5 and under $10 per month.......643　　"　　or 28.7　　"
$10　　"　　$15　　"　　.......380　　"　　or 17.0　　"
$15　　"　　$20　　"　　.......252　　"　　or 11.3　　"
$20　　"　　$30　　"　　.......375　　"　　or 17.0　　"
$30 and over.......................95　　"　　or 4.1　　"

---

[1] Not taking into account sub-rent repaid by sub-tenants; subtracting this and the sum would be, perhaps, $1,000,000—see infra, p. 291. That paid by single lodgers ought not, of course, to be subtracted as it has not been added in.—The Philadelphia Negro, p. 287.　　　　[2] Ibid., p. 290.

Families owning or renting their homes and living alone ....738, or 31 per cent.

Families owning or renting their homes, who take lodgers or sub-renters ....937, or 38 per cent.

Families sub-renting under other families ....766, or 31 per cent.

Total individuals......	7751	100 per cent.
Total families...	2441	
Individuals lodging with families	1924	
Total individuals..	9675	

Families Owning and Renting Homes, by Number of Rooms to a Dwelling
Negroes of Xenia, Ohio

TENURE	FAMILIES OCCUPYING DWELLINGS OF												Total Families
	One Room	Two Rooms	Three Rooms	Four Rooms	Five Rooms	Six Rooms	Seven Rooms	Eight Rooms	Nine Rooms	Ten Rooms	Eleven Rooms	Twelve Rooms	
Owners	2	25	67	74	62	43	24	8	5	3	4	1	318
Renters	14	32	61	40	17	5	6	3	....	....	....	....	178
Not reported	....	....	2	3	....	....	....	....	....	....	....	....	5
Total	16	57	130	117	79	48	30	11	5	3	4	1	501

Rents Paid by Families, by Size of Dwelling
Negroes of Xenia, Ohio

MONTHLY RENT	FAMILIES OCCUPYING DWELLINGS OF								Total Families	Total Annual Rent Paid
	One Room	Two Rooms	Three Rooms	Four Rooms	Five Rooms	Six Rooms	Seven Rooms	Eight Rooms		
Free	2	....	1	1	1	....	....	......	5	....
$1.00	6	1	1	....	....	....	....	......	8	$96
1 50	1	1	..	....	....	....	....	......	2	36
1.75	1	....	1	....	....	....	....	......	2	42
2.00	1	10	3	....	....	....	....	......	14	336
2.25	....	1	....	....	....	....	....	......	1	27
2.50	1	10	4	1	....	....	....	......	16	480
2.75	1	1	2	....	....	....	....	......	4	132
3.00	1	4	20	10	....	....	....	......	35	1260
3.25	....	....	5	....	....	....	....	......	5	195
3.50	....	1	10	4	2	....	....	......	17	714
4.00	....	....	....	....	....	2	....	......	2	96
4.25	....	....	11	11	1	....	....	......	23	1173
4.50	....	2	1	....	....	....	....	......	3	162
5.00	....	1	1	1	....	1	2	1	7	420
5.50	....	....	1	8	4	1	....	......	14	924
6.00	....	....	....	....	....	1	....	......	1	72
6.50	....	....	....	4	6	....	1	......	11	858
7.00	....	....	....	....	2	....	2	......	4	336
7.50	....	....	....	....	....	....	1	......	1	90
8.00	....	....	....	....	....	....	....	1	1	96
8.33⅓	....	....	....	..	1	....	....	......	1	100
10.00	....	....	....	....	....	....	....	1	1	120
Total	14	32	61	40	17	5	6	3	178	$7765

Washington, D. C. The block of houses erected by the Washington Sanitary Improvement Company on O street, between North Capitol and First streets northwest, is rented to colored tenants. These houses contain three and four-room flats; each flat has a bathroom, with hot and cold water; a back yard with exit to an alley, and a cellar. The monthly rental (for eleven months) averages $3.18 per room. These flats have been continually occupied since their completion in 1902 by a good class of tenants, and losses as a result of vacancy or failure to pay rent have been insignificant.[1]

If we examine groups 14, 15, 16, 27, 42, 43, and 44, all occupied by colored people of the better class of laborers, except Group 43 occupied by whites, we find that there are 29 such dwellings, 13 of six rooms, 5 of five rooms, and 11 of four room. These houses are unpapered, some have no gas supply, and some have no supply of hot water; 5, Group 43, are in bad repair. The average cost of these dwellings was $1235.70 each; to which if we add 95 per cent for lot, grading, water connection, etc., we arrive at $2409.67 as the total investment. The average rental of these dwellings was $16.60; thus the gross returns on the investment may be set at 8.37 percent, practically identical with the gross returns from the better houses. It would appear, if these figures be approximately correct, that since the average rental of $16.60 for a four or five-room house, without gas, and often without hot water, furnishes only the usual return on the investment, to venture below that figure could be attempted in single brick dwellings only with the sacrifice of necessary hygienic space or sanitary equipment.[2]

Number of Dwellings	Cost per House	Sold for or Held at	Rent	Tenants
2	$2000	$3550	Owned	Colored
6	2600	....	$30.00	....
2	2000	....	$20.00 (4-room)	....
5	2000	....	$22.50 (corner)	....
....	....	....	$20.50 (inside)	....
5	2000	....	$20.50	....
19	1850	....	$25.00	....
1	1700	....	$20.00	....
2	1500	....	$20.50	....
4	1400	....	$16.50	....
7	1250	....	$16.30 (4-room)	....
2	1200	....	$14.00 (4-room)	....

Sternberg, pp. 82-83.

Other houses with Negro tenants rented as follows:

Number of Houses	Cost per House	Rooms contained	How Heated	Rent
6	$2500	4 and bath	Latrobe and range.	$20 50 / 21 00
3	2400	5 and bath	Latrobe and range.	20 50
4	2000	4 and bath	Stove and range....	15 50
7	2500	4 and bath	Latrobe and range.	15 50
8	2500	4 and bath	Latrobe and range.	15 50
5	1600	4 and bath	Latrobe and range.	15 50

Sternberg, p. 86.

Baltimore. There is no building of new dwellings for colored people in Baltimore; they occupy dwellings abandoned in the march to more fashion-

[1] Sternberg, p. 78.   [2] Sternberg, p. 184.

able or newer residence districts. In a section of Baltimore occupied chiefly by Negroes (Druid Hill avenue, and cross streets and alleys opening upon it) the rents were found to be comparatively high. On the larger streets, the 8, 10, or 12-room houses were occupied by very respectable and well-to-do colored people, who paid from $25.00 to $35.00 in rent. The "room to rent" sign was frequently seen, and it was thought there may be overcrowding here. In the minor streets and alleys, giving upon Druid Hill avenue, are very many houses of one type, all occupied by Negroes. These are two and three stories in height, all with basements and all two rooms deep. Occasionally such houses have running water in the kitchen, but usually there is only a hydrant in the yard. An eight-room house of this type (two rooms in the basement) rents for $15.00; a five-room house (one room in basement) rents for $12.00.

There is, also, an old type of four and five-room and cellar house to be seen in the alleys, most dark, dismal and unsanitary, which rents by the week at from $1.50 to $2.50; but even these houses seemed better structurally than the old frame houses on our main streets which bring from $12.00 to $15.00. The Baltimore house of this type is, however, so small and situated in such narrow alleys that area congestion must enter into the equation.

In general it may be said that in Baltimore, housing of the Negroes is a problem awaiting solution; the homes available for the least resourceful are unfit in many respects, and there is no building of new dwellings for colored people. [1]

Section 22. Food. Two scientific studies of Negro food have been made by the United States Department of Agriculture, from which the following examples are quoted:

Two Weeks' Food of an Alabama Field-hand Family of Four

KIND OF FOOD MATERIAL	Composition			Total Cost	Weight Used				
	Protein	Fat	Carbo-hydrates		Total Food Material	Nutrients			
						Protein	Fat	Carbo-hydrates
Animal Food	Per Cent	Per Cent	Per Cent		Grams	Grams	Grams	Grams
Bacon [1]	8.0	63.2		$3 16	17,915	1,433	11,322	....
Total animal food				$3 16	17,915	1,433	11,322	....

Vegetable Food, Cereals, Sugar, Etc.

KIND OF FOOD MATERIAL	Composition			Total Cost	Weight Used				
Corn Meal [2]	7.3	4.1	66.7	$1 26	21,005	1,533	861	14,010
Wheat Flour [2]	9.6	.8	78.3	58	19,050	1,829	152	14,916
Molasses [2]	1.3	.1	68.3	54	5,430	71	5	3,709
Total vegetable food	....	....	....	$2 38	45,485	3,433	1,018	32,635
Total food	....	....	....	$5 54	63,400	4,866	12,340	32,635

[1] Sternberg, p. 45.   [2] Average of analyses of similar Alabama foods.

Two Weeks' Food of a Negro Carpenter's Family of Six

KIND OF FOOD MATERIAL	Food Material	Nutrients			Cost
		Protein	Fats	Carbo-hydrates	
For Family, 14 days.	Grams	Grams	Grams	Grams	
Beef, veal, and mutton.........	2,495	392	328	....	$0 64
Pork, lard, etc.	5,655	269	4,433	....	90
Poultry	905	133	59	....	10
Eggs	595	79	55	....	10
Butter...........................	990	12	816	....	44
Milk...........................	57,140	2,000	2,400	2,971	5 04
Total animal food...........	67,780	2,885	8,091	2,971	$7 22
	Lbs.	Lbs.	Lbs.	Lbs.	
Beef, veal, and mutton	5.50	0.90	0.70	....	....
Pork, lard, etc.	12.50	.60	9.80	....	....
Poultry	2.00	.30	.10	....	....
Eggs...........................	1.30	.20	.10	....	....
Butter...........................	2.20	....	1.80	... .	....
Milk...........................	126.00	4.40	5.30	6.50	....
Total animal food	149.50	6.40	17.80	6.50	
	Grams	Grams	Grams	Grams	
Cereals, sugars, starches.......	38,050	2,838	619	29,713	$2 51
Fruits.........................	975	12	12	235	18
Total vegetable food........	39,025	2,850	631	29,948	$2 69
Total food	106,805	5,735	8,722	32,919	....
	Lbs.	Lbs.	Lbs.	Lbs.	
Cereals, sugars, starches.......	83.90	6.30	1.40	65.50	....
Fruits	2.20	....	....	.50	....
Total vegetable food	86.10	6.30	1.40	66.00	....
Total food	235.60	12.70	19.20	72.50	$9 91

Part 4.   The Family Group

Section 23.   Differentiation of Classes. Few modern groups show a greater internal differentiation of social conditions than the Negro American, and the failure to realize this is the cause of much confusion. In looking for differentiation from the past in Africa and slavery, few persons realize that this involves extreme differentiation in the present. The forward movement of a social group is not the compact march of an army, where the distance covered is practically the same for all, but is rather the straggling of a crowd, where some of whom hasten, some linger, some turn back; some reach far-off goals before others even start, and yet the crowd moves on. The measure of. the advancement of such a throng is a question at once nice and indefinite. Measured by the rear guard there may be no perceptible advance. Measured by the advance guard the transformation may be miraculous. Yet neither of these are reasonable measurements, but rather the point which one might call the center of gravity of the mass is the true measuring point, and the determination of this point in the absence of exact measurements may be for a long time a matter of opinion rather than proof. So with the Negro American. It is easy to prove the degradation of thousands of Negroes on the back plantations of Mississippi and the alleys of Washington; it is just as easy to prove the accomplishments of the graduates of Atlanta University, or the members of St. Thomas Church, Philadelphia. The point is where, between these manifest extremes, lies today the cultural center of gravity of the race. It is begging and obscuring this question to harp on ignorance and crime among Negroes as though these were unexpected; or to laud exceptional accomplishments as though it was typical. The real crucial question is: What point has the mass of the race reached which can be justly looked upon as the average accomplishment of the group?

The exact location of this point is impossible to locate beyond doubt. Yet certain facts about it are certain: it is moving forward rapidly; this is proven by the decrease of illiteracy and the increase of property holding, both on such a scale, covering so long a period of years as to be incontrovertible evidence.

To illustrate this differentiation there follow four sections on the Negro country families, the social life of the country, the Negro Northern city home, and a study of thirteen select homes representing mostly the upper class of Negroes.

Section 24. The Negro Families of Dougherty County, Georgia. The plantations of Dougherty in slavery days were not so imposing as those of Virginia. The Big House was smaller and one-storied, and the slave cabins set closer to it. Today the laborers' cabins are in form and disposition the same as in slavery days. They are sprinkled in little groups all over the land clustering about some dilapidated Big House where the head-tenant or agent lives. Out of fifteen hundred homes of Negroes only fifteen have five or more rooms; the mass live in one or two-room homes. The one-room cabin is painfully frequent— now standing in the shadow of the Big House, now staring at the dusty road, now rising dark and sombre amid the green of the cotton-fields. Rough-boarded, old and bare, it is neither plastered nor ceiled, and light and ventilation comes from the single door and perhaps a square hole in the wall. Within is a fireplace, black and smoky, unsteady with age; a bed or two, high, dark and fat; a table, a wooden chest and chairs or stools. On the wall is a stray showbill or a newspaper for decoration.

It is not simply in the tenement abominations of cities like New York that the world's flesh is crowded and jammed together, sometimes twenty-two persons to every ten rooms; here in Dougherty county there are often over twenty-five persons to every ten rooms of house accommodation. To be sure, the rooms are large—fifteen to twenty-five feet square. And there is the fresh air and sunshine of all outdoors to take refuge in. Still I met one family of eleven eating and sleeping in one room, and thirty families of eight or more. Why should there be such wretched tenements in the Black Belt? Timber is rotting in the forest, land is running to waste and labor is literally cheaper than dirt. Over nine-tenths of the cabins belong to the landlords yet nearly all of them let the quarters stand and rot in rude carelessness. Why? First, because long custom born in slavery days, has assigned this sort of house to Negroes. If the landlord should hire white men he would not hesitate to erect cosy three-room cottages such as cluster around the Carolina cotton-mills. Small wonder that the substitution of white for Negro labor is often profitable, since the white being better paid and better cared for often responds by doing better work. Again, the Negroes themselves, as a mass, do not demand better homes; those who do, buy land and build their own homes, roomy and neat. But the rest can scarcely demand what they have seldom thought of. As their fathers lived so they live, and the standard of the slave still lowers the standard of the quasi-freeman. In the third place, the landlords fail to see that in an increasingly large number of cases it would be a distinctly good investment to raise the standard of living among the black laborers; that a man who demands three rooms and fifty cents a day may in the end be much cheaper than a listless, discouraged toiler herding in one room at thirty cents a day. Lastly, amid such conditions of life there is little to inspire the laborer to become a better farmer. If he is ambitious, he moves to town or tries other kinds of labor; as a tenant-farmer his outlook in the majority of cases is hopeless, and following it as a makeshift or in grim necessity, he takes its returns in shelter, meat and bread, without query or protest.

That we may see more clearly the working out of these social forces, let us look within the home and scan more nearly the family that lives there. The families are large and small: you will find many families with hosts of babies, and many young couples, but few families with half-grown boys and girls. The whole tendency of the labor system is to separate the family group—the house is too small for them, the young people go to town or hire out on a neighboring farm. Thus single, lone persons are left here and there. Away down at the edge of the woods will live some grizzle-haired black man, digging wearily in the earth for his last crust; or a swarthy fat auntie, supported in comfort by an absent daughter, or an old couple living half by charity and half by odd jobs.

The boys and girls cannot afford to marry early, nor until most of the men are over twenty-five and the girls over twenty. There is little or no actual prostitution among these people and most of the families are honest, decent people, with a fairly good standard of family morals. Nevertheless the influence of the past is plain in customs of easy marriage and easy separation. In the old days Sam "took up" with Mary by leave of his master. No ceremony was necessary, and in the busy life of the great plantations of the Black Belt it was usually dispensed with. If the master needed Sam on another plantation, or was minded to sell him, Sam's married life with Mary was unceremoniously ended, and just as unceremoniously begun with Jane or Matilda elsewhere.

This widespread custom of two centuries has not disappeared in forty years. Between three and four per cent of the families are today separated, others have been and are remarried usually without the trouble of a divorce, while others will separate in the future. Here is the plague spot of the Negro's social relations, and when this inherited low standard of family life happens to be in the keeping of lustful whites, as it sometimes is, the result is bad indeed.

Section 25. The Social Life of the Country. A sketch of the social life of Negroes in the rural districts of the South is almost like an essay on the snakes in Ireland: it is the lack of social life that tends to depopulate the rural black belt and does draw off its best blood.

There are, however, many occasions of meeting and intercourse which may be set down thus in the order of their importance.

1. *The Saturday Visit to Town.* Practically throughout the rural South the black laborers and farmers come to town on Saturday. This is more than an occasion of marketing; it is a time of holiday, and is spent in chatting and loafing, with some liquor drinking. To thousands this forms the one glimpse of the larger world, and the merchants of many towns, indeed the towns themselves depend on the weekly pilgrimage. It reduces the working week of the rural South practically to five days save in very busy times.

2. *The Sunday Church Service.* "The Negro Church is the only social institution of the Negroes which started in the African forest and survived slavery; under the leadership of priest or medicine-man, afterward the Christian pastor, the Church preserved in itself the remnants of African tribal life and became after emancipation the center of Negro social life. So that today the Negro population of the United States is virtually divided into church congregations which are the real units of race life."[1] The typical Negro country church stands at some cross-roads and holds services once or twice a month. These meetings are great reunions and are the occasions of feasting, country gossip and preaching. The people gather from 9 a. m. to 1 p. m., and remain usually till late in the afternoon. Christenings and baptizing take place at this time.

3. *"The Christmas."* The week between Christmas and New Year's, including both days, is the great time of social rejoicing among country Negroes. Historically it was the time when the master gave his

---

[1] Atlanta University Publications, No. 3.

slaves time and license. Today it is the time when the serf receives his annual accounting with his landlord and collects his small balance due in cash. This he often spends in carousing and drinking, to pay for the hard year's work. Many honest, hard-working sober men get drunk religiously and regularly every Christmas. There are always many parties, church entertainments and excursions, together with fights and quarrels.

Later years have of course brought improvement. A resident of New Orleans writes: "Possibly there is less idleness at Christmas in Louisiana at present than formerly. My impression is that the influence of our better ministers and graduates or students from our higher institutions of learning is gradually modifying the character of the festivities and conduct of the people at the Christmas season."

4. *The "Frolic."* The occasional party given at the cabin is often called "the frolic"; it varies all the way from a pleasant little gathering with games and feasting as portrayed by Dunbar, to a scene of wild drinking and debauchery as is often the case in lumber camps.

5. *The Wedding and the Funeral.* The only distinctly family festivity is the wedding. This is celebrated with varying emphasis, being a ceremony only a generation old in the country districts. In the newer Southwest it seems to be more of a general occasion of rejoicing. A correspondent says:

The two things that interrupt our community life more than anything else in the way of home duties are the weddings and funerals, both of which seem to give the people more actual happiness and joy than anything they enter into during the whole year, but I suppose these hardly come under the head of social life. We have in our community a good many of the quiltings which appeal to the hearts of the women and during the winter is our regular form of festivities for them. This is an all-day affair with a luncheon served at midday, and sometimes we hear of as many as three or four in a single week.

6. *The Revival.* Connected with the church services comes the revival. This is a recruiting of church membership, and usually takes place in the fall after the crops are "laid by." It consists of protracted nightly meetings and brings together large numbers.

7. *School-closing.* Where the country schools are good and regular, as in Texas, there is considerable social life connected with the closing of schools; often there are examinations on this day with a free spread and an "exhibition" at night which attract large numbers.

8. *The Circus,* which visits the county-seat once or twice a year, is largely attended. So much so that such exhibitions are taxed as high as $500 for each county.

9. *Secret Societies.* In parts of Virginia and Georgia and some other States the benevolent societies, with their halls, are fast becoming the chief centers of the rural Negroes' social life. The annual installations of officers are the great social events of the year.

10. *Miscellaneous.* Besides the occasions mentioned there are summer excursions by train which take those who can get to town, the Methodist Conference and Baptist Convention which attract many to town, and a very few annual holidays like Emancipation Day, January 1st, which is often celebrated by a speech from some visiting celebrity. There are also some local celebrations, like those due to the influence of the Catholic Mardi Gras in Louisiana.

Section 26. The Negro Family in New York. (Miss Mary W. Ovington in Charities, October 7, 1905. Reprinted by permission.)

The great majority of the Negroes of New York live in poverty. Sixty-two per cent of the men, according to the last census, are in domestic and personal services, and in large stores and factories they do the work of porter or general utility man, not the better paid tasks. Only a few practice a trade. The women have not been able in any numbers to gain entrance to the factory or the shop. The result is a group of people receiving a low wage, and the character of their homes must be largely determined by their economic position.

Like all the New York poor the Negro lives in a tenement. The lower East side, famed for its overcrowding, does not know him. His quarters are West, but there he finds conditions that are often quite as bad as those among the Italians or the Jews. In the most thickly segregated Negro section, that between West Fifty-ninth and West Sixth-fourth streets and Tenth and West End avenues, the tenements are of the old double-decker and dumbbell types, with no thorough ventilation and with twenty and twenty-two families to a house. The air-shafts in these tenements are so small as to be only "culture tubes" except on the top story, where the rooms gain something of air and light. In the lower part of town, about the thirties, we still find a number of rear tenements occupied by the colored race. The sunlight enters these houses, but they are very old, impossible to keep clean, and dangerous because of their distance from the open street. Again still further south, about Cornelia street, the race lives in dilapidated former dwelling-houses. These West Side districts have little of the picturesqueness of the lower East Side, and have been more or less neglected by those interested in the moral and civil welfare of the community.

Rents are high for everyone in New York, but the Negroes pay more and get less for their money than any other tenants. Every week in the warm weather hundreds of them come from the South. They must find shelter, and the places that they may rent are few and those not tenements of the better sort. The many attractive and healthful houses that have been built since the creation of the Tenement House Department are not open to them. They are confined to certain localities, and usually to only a few houses in each block. Forced to crowd into small and uncomfortable rooms, their opportunities for making a home are much restricted.

Like the dweller on the East Side, the Negro knows enough to get out of his house and into the fresh air when he can. In the summer the streets, while not so filled with people as in the neighborhood about Rivington and Delancey streets, are well crowded. The roofs, too, offer breathing-places. Day as well as night many men and women are to be seen about, especially in the vicinity of the Sixties. The presence of men in the daytime gives an appearance of idleness among the population that is not as great as it seems, as about fifty per cent of the colored men of this city are engaged at jobs that give them leisure when other people are at their tasks.

Study closely the tenants in any of these streets and you will find every grade of social life. Their difficulty in procuring a place to live compels the colored people to dwell good and bad together. Ten families of pure and upright lives may be forced to rent rooms in a house where there are other ten families who are rough and noisy, often immoral. This is true of all over-crowded districts, but it is especially true in the Negro quarters; for the land-lord of a colored tenement rarely makes any attempt to discriminate among his applicants, but takes in anyone who will pay his rent. Complaints against objectionable tenants are unheeded, and the mother and father in the respect-able home have the difficult problem of rearing children in a few rooms from which there is no escape, save to the stairway and street where undesirable companions are numerous. Lines need to be drawn very sharply by such parents, and factions arise among the children that are the despair of the club worker, who gathers in her boys and girls believing that propinquity makes a harmonious group.

It is impossible to give an idea of the home of the Negro in New York without touching upon his relations with the rest of the city's population. He comes to make his home among a people who are foreign to him. He is not, to any appreciable extent, with the descendants of the men who years ago fought for his freedom; he speaks mournfully of wishing that he might take his chances with the American, but he is living among many races, the most of whom have but lately found their way to this country and are without tradition of friendliness. He has to meet the Irish, the German, the Hebrew, the Italian, the Slav. These maintain varying attitudes of animosity and friendliness. The Irish is the most boisterously aggressive, though when once the Irishman really knows the Negro he can be a very good comrade. New York seems to demand that all the laborers who come to her must endure a period of abuse and ridicule; there must be street fights and biting nick-names and the refusal to work with the detested race. All this the Negro must endure, as other races have endured before him, but his case is an exag-gerated one. There are those who wish to deny him opportunity because they believe in his inherent and eternal inferiority. This minority, for I believe it to be a minority, can prevent his obtaining a position. For where the majority of men and women will consent to have a Negro work with them, a strong caste sentiment on the part of a few will prevail against this friendly feeling which, after all, is little more than indifference.

While the Negro is an able and respected member in some of the labor unions, and while his children occasionally have playmates among the boys and girls of other races in the schools, he does not usually see the white work-ingman at his best. Too often white and colored meet only in the saloon of a low type or in the rough jostle of the street. This is a misfortune for a peo-ple who are in the process of creating a social life. To see the best among those of the same economic position as themselves would be a help and profit to them.

The contact that the colored people have with the monied people of the white race is varied. In the domestic service Negro men and women often have the opportunity to live in good and honorable homes, but it is not always so; and from people whom they are taught to regard as belonging to the upper class they learn low standards of married life. Those who are not in domestic service see from their tenement streets much that is base in the dominant race. There must be a world of irony in the heart of the seeing Negro who reads in the papers the lurid descriptions of his own crime, while he lives in the Tenderloin district and looks out upon its life. He sees the daily danger attending the attractive women of his own and other races, and he sees temptation offered where he should see high ideals. The Negro is imitative, and all this must and does have an effect upon his own home.

Yet, despite these handicaps, there is much of good and honorable living in the homes of the race. Choosing at random fifty families living in the most demoralizing neighborhood of New York, I found that seventy per cent of the mothers are known to be moral by those charitable workers who for many years had been in close touch with them. These people live a life apart from the roughness about them, but close to their church and their children. Such loose unthinking statements are made regarding the Negro and his morality that no better service could be done the race than to show us all of his homes, just as they come. For, where one would be revolting, the next would carry with it so much of worthy relationship between man and wife and parents and children that the first might be forgotten. And yet, I doubt if this would be so; for modesty like charity does not vaunt itself, and the loud colored woman who parades the streets counts for more in the minds of most of us than a dozen of the quiet women of her race who pass by without our noticing them. But for those who wish to see the whole and not merely the part that calls for censure, the majority of Negro homes, like the majority of homes of all working people, are places where good and honest men and women are striving, often against great odds, to bring up their children to lead moral and useful lives.

There is in New York, in proportion to the population, a fairly large class of professional colored men and women; and also a class of business men of some means. The homes of these do not differ essentially from the homes of all good Americans in the city. There is nothing by which to especially characterize them. Their hospitality is very pleasant and their family life is very harmonious and sweet. The young women are, perhaps, brought up in more sheltered fashion than those of the white race. Very much emphasis is laid upon education, both for the boy and for the girl. The music-loving character of the race is shown in these homes, as indeed it is in all colored households; but here we have much ability, for there are among the race in New York musicians of no mean gifts. These homes are too little known among the people of the city. Occasionally some colored high-school girl or college student will show her classmate her family circle, and thus a few in our population learn something of the wholesome life of a class of Negroes of whom one Southern woman told me that she knew less than she did of the Esquimaux. Perhaps there has never before been a race concerning which so many opinions have been written and yet of whose best life we are so ignorant. If "highest is the measure of the man," we know the highest of the New York Negro when we know the homes of the best of his race. And while from the South there comes an idle, criminal class, the industrious and intelligent come as well, and their homes are increasing and are an honor to the commonwealth.

Section 27. A Study of Thirteen Families. To illustrate this emergence of better classes, a careful description of thirteen Negro families follows. Number one represents one of the lowest type of a country family and number seven a common type of city family. The other eleven are of the higher types of Negro families. The incomes are given by the families themselves and are probably exaggerated in some cases.

No. 1. *A country family living in two rooms, with an income of $700 per year.* The whole family is very ignorant and consists of twelve members. None have had the advantage of school. A few of the younger children can write their names. No books or papers can be seen in the house.

The parents are religious fanatics; they believe in praying night and morning. The father can be heard praying on a still night for two miles. The elder boys are rough characters. They get drunk and fight, especially at church. The older girls are not wholesome characters; the two eldest have had illegitimate children, one by a white man and the other by a Negro; both children were given to relatives. The entire family is given to petty thefts, and is especially high-tempered. They do not get along with the neighbors, but tattle and tell lies and carry news to white people and Negroes.

The family consists of father, age 62 years; mother, age 61 years; six sons, ages respectively 28, 26, 22, 20, 14 and 11 years; and four daughters, ages respectively 24, 18, 16 and 8 years.

The entire family work in the field. The mother and one of the daughters leave each day in time to cook dinner. They work from sunrise or earlier until twelve, and from one until dark. The heavy farming work is done by the men and boys, the light work by the girls. The girls work from February to August and from September to December. The men and boys work the year round. When there is no work to be done on the farm, they have to report to the landlord for something to do. When it rains the bell taps and all must report at the barns to see what "Cap" wants done. For this kind of service they get no pay. The house is near the pasture and is partly surrounded with woods. The landlord's house is 300 yards away. The yard is very small, with weeds growing in the summertime into the window on the back side. The water is brought from a spring in the pasture. The house is dirty within. The bed-clothes are dingy and the doors are black with dirt. They have no bathing facilities. All bathe in a washpan, about three-quarts size, once a week. A peculiar odor is prevalent in spring and summer. They dress in gaudy colors. Their clothes are fairly good, but not well made and do not fit properly. In fact, they do not know how to wear what they have and are very hard on clothes. Only a low class of people visit them. Any decent person visiting there is branded as bad. Four of the family are members of the Baptist church. The two older daughters were members but were expelled on account of conduct. The only property is one buggy, an organ and twenty-five chickens.

Both sides are of African descent. They are very black, and it is said that their forefathers were all similarly high-tempered and immoral. Both sides of the family were in slavery, and after the war were held in peonage twenty-two years. They are much different from other colored people around in the structure of head and mouth, and in general appearance. They have three meals: breakfast before sunrise, of biscuits, pork, syrup and coffee; dinner at noon, of cornbread, syrup and pork; supper after dark, of cornbread or biscuits, and syrup. The table is too small to accommodate the entire family—seven by three feet. Some take their meals in their hands—children especially—and sit in a chair and sometimes in the door. Some of the time the food is served from the table and at other times from the cooking vessels. The dishes are common china, with some tin plates and cups. There is no tablecloth. There are two benches the length of the table on each side of the table.

No. 2. *A country family living in three rooms, with an income of $625 per year.* This family consists of eleven persons: a man and his wife and nine children; six girls and three boys. The man and his wife are both 43 years old. The oldest child is a girl of 19, the next a girl of 17, then a girl of 16, a girl of 15, a girl of 13, a boy of 11, a boy of 9, a boy of 6, and the baby, a girl of 3 years old. The people work a farm; they have never done anything else. The father is a man small in stature, about medium height, slender, with a dark brown skin, crinkly black hair and thick black mustache. He is a genial, cheerful man, always full of fun. He is very intelligent and business-like, ambitious and eager for knowledge. He is the main stay of the whole family. The mother is about medium height and corpulent. She is lighter brown than her husband, with soft and once abundant black hair. She is kind and motherly, but rather slow and sleepy; in fact, much given to deep trance-like spells of sleeping. She oversees the housework. The oldest daughter is below the medium height, with dark-brown skin and soft black hair. She is plump and vivacious, and rather restless and fidgety. She does not work much in the field, but sews and helps about the house. The next girl is about medium height, small but solid, a little lighter brown than the first, with crinkly black hair. She is strong and full of life, quick to make friends, kind-hearted, frank and winning. She does harder work in the field than any of the others. The next girl is below the medium height, about the same shade of brown, with very crinkly hair; she is somewhat inclined to be "airish" but she is lively and good-natured. She also works in the field. Next comes her inseparable companion, the girl of 15. She is of medium height and plump. She has the good looks of the family. She is the same shade of brown, with soft black hair. She has a very good opinion of herself and is somewhat high-tempered. She works in the field at the busiest season, but usually stays in the house. The girl of 13 is the scapegoat of the family. She is far below the medium height, very plump, a lighter brown than any of the others, with very crinkly black hair. She is very quiet and seldom grumbles. When she speaks she usually says something worth while. She does most of the things which the others refuse to do. She is housemaid, nurse and errand-girl. The oldest boy is about the size of the usual eleven-year-old boy. He is dark brown, with crinkly black hair; he is decidedly jolly and boyish. The next boy is his boon companion; he is nearly as large and has the same general appearance and disposition; they are often mistaken for twins. The oldest boy is his father's chief dependence in the field. He can plough as well as any man. The other one does lighter field work. The last boy is a fat child of six, dark brown, with soft black hair, and an unusually large and well-shaped head. He is very sly and quiet, but when drawn out shows great intelligence. He romps and plays all day with his baby sister. She is small, dark brown, with crinkly reddish hair. She is very droll and demure, and is well-spoiled by the whole family.

The whole family dress very simply. The girls all have calico working dresses, and the boys have calico home-made jackets and breeches. Each of the boys has a suit and cap for Sunday wear. The girls have neat, inexpensive dresses for Sunday wear. The older girls keep themselves neat and clean, but the younger members are never clean except on Sundays. The mother is not very tidy. Very few colored people live in the part of the country where these people live, and the few who live near are related to them. They often go visiting their people and receive visits from them in turn. They go to church every Sunday, unless the weather is very bad. The father, the mother and the three oldest girls belong to secret orders. There are none of the family absent except a boy who died. He came in between the boy of nine and the boy of six.

They own 165 acres of land, the house in which they live, two mules, two cows and four hogs. The family have lived in this place for sixteen years. Before that they lived about five miles away. The mother came from a family of twelve children, seven boys and five girls. All the boys are dead except one, who lives out West. Four of the girls are living, all in the same part of the country. The other is dead. The father came from a family of eight children, five boys and three girls. One of the boys is dead; all the others live in the country around. Two of the girls live near by and the other is in Milledgeville in the insane asylum. There is no school near for the children to attend.

This family has three meals every day. The food is well cooked, and they have very nice dishes but no silver. During the working season they have breakfast at 6 o'clock, dinner at 12 o'clock and supper at 6:30. During the season of rest and on Sundays they have breakfast at 7 o'clock, dinner between one and two o'clock and supper at 7:30. They raise nearly all their food. In summer they have for breakfast wheat bread and butter, milk, syrup and salt pork, varied occasionally by beef, chicken and eggs. For dinner they have vegetables, cornbread, milk, and sometimes soup and some kind of dessert. For supper they have wheat bread, butter, syrup, milk, and salt pork. In winter the breakfasts are about the same, but they have for dinner such things as peas and sweet potatoes, varied with beef and chicken. Dried fruit also plays an important part. They have tablecloths, but no napkins. They always sit at the table, and the younger ones have to wait until the older ones eat.

No. 3. *A country family living in 7 rooms with an income of $650 per year.* The family consists of six persons: the parents, two boys and two girls. The father is yellow, of moderate build—five feet four inches—weighs 156 pounds, and is 47 years of age. He has been engaged in farming since he was 19 years of age. He has a common-school education, chews tobacco but uses no intoxicants, and has good health. The mother is light brown in complexion and is rather large in build; she is 45 years of age and was born and reared in the country. She has part of a high-school education, and taught school previous to marriage. The eldest boy is 20 years old; he is five feet four inches in height, of good build, weighs 140 pounds, and has lived in the country all his life; he has a high-school education, and is still in school. The youngest boy is 19 years of age, height five feet and six inches. He is now in school and is a fairly good student; he has a high-school education. The eldest girl is 17 years of age, weighs 140 pounds; height five feet and four and a half inches, and has almost completed a high-school course. The youngest girl is 11 years old, four feet in height, and has almost completed a grammar-school course; she has some ability in instrumental music. The father supervises the farm, prepares the soil, plants the crop in the spring and during the summer superintends the working of the farm, the crop-gathering in the autumn and marketing the crop, and fertilizing the soil during winter. Also he cares for the live stock, markets $2.00 worth of wood a week, and the dairy and the poultry products ($2.00 a week). The mother does about half of the family cooking (that is, the mother and girls do the cooking by turns), sews and makes the working garments of the whole family, and all the garments of herself and girls; she cares for the poultry, cultivates the garden and supervises the garden, dairy and poultry products to be marketed; also she preserves and cans fruits. The boys prepare the fuel for family cooking and the wood for market, and assist in the farm work; also in crop-gathering during September. The girls do half of the family cooking (by turns), all of the family washing, and clean the house; and they assist some in the farm work during summer and autumn, also in gathering. The rising hour is 5:30 a. m., breakfast at 6:30. Work period from 7 to 12 o'clock; dinner at 12 m.; work hours 2 to 6 o'clock p. m., supper at 7 p. m. At 7:30 the family, except the girls who remain for dining-room duties, retire to the sitting-room for reading, study, conversation, writing, etc.; the girls join the other members of the family in the sitting-room at 8 o'clock. National holidays and family birthdays are the days of special festivity, also the first fifteen days of August, when cropmaking is over—generally called the summer lay-by. There is usually company on Sunday. The Sunday routine for the family is: Breakfast, 8:30 a. m.; bath hour, 9 to 9:30 a. m.; Sunday-school, 9:45 to 11 a. m.; church services, 11 a. m. to 1 p. m. (church three-quarters of a mile distant); dinner, 2 p. m.; company, 3 to 5 p. m.; supper, 7 p. m.; song practice, 8 p. m.; retire at 9:30. The dress of the family is as moderate as possible; the mother being a seamstress reduces the cost to a low figure. Fifty dollars ($50) is the amount which the boys find themselves together provided with in order to be clothed, and the amount for the two girls is thirty dollars (30); forty dollars clothes the parents.

The family owns $2200 worth of real estate, the estate has only been of present number of acres for six years; the original farm as owned by the father before marriage was thirty acres; six years ago at the death of the father's father he bought his father's farm of sixty acres, which adjoins his own. The land value was not as great then as now, so he profited quite a deal. At the same time, at the death of the mother's mother, her father's estate of eighty acres was sold and her realizations from the land was also used in the aforesaid transaction. The live stock value (one horse and four head of cattle) is $300; vehicles, $125; house furnishings and other incidentals, $350. So the whole value of the farm plant is approximately $3000. The estates of the grandparents were acquired by each about 1880, and was kept intact by each until their death, when they were disposed of at auction and proceeds went to their children.

At the meals the following food is used at different times: Breakfast, 6:30 a. m., bacon, ham, steak, pork, eggs, butter, hash, chicken, rabbit, liver, sausage, squirrel, etc., fish, mutton, bread-pancakes, muffins, eggbreads, rice, hominy, grits, buckwheat cakes and oatmeal. Fruits, preserves, apples, peaches, strawberries, potatoes, pears, bananas, syrup, etc. Drink: Postum and milk. Dinner, 12:00 m., Cabbage, collards, salad, peas, turnips, onions, celery, lettuce, radish, beets, soups, spinach, thyme, tomatoes, cucumbers, beans, squashes, ham, fish, beef, pork, rabbit, opossum, potatoes, chicken, partridge, duck, geese, turkey, apples, peaches, berries, lemon pies and drinks, egg custards, jams and jellies, puddings. Supper, 7:30 p. m., Postum, milk, chocolate, tea, etc. Apples, peaches, pumpkins, grapes, strawberries, blackberries, etc. Ham, eggs, chicken, rice, macaroni, cheese. Gelatine, cream, pudding, cakes, candies. Meals are cooked and served by the mother and daughters.

No. 4. *A country family occupying 9 rooms, with an income of $2500 per year.* The eleven members of this family are especially intelligent. They consist of mother and father, ages 50 and 60 years respectively, two daughters, ages 15 and 19 years, and seven boys, ages 29, 27, 25, 23, 21, 11 and 8, respectively. The deceased members of the family are two sons and two daughters; all died soon after birth. The whole family is peaceful and agreeable. The father is head, and what he says is law. The entire family is subjected to a strict discipline. The boys are allowed to visit, but they must return by sundown; if late, an excuse must be given beforehand. The girls do not leave home unless accompanied by some male member of the family. Every one on Sunday must go to Sunday-school, but there is no family prayer. No swearing is allowed. All the members of the family work on the farm excepting the mother. The boys and father do all the cutting, plowing, sometimes hoeing, repair work, and ditching, etc. The girls do the light work, such as hoeing, picking cotton, housework in general, and laundering. The mother stays at home, cooks, and looks after the children. From July 28th to August 24th they do nothing. This is called "laying-by time." From August 24th to December 1st they gather cotton, corn, potatoes, etc. From December 1st to January 15th they do practically nothing except keep fires and hunt.

This family is situated in a peaceful community composed of white and colored people. About two hundred yards from the house on one side are woods. The house is built on a high spot with a splendid drainage. The entire yard is filled with flowers and shade trees. The barns are a convenient distance from the main building, and there is an orchard. The best people of the community visit these people, and some white people from town and the neighborhood. Everything about this house is neat and clean. Their clothes are plain and simple and well cared for. The father is a member of the Masonic order. All are members of C. M. E. Church and of all its societies. The property owned consists of 175 acres of land, 5 mules, 5 milk cows, 7 heads of cattle, 25 hogs and pigs, 3 wagons, 2 buggies, 1 syrup mill, 1 disc harrow, 1 mower and rake, and other tools; there are also 150 chickens, 8 turkeys and 12 guineas.

On the father's mother's side the descent is direct from Africa, without any mixing of blood; on the father's father's side there has been an intermingling of white blood somewhere which makes the father a shade between black and light brown, or a ginger-cake color. On the mother's side the grandfather was a white man and her father was yellow. The mother's mother had a strain of Indian blood in her, making her dark red. This makes the mother yellow. Both sides were in slavery except the mother's grandfather. Breakfast is usually about or before sunrise, with coffee, milk, butter, syrup, meat, grits or rice, chicken or beef on Sunday mornings and biscuits and eggs. Dinner comes at 12 o'clock, with boiled vegetables, cornbread, pies, syrup, milk, butter, biscuits, potatoes, etc., are served. Supper is a little after sundown, with cornbread syrup, meat, milk, butter, and cold vegetables from dinner. Of course these meals vary on different occasions, especially when company is present and on Sundays. All the members of the family assemble around one large table and the father and mother serve the food, which is put on the table before the meal. The knives, forks and spoons are made of plated silver. The dishes are china, plain, with glasses for milk and water.

No. 5. *A country family living in 8 rooms, with an income of $2000 per year.* The family which occupies this house consists of four brothers, a wife of the oldest of the brothers and his child, a boy two years of age. The oldest brother is twenty-five years of age, and tends the farm. He is a reddish-hued mulatto. The next brother, a man of twenty-three, is the life of the family. He is short and reddish, with sandy hair. The next brother, a man of twenty, is like his oldest brother. The youngest brother, of seventeen, is darker than the rest, and has straight black hair. The mother and father are both dead; they died some time ago—the mother in Augusta, the old family home, the father after they had moved to the present quarters to better family conditions. The whole family now consists of two sisters, married, living in Augusta, one brother, married, in New York city, two brothers in Atlanta, and the four brothers at home. The brother of twenty-three is the center of home life. It is he who sells the cotton, sees after all expenses, and pays the others what they have made. He does not eat at home, he runs the only down-town restaurant in the business district of a near-by town. He and his youngest brother rise about five o'clock on mornings and go to town, two miles distant, to open up and start business. There he looks after the buying of provisions, and sees that the orders are filled. The youngest brother runs errands; the other two stay at home and supervise the farm, and attend to all outdoor domestic work—sweeping, cleaning, milking, and the like. The wife cooks at home, churns, makes beds, washes, patches and scrubs. Company from town is entertained with the greatest hospitality, including buggy rides. The whole family goes to church on the second and fourth Sundays of every month. They belong to two secret orders, which meet every second and fourth Tuesday and every second and fourth Thursday nights. The farm is eighty acres in extent and is owned by the family. When dressed-up the woman wears gay-colored dresses, ordinary shoes and fancy country hats, with her hair tied with blue and yellow ribbon. All the brothers wear on Sundays red shoes, striped trousers, black coats, gay socks, and colored shirts with collars attached. The main foods are syrup, potatoes, milk and butter. As much cornbread is eaten as wheat bread, and vegetables in season. Fish comes in whenever they are caught in the near-by creek or are brought from town. Cured meat is eaten two meals a day, together with chicken and eggs. There are three meals per day: breakfast at five in the morning, dinner at twelve and supper at five. At breakfast they have corn cakes, biscuit, fried meat, coffee, and perhaps eggs. The food is served in plain semi-porcelain dishes, and sit upon the table which the family surrounds. Knives, forks and spoons are used. The dinner consists of potatoes, baked, some sort of vegetables boiled with cured meat, and cornbread served upon appropriate dishes. Supper consists of coffee, perhaps chicken or eggs, biscuit and cornbread, together with the staples, that is, syrup, butter and milk, which always have a place on the table at all meals. The table is made of white pine, and is kept well-scrubbed, for no cloth is used. The chairs are plain cane-bottom, and are also kept white with soap and water. I hardly believe that napkins are used at all meals, but they produce, when company comes, some napkins about six inches square ironed as stiff as boards.

No. 6. *A country family living in 9 rooms with an income of $1500 per year.* There are fourteen members in the family: father 58, mother 54, mother's mother 70, five sons, respectively, 35, 33, 31, 24 and 18 years of age; and six daughters, respectively, 29, 28, 26, 22, 20 and 15 years of age. Eight of the older children do not live at home. As a family they are loving and congenial. The father is a man who takes care of his family. The mother will do anything for her children. All the children do well in school and are quick to learn. The whole family dress well, and especially the girls keep up with the style. The girls have been off to school and have put aside the old-fashioned way of dressing of the community in which they live. There is not much time for dressing during the week, however, owing to household duties, but on Sunday they all appear in white dresses and straw sailor hats, or perhaps in a black skirt, a white waist and a hat trimmed in flowers. Some of the older girls have black and white silk parasols. The father wears a black suit, or sometimes a pair of striped trousers and a black coat. The mother always dresses in a plain white suit or a white waist and a black skirt. Everything is kept clean and tidy. Company call very often, sometimes to stay two or three weeks, and the guests come from neighboring cities. The family goes to church regularly. The property owned consists of 325 acres of land, very fertile, and worth fifty dollars an acre. The family has been living in the present locality for the past thirty-one years. Neither of the parents have had any education except what they have picked up themselves. All the children have been educated. Two daughters and one son are married.

Breakfast is at seven and consists of hot biscuits, cornbread, fried meat, butter and coffee. Dinner is at twelve and consists of cabbage, greens, corn (fried), pepper, fried meat, sweet potatoes, white potatoes, cornbread and squashes. For Sunday dinners there is often macaroni, cheese, chicken, and pudding in addition. Supper is at sundown, and consists of cornbread, biscuits, fried meat and syrup. Dishes and plates are all of porcelain, with steel forks and knives with wooden handles. The table is set in the week with a tablecloth of red and white flowers, on Sunday with a linen cloth. Two benches stand, one on each side of the table, and a chair is at either end.

No. 7. *A city family living in 3 rooms, with an income of $200 per year.* There are three members in this family, a mother and two daughters. The mother is fifty-one years old and wholly illiterate; she is a washerwoman and not at all neat or clean in her dress; she looks like an Indian and is very quick-tempered. The elder daughter is twenty-two years of age, very slow in thought and action. She finished the grammar schools and got as far as the second year in high school. In summer she washes and irons, in winter she cooks for a white family. Her dress is sometimes clean and neat, and sometimes just the opposite. The younger daughter is thirteen years of age and goes to grammar school. She has a very even temperament and is usually clean. They own no property except the house and lot where they live. Both daughters belong to the church, but the mother does not. They belong to no societies, and have no social life to speak of. They usually go together, except that the younger girl has some young girl friends. The father is dead. The mother's father was a white farmer and her mother a slave. The father's father and mother were slaves. He had two brothers, one of whom is dead. They know of no other relatives.

Breakfast, consisting of coffee, wheat bread, meat, bacon, sometimes beef, is eaten at half past six, and dinner, with cornbread, vegetables, now and then meats, is eaten about eight at night; except on Sunday, when breakfast is eaten at nine o'clock and dinner at half past two or three o'clock. The meals are eaten from miscellaneous dishes. The table upon which the family eats has no tablecloth upon it. The food is taken from the cooking utensils and put on a plate—some of everything they have is put on a plate—and each member of the family takes her plate and sits to the table in the kitchen and eats. There are only two meals cooked. Between meals they eat what is left from the previous meal.

No. 8. *A city family living in 3 rooms, with an income of $800 per year.* This family is seven in number: husband, aged 34; wife, aged 29, their two children, both girls, ages ten and six; the husband's mother, about seventy; husband's brother, aged eighteen, and a nephew of the husband, aged fourteen. The wife before being married was orphaned and reared by her sister. She has a grammar-school education; she is red brown in color. The husband, a brown man, got a little education and then came to town in search of work. He found employment with the railroad as hostler; he was at this employment until after marriage when, under the influence of his wife, he became a brickmason. The husband's mother lived in the country until her husband died and several children, after which she moved to the city with her youngest son, a boy of eighteen, and her orphaned grandson, a boy of fourteen. The duties of the wife and the mother are to keep the home in order. The children go to school. The boy of fourteen cuts wood, brings up coal and kindling, goes to school, and spends two hours in the service of a small dairy, delivering dairy products to the neighbors, for which he receives fifty cents a week. The boy of eighteen drives a furniture wagon for a local furniture store, receiving six dollars per week for his services. The husband works at his trade, averaging about five hundred dollars a year. There have been born into this family since marriage six children, four of whom died in infancy, two of whom were twins. The dress of this family is common city dress with nothing extra. The men's suits average fifteen dollars per suit; the women's clothes, averaging five dollars per suit, being made at home. All belong to the church, although to different ones; all attend very regularly. The husband is a Mason and the wife a True Reformer. The home is now being paid for. The family is very genial in disposition, and receives some company.

The staple foods are meat, grits, rice, syrup, butter and jelly. All of this is bought from stores except the jelly, which is made in the summer. At breakfast there is rice, grits, coffee, biscuit and some sort of steak, sausage or liver, bought from the near-by market. Red damask tablecloth covers the table, with china dishes. The food is served on appropriate dishes. Common napkins are used. The whole family eat at the same time. At dinner they have baked beans, or roast, together with white potatoes, rice, and wheat bread, coffee, and some sort of cheap dessert, like pie. At supper there is something fried from the market, wheat bread, grits, cheese, coffee and tea. Breakfast is at six in the morning, dinner at twelve, and supper at six in the evening.

No. 9. *A city family living in 5 rooms, with an income of $864 per year.* The family is composed of five members: mother, father and three sons. The father, fifty-four years of age, a portly man, light yellow, with straight black hair. The mother, fifty years of age, is a heavy-built woman, with a stately and erect form, dark-brown complexion and coarse hair. The sons, of 22, 27 and 29 years, are very much alike; they have straight black hair and Indian complexion and features. The mother and father belong to the Baptist church; the sons are not church members. The mother and father are well thought of by the neighbors. The sons' habits on the whole are not of the best. The two oldest do not live at home. The mother and father wear plain clothes, the sons dress moderately and keep clean. The house is kept very clean and neat. The windows, floors and furniture are kept neat; the bedclothes are always clean and comfortable. The rooms are well-ventilated daily, and the yard is kept in good condition. The father was a country schoolteacher up to twenty-nine years ago, but from that time up to the present he has been employed as a cotton classer. The oldest son has always followed the profession of embalming; the youngest boy is a special delivery messenger at the post-office. The other boy is a common laborer. The mother and father belong to secret societies. The boys live with their parents when they are in the city. They own the house and lot they live on.

The principal foods are bread, meat, rice, grits, coffee, tea and vegetables. They cook twice a day, morning and evening, between six and seven o'clock in the morning and five and six in the evening, and serve a light cold lunch at noon. The dishes are of various sets, few in number. Common silver-plated spoons, knives and forks of different kinds are used. The mother does the cooking; at mealtime all the food is put on the table at the beginning. After the meal she clears the table and washes the dishes.

No. 10. *A city family living in 4 rooms, with an income of $560 per year.* This family is composed of nine members: father, 38 years; mother, 35 years; four girls, 16, 13, 11 and 8, respectively, and three boys, 6, 4 and 2 years, respectively. The father's father was a farmer. The man himself is a brickmason. In recent years he has been studying theology, and is now pastor of three churches. The mother's mother has been, since emancipation, a servant in the house of white families for the most part, and her daughter did the same thing until she was married. The family is thoroughly Christian, and very highly thought of in the community where it is. The dress of this family is very plain and clean. This family has no family gatherings except birthday parties. The usual company are those who belong to the same church, the same society and the school friends of the children. The older members are members of the A. M. E. Church. The four oldest children go to Sunday-school regularly, and the father is a regular church goer. The man is an Odd Fellow and a Knight of Pythias also. All the children except the youngest belong to an insurance company that collects the dues every week. This family owns three-eighths of an acre of land; one-quarter is in one place and one-eighth of an acre in another. They have a cow, a hog, chickens and ducks. The house and everything around it is kept fairly clean. The family has lived near where they now live all of their lives. When this couple was first married they rented, then they moved to a home that belonged to the mother of the man. When the family became too large to live in that three-room house, the man bought land and built the house in which the family now lives.

For breakfast the family usually has ham or bacon, grits, tea or coffee, sometimes eggs, sweet potatoes in their season, cornbread and biscuits. For dinner they usually have two kinds of vegetables—peas, collard greens, cabbage or beans—and white potatoes or rice, cornbread or biscuits; either peach, pear, apple or blackberry pie, or bread pudding for dessert; sweet potatoes for dinner in their season. For supper they have beef stew, or soup sometimes, and at other times they have ham or bacon, and rice, coffee or tea, and milk when the cow is giving milk. Syrup may be had at almost any meal, if any one desires it. This is the regular course of eating, but many times they have fish or pork for breakfast or supper. This family usually has breakfast between 5:30 and 6:30 o'clock. The man has to be at his work at seven o'clock and the children leave for school at seven-thirty o'clock. In the winter the children take their lunch to school with them, but when they get home in the afternoon they usually eat what has been left from the morning cooking, and they have supper about six o'clock when the man comes home from his work. The dishes are all very plain, but there are some silver knives, forks and spoons that are used on special occasions, or when there is special company. As a rule, everything is put on the table at one time and everybody sits down together. When the mother is at the table she usually does the serving, and when she is not there the oldest girl does it. The man serves himself, and as soon as he is through he gets up and begins reading the newspaper or a book. The table is of rectangular shape, made of pine lumber, rather small for nine people. A linen tablecloth is used all the time.

No. 11. *A city family living in 4 rooms, with an income of $1200 per year.* This is a family of three: a man 57 years old, his wife, 41, and an adopted girl 10 years old. The man is a janitor, superintending several flats. The owner furnishes him a house and all of his fuel, besides his wages in money. He was coachman for the same man before he became janitor. The woman is a fine dressmaker, and she sews and keeps house. The man is a little above medium height, slender, with dark brown skin and crinkly black hair, mixed with gray; he has a black mustache. He is jovial, usually cheerful, generous, kind-hearted, prudent and business-like. The woman is of medium height and

heavy build. She might easily pass for a white woman. She has very
fair skin and straight chestnut hair. She is industrious and also business like. The little girl is about the size of the average child of ten.
She is a very light brown, with closely-waved reddish hair. She is
the woman's niece. She goes to school, and when at home runs errands,
etc. They all wear good clothes, well-made, of good material. They
are very neat and clean. They are very fond of staying at home, but
have friends whom they visit and who visit them. They go to church
dutifully, and each one belongs to some society, insurance or secret
order. There was one child, which died while an infant. Since the
owner of the flats furnishes them a house, they rent out their own
house, which is a wooden structure of four rooms, with a lot 25 feet by
200 feet. The woman came from a family of seven girls. The father
and four of the girls are dead; the mother lives sometimes with this
daughter and sometimes works out and stays where she works. Of the
three other girls one—the mother of the little girl—lives in the North.
She has one of her children with her, a boy, and the third child has
been adopted by one of her friends. The other sister is unmarried, and
teaches. The man came from a family of five children. His mother
and father are dead. His three brothers live near him, and his sister
lives in another city. He was reared from a small boy by the man for
whom he now works and has always worked.

This family has three meals a day. The food is well-cooked and
well-served. They have nice dishes, silver, and good table linen. They
have breakfast at seven o'clock, dinner between two and three o'clock
and a cold supper about seven-thirty o'clock. In summer they have
for breakfast a cereal, fruit, flour bread, and some kind of meat (beef,
fish, chicken, mutton, fresh pork). For dinner they have cornbread,
vegetables, or sometimes flour bread and baked meats, rice and tomatoes, potatoes, iced tea, and some kind of dessert. For supper they have
fruit, iced tea, bread and butter, and sometimes meat. In winter they
have for breakfast a cereal, bread, meat, and coffee or cocoa. The dinner is about the same as that of summer, with the exception of the
summer vegetables and the iced tea. They often have soup. For supper they have bread and butter, cold meats, and sometimes stewed fruit
and cocoa.

No. 12. *A city family living in 9 rooms, with an income of $1300 per
year*. The father's father's birthplace and age is unknown. He was
a slave of some wealth when freed. He belonged to a very good task-
master and had considerable amount of cattle and other property.
Some of his money he intrusted to his master for safety, but he died
without ever getting it back again. The father's mother's birthplace
is unknown. She had about three-fourths Indian blood, and was married three times. She was the mother of six children: five boys and
one girl. One boy died while a very small child. The mother died in
1891. The father was born December 24, 1865, and is the oldest of the
six children. He has been the main breadwinner for the family since
the death of his father, when he was a boy, and has had a very little

chance for schooling. He had to raise the four remaining children after his mother's death. He married at twenty years of age, and has farmed fourteen years. He owns a house and a four-acre lot at —— Texas. He moved from —— to —— Texas, in 1900, and was porter in a hardware store for three years, with wages at $9.00 per week. Since then he has been a porter at the depot, with wages at $35.00 per month. He has one child, a boy, age 22 years. He is now buying a quarter block at $1500. The wife was born near ——, Texas, July 13, 1867. Her father died before her birth. Her mother's birthplace was in ——, Texas, and she is still living. The mother's mother has been married twice. First husband died soon after marriage; the second husband is still living. She is the mother of two children; both are married, and both girls. The mother sells vegetables, chickens and eggs, milk and butter, to neighbors, washes and irons and sometimes cooks. She had very little chance for education, and was married at eighteen years. Neither husband nor wife possessed any property at their marriage. The boy was born at ——, Texas, and he has been in school ever since he reached school age. Only works during the summer, averaging about $5 per week. Husband belongs to Odd Fellows Lodge, and has an accident life insurance policy of $1500.

No. 13. *A city family living in 7 rooms, with an income of $1344 per year.* There are eight members in the family; father, 53 years of age; mother, 49 years of age; grandmother on the father's side, 80 years of age; eldest daughter 21, eldest son 19, younger daughter 17, youngest son 15 and the youngest girl 12. The father is a railway mail clerk and has been for years. The mother only carries on the household affairs with the aid of the three girls. The grandmother attends to the cow and sells the milk. The eldest daughter teaches in one of the public schools of the city. The oldest son works in a barber shop. The younger son attends college in the winter and works as messenger boy in one of the factories in summer. The other two girls attend school and also assist in the house work.

During vacation three meals are served: breakfast at 7:30 a. m., and dinner at 12:00 p. m. and supper at 6 p. m. But when school begins only two meals are served: breakfast, and late dinner about 4:30 p. m. They raise none of the food, everything is bought. The meals are served by the girls of the family. The dishes used on the dining-room table are china, the knives and forks silver, but those used in the kitchen are not so expensive. The table used in this kitchen is comparatively small, being only for family use. But when there is company the larger dining-room is used.

For breakfast they always have some kind of cereal, biscuits, tea and coffee; either fried steak, ham, or the like, and home-made butter. For dinner they generally have something boiled, and dessert, either pies or pudding. They always dress well and are always very neat and clean. This family was once accustomed to spending Christmas day with the grandparents—the mother's parents—but since their death they spend the holidays at home. They attend church regularly, and the mother belongs to one of the largest Methodist churches of the city. The mother and father own quite a deal of property; the mother's was left to her by her parents, the father acquired his by his own labor.

Section 20A. Expenditures of Laborers. Just before going to press the following budgets of Negro laboring people of Atlanta have been collected. Logically this section should follow Section 20 which it serves to complete, and represents more nearly the expenditures of the mass of Negroes These budgets were collected by students of Atlanta University during the current year.

No. 1. *A Wood Chopper.* Two adults. Weekly earnings: Head, $2.50; wife, 75 cents; total, $3.25. Rent, $3.00 per month, two rooms. Weekly expense: Flour, wheat, 10 lbs., 40 cents; corn and cornmeal, 2 lbs., 5 cents; potatoes (Irish, etc.), 1 quart, 5 cents; sweet potatoes, yams, etc., 1 quart, 5 cents; green vegetables, 10 cents; meat: beef (fresh), 1 lb., 10 cents; bacon, 10 cents; fish of all kinds, 10 cents; lard, 10 cents; coffee, ½ lb., 10 cents; sugar, 1 lb., 10 cents; molasses and syrup, ½ pt., 5 cents; coke, 1 bu., 10 cents; wood, 25 cents; kerosene, ½ gal. 10 cents. Total, $1.75.

No. 2. *Laborer in Paper Mill.* Seven members in family, parents and five children, two boys and three girls; ages, respectively, 19 and 15 and 18, 14 and 10 years. Weekly earnings: Head, $22.00; one boy $7.00 and one girl $1.75; total, $30.75. House owned (rent of a similar house, $10.00), four rooms. Weekly expense : Flour, wheat, 50 lbs., $1.80; corn and cornmeal, 10 lbs., 25 cents; macaroni, 2 lbs., 20 cents; rice, 3 lbs., 25 cents; Irish potatoes, 1 peck, 30 cents; sweet potatoes, yams, etc., 1 peck, 30 cents; green vegetables, 35c.; meat (fresh beef), 20 lbs., $1.75; sausage, 3 lbs., 20c.; fish of all kinds, 6 lbs., 50c.; lard, 4 lbs., 50c.; butter, 2 lbs., 40c.; cheese, 2 lbs., 40c.; milk, fresh, 8 quarts, 30c.; milk, condensed, 2 lbs., 20c.; eggs, 1 doz., 25c.; coffee, 2 lbs., 40c.; sugar, 8 lbs., 50c.; molasses and syrup, 2 pts., 20c.; coal, 480 lbs., $1.50; wood, 25c.; kerosene, 2 gal., 30c. Total, $11.20.

No. 3. *Truckman.* Parents and one child. Weekly earnings: Head $6.00, wife $3.00, total $9.00. Rent $5.00 per month, three rooms. Weekly expense: Flour, wheat 12 lbs. 50c, corn and cornmeal 10 lbs. 25c, dried peas and beans ⅓ lb. 5c, tomatoes, etc. 25c, meat, beef (fresh and corned) 2 lbs. 25c, pork (fresh and salt) 7½ lbs. 75c, bacon, ham, head cheese, etc. 6 lbs. 75c, fish of all kinds 2 lbs. 25c, lard, suet dripping 2½ lbs. 25c, cheese 1 lb. 20c, milk (fresh) 1 qt. 20c, tea 2½c, sugar 4 lbs. 25c, coal 50c, wood 50c, kerosene ⅓ gal. 10c. Total, $5.08.

No. 4. *Brickmason.* Parents and six children, four boys and two girls; ages, respectively, 19, 13, 4 and 1, 9 and 7 years. Weekly earnings: Head, $20.00. Home owned (rent of similar house $8.00), five rooms. Weekly expense: Bread, of wheat, 6 loaves, 30c.; flour: wheat 24 lbs., 90c.; rye, 5 lbs., 35c.; crackers, 2 lbs., 25c.; macaroni, 1 lb., 10c.; rice, 6 lbs., 25c.; potatoes (Irish, etc.), 3 qts., 15c.; sweet potatoes, yams, etc., 1 pk.. 30c.; dried beans, 1 qt., 15c.; tomatoes, 18 lbs., 45c.; meat: beef (fresh), 10 lbs., $1.00; ham, 2 lbs., 40c.; sausage, 1 lb., 10c.; fish of all kinds, 3 lbs., 30c.; lard, 4 lbs., 50c.; butter, 2 lbs., 40c.; cheese, 1 lb., 20c.; milk, fresh, 8 qts., 30c.; milk, condensed, 1 lb., 10c.; eggs, 1 doz., 25c.; tea, ¼ lb., 20c.; coffee, 1 lb., 20c.; sugar, 9 lbs., 50c.; syrup, 1 pt., 10c.; jams, 1 pint, 25c.; coal, 3 bu., 75c.; coke, 2 bu., 20c.; kerosene, 2 gal., 30c. Total, $7.95.

No. 5. *Railroad Employee.* Parents and one child, boy three years old. Weekly earnings: Head, $25.00. Home owned (rent of similar house, $20.00 per month), seven rooms. Weekly expense: Bread, of wheat, 8 lbs., 25c ; flour: wheat, 6 lbs., 25c.; corn and cornmeal, 6 lbs., 15c.; spaghetti, 1 lb., 10c.; rice, barley, sago, etc., 3 lbs., 25c.; oatmeal and breakfast cereals, 2 lbs., 10c.; potatoes (Irish, etc.), ½ pk., 20c.; sweet potatoes, yams, etc., ½ pk., 15c.; dried peas and beans, 1 qt., 20c.; sweet corn, 14 lbs., 35c.; green vegetables, salad, tomatoes, etc., 35c.; meat: beef (fresh), 4 lbs., 60c.; bacon, ham, head cheese, etc., 10 lbs., $1.50; fish of all kinds, 3 lbs., 45c.; lard, suet dripping, 2½ lbs., 28c.; butter, 2 lbs., 40c.; olive oil, 1 pt., 30c.; cheese, 1 lb., 20c.; milk, condensed, 2 ibs., 25c.; eggs, 6 doz., $1.20; tea, ¼ lb., 15c ; coffee, ½ lb., 15c. ; sugar, 4 lbs., 25c.; molasses and syrup, 1 pt., 10c. ; Ice, 70c.; coal, 6 bu., $1.50; wood, 60c.; kerosene, 1 gal., 15c. Total, $10.88.

No. 6. *Insurance Collector.* Parents and one child, a girl, 18 years. Weekly earnings: Head $17.90, total $17.90. Home owned (rent of similar house $10.60), five rooms. Weekly expense: Bread of wheat, 10 lbs., 55c., flour: wheat, 12 lbs., 45c., corn and cornmeal 7½c., spaghetti 1 lb. 10c., rice 1½ lb. 8c., potatoes (Irish), 1 qt. 5c., sweet potatoes, yams, etc., 1 peck 20c., meat: beef (fresh), 3 lbs. 30c., pork (fresh), 2 lbs. 20c., bacon 3 lbs. 25c., lard 2½ lbs. 35c., butter 1 lb. 35c., cheese 1 lb. 20c., milk, fresh, 1 quart 5c., milk, condensed, 1 lb. 10c., eggs 1 dozen 22c., coffee ½ lb. 12½c., sugar 4⅓ lbs., 25c., coal 3 bu. 75c., wood 25c, kerosene 1 gal. 15c.   Total, $4.05.

No. 7. *Brickmason.* Parents and two children, ages 10 and 7 years. Weekly earnings: Head $12.00, wife $5.00; total $17.00. House owned (rent of similar house $8.00 per month), three rooms. Weekly expense: Bread of wheat, 2 lbs. 10c, flour: wheat, 12 lb. 45c, corn and cornmeal, 2 lb. 5c, crackers, 1 lb. 10c, macaroni, 1 lb. 10c, rice, 2 lb. 15c, potatoes (Irish, etc.), 1 qt. 5c, sweet potatoes, yams, etc., 2 qts. 10c, green vegetables, 10c, meat: beef (fresh), 3 lb. 25c, pork (fresh) 2 lb. 30c, ham, 1 lb. 20c., sausage, 1 lb. 10c, fish of all kinds, 3 lb. 25c, lard 2 lb. 25c, butter 1 lb. 20c, cheese, 1 lb. 20c, milk (fresh) 4 qts. 15c, milk (condensed) 1 lb. 10c, eggs, 1 doz. 25c, coffee, 1 lb. 20c, sugar, 4 lbs. 25c, molasses and syrup, 1 pt. 10c, coke 30c, wood 25c, kerosene, ½ gal. 10c.   Total, $4.65.

No. 8. *City Cart-driver.* Two adults and one child, a boy one year old. Weekly earnings: Head $6.00, total $6.00. Rent $3.00 per month, two rooms. Weekly expense: Flour, wheat 24 lbs. 90c, corn and cornmeal 2 lbs. 5c, rice 1 lb. 10c, potatoes (Irish) 1 qt. 5c, sweet potatoes, yams, etc., ½ pk. 15c, dried peas 2 qts. 20c, meat: beef (fresh and corned) 6 lb. 60c, pork (fresh and salt) 1 lb. 15c, bacon 2 lbs. 25c, sausage 1 lb. 10c, lard 1 lb. 15c, butter ½ lb. 10c, coffee ½ lb. 15c, sugar 2 lbs. 15c, molasses and syrup 1 pt. 10c, vinegar, pickles and condiments 5c, nearbeer 4 pts. 20c, coal 1 bu. 25c, wood 15c, kerosene ½ gal. 10c. Total, $3.35.

No. 9. *Drayman.* Two adults. Weekly earnings: Head $8.00, wife $1.75; total $9.75. Rent $5.00 per month, three rooms. Weekly expense: Flour, wheat 12 lbs. 45c, corn and cornmeal 4 lbs. 10c, rice 1 lb. 10c, potatoes (Irish, etc.) 2 quarts 10c, sweet potatoes, yams, etc., 3 qts. 15c, dried peas and beans 2 qts. 20c, green vegetables 30c, meat: beef (fresh and corned) 6 lbs. 60c, pork (fresh and salt) 2 lbs. 30c, ham 2 lbs. 40c, sausage 2 lbs. 20c, fish of all kinds 2 lbs. 15c, lard, suet dripping 2 lbs. 20c, butter 1 lb. 20c, eggs 1 doz. 25c, coffee 1 lb. 20c, sugar 3 lbs. 20c, vinegar, pickles and condiments 5c, spirits 2 pts. $1.60, coal 1 bu. 25c, wood 25c, kerosene ½ gal. 20c.   Total, $6.40.

No. 10. *Drayman*. Two adults and two children, girls, ages 12 and 6 years. Weekly earnings: Head $6.00, wife $1.50; total $7.50. Rent $4.50 per month, two rooms. Weekly expense: Flour, wheat, 8 lbs., 30c., cornmeal, ½ pk., 15c., dried beans, 1 qt. 10c., green vegetables—salad, tomatoes, etc., 20c., meat: beef (fresh and corned) 2 lbs. 20c., pork (salt) 4 lbs. 50c., sausage 1½ lbs. 15c., lard 15c., tea 5c., coffee 5c., molasses and syrup 2 qts. 15c., sugar 3 lbs. 15c, beer $1.00, wood 50c., kerosene ½ gal, 10c. Total, $3.85.

No. 11. *Porter in Store*. Two adults and three children, girls, ages 11, 9 and 7 years. Weekly earnings: Head $6.00, wife 75 cents, total $6.75. Rent $2.50 per month, one room. Weekly expense: Flour, wheat 24 lbs. 90c., cornmeal 1 pk. 30c., sweet potatoes 1 pk. 20c., green vegetables, salad, tomatoes, etc., 20c., pork (salt) 8½ lbs. $1.00, sausage 1 lb. 10c, fish of all kinds 4 lbs. 25c., lard 35c., butter ½ lb. 15c., coffee ½ lb. 10c., sugar 4 lb. 25c., wood 50c, kerosene 1 quart 5c. Total, $3.35.

No. 12. *Carpenter*. Three adults and one child, a girl five years old. Weekly earnings: Head $18.00, total $18.00. Rent $8.00 per month, four rooms. Weekly expense: Flour, wheat 8 lbs. 30c., cornmeal 2 qts. 10c., macaroni 1 lb. 10c., rice 1 lb. 10c., potatoes (Irish) 3 qts. 15c., sweet potatoes, yams, etc., 2 qts. 10c., dried peas and beans 1 qt. 10c., green vegetables, salad, tomatoes, etc., 40c.; meat: beef (fresh and corned) 4 lbs. 50c., pork (fresh and salt) 2 lbs. 30c., bacon 2 lbs. 25c., sausage 4 lbs. 40c., lard 3 lbs., 30c., butter 1 lb. 35c., cheese 1 lb. 20c., milk (fresh) 2 qts. 20c., milk (condensed) 1 lb. 12c., eggs 1 doz. 25c., tea ¼ lb. 15c., coffee ½ lb. 15c., sugar 5 lbs. 25c., molasses and syrup 1 pt. 5c., vinegar, pickels and condiments 1 pint 5c., fruits (fresh, dried and canned) and jams 50c., coal 250 lbs. 63c., charcoal 1 bu. 13c., kerosene 1 gal. 15c. Total, $7.68.

No. 13. *Common Laborer*. Two adults and two children, a boy and girl, ages 6 years and 9 months, respectively. Weekly earnings: Head $6.00, wife 40 cents; total $6.40. Rent $2.50 per month, one room. Weekly expense: Flour, wheat 24 lbs. 90c., cornmeal 2 qts. 10c., rice 1½ lbs. 15c., potatoes (Irish, etc.) 1 qt. 5c., sweet potatoes ½ pk. 15c., green vegetables, salad, tomatoes, etc. 25c.; pork (salt) 8 lb. $1.00, lard 3 lb. 30c. coffee ½ lb. 10c., sugar 3 lbs. 15c., coke 2 bu. 20c., wood 35c., kerosene 1 qt. 5c. Total, $3.75.

No. 14. *Stableman*. Two adults and three girls. ages 9, 4 and 2, respectively. Weekly earnings: Head $7.00, wife $2.00, total $9.00. Rent $7.60, three rooms. Weekly expense: Flour, wheat 12 lbs. 45c., rice 3 lbs. 30c., potatoes (Irish, etc.) 2 qts. 10c., dried peas and beans 2 qts. 20c., green vegetables, salad, tomatoes, etc. 30c., meat: beef (fresh and corned) 6 lbs. 60c., pork 4 lbs. 50c., butter 1 lb. 25c., coffee ½ lb. 10c., sugar 3 lbs. 25c., vinegar, pickles and condiments 1 pint 5c., coal 2 bu. 50c., wood 60c., kerosene 1 gal. 15c. Total, $4.95.

No. 15. *Drayman*. Two adults and four children, two boys and two girls, ages respectively 4 and 1½, and 5 and 8 years. Weekly earnings: Head $5.00, wife $1.50; total $6.50. Rent $3.50, two rooms. Weekly expense: Flour, wheat 12 lbs. 40c., cornmeal 1 lb. 30c., rice 1 lb. 10c., dried peas and beans 20c., green vegetables, salad, tomatoes, etc., 10c., pork (fresh and salt) 9¼ lbs. $1.25, fish of all kinds 3½ lbs. 25c., lard 3 lbs. 30c., tea 10c., sugar 5 lbs. 25c., fruits (fresh, dried and canned) and jams 1 lb. 10c., coke 3 bu. 30c., wood 35c., kerosene 1 qt. 5c. Total $4.05.

No. 16. *Street Sweeper*. Two adults and four children, two girls and two boys, ages respectively 14 and 3, and 17 and 10 years. Weekly earnings: Head $6.60, wife 75 cents, 1 boy $4.50; total $11.85. Rent $5.00 per month, two rooms.

Weekly expense: Flour, wheat 24 lbs. 90c, cornmeal 1 pk. 30c, rice 1 lb. 10c, sweet potatoes 1 pk. 25c, beans 2 qts. 20c, green vegetables, salad, tomatoes, etc., 25c, meat, beef (fresh) 2¼ lbs. 30c, fish of all kinds 3 lbs. 40c, lard 4 lbs. 50c., butter 1 lb. 25c, coffee ½ lb. 10c, sugar 5 lbs. 25c, syrup 3 pts. 15c, beer 60c, coal 1 bu. 25c, wood 50c, kerosene ½ gal. 10c. Total, $5.90. Meals away from home 60 cents.

No. 17. *Head Porter for Insurance Company.* Four adults and two children, one boy and a girl, ages respectively 18 and 20 years. Weekly earnings: Head $15.00, wife $4.00, total $19.00. Rent $12.60 per month, six rooms. Weekly expense: Flour, wheat 12 lbs. 55c, buckwheat and other 1 pkg. 10c, cornmeal 2 qts. 10c, macaroni 1 lb. 10c, rice 2½ lbs. 25c, oatmeal 2 pkgs. 25c, potatoes (Irish etc.) ½ bu. 60c, sweet potatoes, yams, etc. 3 qts. 15c, dried pease and beans 1 qt. 10c, green vegetables, salad, tomatoes, etc. 50c, meat, beef (corned) 2 tins 30c, pork (fresh) 6 lbs. 90c, bacon and ham 4 lbs. 60c, poultry 1 chicken 65c, fish of all kinds 2 lbs. 25c, lard 3⅓ lbs. 40c, butter 1⅓ lbs. 45c, cheese 2 lbs. 40c, milk (fresh) 4 qts. 40c, milk (condensed) 1 lb. 12c, eggs 1 doz. 25c, tea ¼ lb. 10c, coffee 1 lb. 25c, sugar 5½ lbs. 40c, syrup 1 pt. 5c, vinegar, pickles and condiments 1 pt. 5c, fruits (fresh, dried and canned) and jams 1 lb. 10c, coal ¼ ton $1.25, coke 1 bu. 10c, wood 25c, kerosene 1 gal. 15c. Total $9.12. Meals away from home 75c; gas 25c.

No. 18. *Drayman.* Two adults. Weekly earnings: Head $5.00, wife $1.00; total $6.00. Rent $4.00 per month, two rooms. Weekly expense: Flour, wheat 5 lbs. 25c, cornmeal 4 qts. 20c, rice ¼ lb. 5c, potatoes (Irish, etc.) ⅓ pk. 20c, green vegetables, salad, tomatoes. etc. 60c, meat, beef (fresh) 3 lbs. 30c, pork (salt) 2¼ lbs. 30c, fish of all kinds 3 lbs. 40c, lard 3 lbs. 30c, butter 1 lb. 25c, coffee 1 lb. 25c, sugar 4 lbs. 20c, wood 40c, kerosene ⅓ gal. 10c. Total $3.60.

No. 19. *Common Laborer.* Two adults and three children, one boy and two girls, ages respectively 6 and 5 and 3 years. Weekly earnings: Head $7.50, total $7.50. Rent $6.00 per month, three rooms. Weekly expense: Flour, wheat 12 lbs. 40c, cornmeal 1 pk. 30c, sweet potatoes 2 qts. 10c, dried peas and beans 2 qts. 20c, green vegetables, salad, tomatoes, etc. 35c, meat, beef (fresh) 5 lbs. 60c, pork (salt) 4 lbs. 50c, fish of all kinds 2 lbs. 25c, lard 3 lbs. 30c, butter 1 lb. 25c, coffee ½ lb. 10c, cocoa 1 box 10c, sugar 3 lbs. 15c, fruits (dried) 15c, spirits ½ pt. 25c, kerosene 1 gal. 15c. Total, $4.55.

No. 20. *Stonemason.* Two adults. Weekly earnings: Head $12.00, total $12.00. Rent $6.50 per month, three rooms. Weekly expense: Flour, wheat 6 lbs. 25c, corn and cornmeal 4 lbs. 10c, sweet potatoes, yams, etc. 15 lbs. 30c, meat, beef (fresh and corned) 2 lbs. 20c, pork (fresh and salt) 1 lb. 15c, bacon, ham, head cheese, etc. 2 lb. 25c, fish of all kinds 3 lbs. 30c, lard, suet dripping 2⅓ lbs. 25c, Butter ½ lb. 15c, milk (fresh) 1 qt. 5c, milk (condensed) 1 lb. 10c, eggs 5, 10c, coffee ½ lb. 10c, sugar 1½ lbs. 10c, vinegar, pickles and condiments 1 pt. 10c, coal 100 lbs. 50c, wood 50c, kerosene ⅓ gal. 5c. Total, $3.55.

Section 28. Conclusion. Judging from family life and other conditions how far, is it fair to conclude, has the Negro American emerged into twentieth century civilization? The United States had, in 1900, 10.7% of illiteracy, 46.5% of home ownership, and perhaps 2% of illegitimate births. The Negro had, in 1900, 44.5% of illiteracy, 20.3% of home ownership and, probably though not certainly, 25% of illegitimacy.

These rough measurements would permit the following assumption: that in the Nation at large four-fifths of the citizens have at least common school training, two-thirds have reached a plane of economic independence, and nine-tenths are observing the monogamic sex *mores*. Among the Negroes probably one-third have at least common-school training, one-third have reached a plane of economic independence, and at least one-half are observing the monogamic sex *mores*.

We may conclude this study by short extracts from the remarks of two of the speakers of the Thirteenth Annual Conference.

Miss Jane Addams said, among other things:

. . . The thing I feel most strongly as the difficulty among the Italians, among the Greeks and among the Russians (for these are the ones whom I constantly see), is the contrast they find between the life they have led at home and the life they are obliged to live in Chicago. All sorts of customs fit them to walk in the old folk ways, the old ways which their ancestors have had for so many years. Now, as I take it, your difficulties are quite unlike that. The habits which you might have had from your ancestors were all broken into, they were all scattered, and especially the habits connected with family life. There are advantages and disadvantages in the lack of tradition and the lack of habits in those directions. The advantages are that you are much more ready to make your adaptation; you are much more ready to bring the results of education and the rationalistic side of life to bear directly upon the refining of the family. And the disadvantages are that you lack some of the restraints of the traditions which the people I have mentioned bring with them.

The Reverend E. L. Henderson, Episcopal Archdeacon of the diocese of Atlanta, said:

While the Negro has made a splendid beginning in the acquisition of homes, a beginning it is, and not the end. For, here and there, in country and in city, we find not only types of the ideal home but tenements and shanties which barely afford protection from wind and storm; dwellings where the laws of health are defied, where the most ordinary sanitary arrangements are unknown, and where boards of health fail to penetrate; beds innocent of clothing; human forms, even those of children, piteously clad; hunger written upon careworn faces and despair everywhere triumphant. What can be expected in such a home as this but that which often exists—an immorality as deep as its poverty; a moral atmosphere as pestilential as the physical. Again, there are homes, so-called, in which the holy ties of human affection are greatly warped, if not broken asunder, and where the old motto, "What is home without a father?" which once served as an adornment and certificate of value, is now replaced by the State's certificate of divorce. For while the Negro, being imitative, has been strengthened by the examples of the good, he has been weakened by the examples of the bad.

If the moral, economic and educational advance of the Negro race be necessary for the well-being of society; if the unit of society is not the individual, but the family; if nothing can take the place of the early influences of a true home, and the function of education be to "Prepare us for complete living," then, the Christian Church, which underlies and upholds all other institutions, and gives to each an immortal power and an eternal significance, must purify the stream at the *fountain head* by sending her ministering angels—her clergy, deaconesses, sisters, teachers, Bible women, and visitors—into the homes of the Negroes, not only to teach the importance of daily family prayer, but, in the language of one of our learned prelates, to teach, also, what is good taste in dress; the part soap and water, liberally used, plays in health and strength of mind and character; the fact that clammy bread and bad coffee are not a necessary incident of poverty; that separate and well-ventilated bedrooms, a clean tablecloth and gentle manners, belong to a polite education; that order and thrift are not a waste of time, but make time for rational enjoyment and brighten life; that nothing is lost by supplanting coarseness, vulgarity, slovenliness, with tidiness, refinement and innocent amusement; that the best elements of the highest civilization in Virginia or Connecticut are wrought in the *home*, and that the sweetness and delight of home are as possible in a plain Negro cabin as in houses of brick or marble with all modern improvements, and that the flowers and the fruits of good living are attainable wherever the disposition exists and a determined effort is made to have them.

FINALLY: If there would be a further transition from ignorance, poverty and moral darkness, to enlightenment, thrift, industry, and improvement of the individual and the Negro family, the Church and the Home must unite in a more vigorous warfare to reduce to a minimum the prevailing evil of divorce. This they must do,

(1) By teaching young women to appreciate the seriousness of marriage, its solemn import and its sacred responsibilities.

(2) By teaching young men to revere womanhood and motherhood, for the sake of their own mothers and the Mother of our Lord, so that their purity may be no mere prudential restraint, but a generous and chivalrous Christian knightliness.

(3) By teaching all that marriage and family life are not dependent upon selfish desire, or mere caprice, but are institutions ordained of God, and designed like other ordinances of God with a view to the education, the formation and discipline of character.

When the Church and the Home receive a clearer vision and use their full power; when the estate of Holy Matrimony, which has a sacramental character, be no longer entered into, as so often now, "unadvisedly or lightly," but "reverently, discreetly, advisedly, soberly, and in the fear of God," then the Church and the Home will have served their mission, and be permitted to look with satisfaction upon "Their sons as plants grown up in their youth, and their daughters as corner-stones, polished after the similitude of a palace."

Index